LIVI...

Ireland

FIRST EDITION

Steenie Harvey

© Steenie Harvey

AVALON
TRAVEL

Introduction 1

Welcome to Ireland 3
Map 2
The Lay of the Land 5
Social Climate 15

History, Government, and Economy 21
History 21
Government 35
Economy 37

People and Culture 41
Ethnicity and Class 41
Traditional Culture 44
Customs and Etiquette 48
Gender Roles 50
Religion 51
The Arts 52

Prime Living Locations 59

Overview 61
Map 60

Planning Your Fact-Finding Trip 69
Preparing to Leave 70
Arriving in Ireland 72
Sample Itineraries 73
Practicalities 84

Dublin 95
Map 94
The Lay of the Land 96
Housing 97
Downtown Dublin Map 100
Getting Around 108

The Western Seaboard 111
Map 110
County Galway 112
County Mayo 119
County Clare 124

The Southwest 129
Map 128
County Kerry 130
County Cork 134

The Southeast 141
Map 140
County Kilkenny 142
County Wexford 146
County Waterford 150
County Tipperary 154

The Northwest and Lakelands 161
Map 160
County Sligo 162
County Donegal 165
The Lakelands: Counties Roscommon, Leitrim, and Cavan 171

Daily Life 177

Making the Move 179
Red Tape **181**
Citizenship **183**
Holding Dual Nationality **187**
Moving with Children **188**
Moving with Pets **189**
What to Take **190**
Customs and Excise **191**

Language and Education 193
Learning the Language **194**
Education **199**

Health 207
Public and Private Medical
Care **209**
Dental Care **211**
Alternative Therapies **212**
Critical Illness Insurance **213**
Pharmacies and Prescriptions **213**
Preventative Measures **214**
Environmental Factors **216**
Disabled Access **217**
Safety **217**

Employment 221
Ireland's Economy **222**

The Job Hunt **224**
Self-Employment **229**
Labor Laws **231**

Finance 235
Cost of Living **236**
Banking **241**
Taxes **243**
Investing **246**

Communications 251
Telephone Service **251**
Email and Postal Service **256**
Media **259**

Travel and Transportation 265
   Map **264**
By Air **265**
By Ferry **268**
By Bus **270**
By Rail **271**
By Car **272**

Housing Considerations 281
Renting **282**
Buying Property **287**

Resources 299

Contacts 300
Consulates and Agencies **300**
Tourist Information Offices **300**
Making the Move **302**
Language and Education **303**
Health **305**
Employment **306**
Finance **307**

Communications **308**
Travel and Transportation **311**
Housing Considerations **315**
Real Estate Agents **316**

Suggested Reading 320

Index 321

Preface

A new life in Ireland. Sounds like a wonderful idea, but is it really possible? Well, I'd just like to tell you that dreams can come true. I should know, mine did. . . .

I haven't always been a writer, you know. And Ireland is my adopted home, rather than my place of birth. Back in the late 1980s, my life was in a rut. I lived in a dreary industrial English town and had an equally dreary job as an office clerk in a printing factory.

Although family life was great—wonderful husband, wonderful daughter—I felt crushed by the sheer grind of my day-to-day existence. I got up, went to work, caught a bus home, cooked dinner, and watched television. Day after day after day. But what's wrong with that? After all, thousands of people were in the same boat as me.

Then a bombshell dropped—my husband, Michael, lost his job. Maybe it was the shock of discovering our income had been cut in half, but we had this crazy idea. Why not move away, try a completely different lifestyle?

We knew Ireland, having spent several vacations there--and Michael has Irish blood passed down from his grandfathers. We had always enjoyed fantastic holidays in Ireland, and it seemed such a *gentle* place, so why not give it a try? I had always yearned to live in the countryside, and Ireland certainly had plenty of that.

To be frank, it was all very impulsive. And maybe if I had thought longer about it, I'd still be serving a life sentence in that wretched old printing works. At that time, 17 years ago, Ireland's unemployment figures were ghastly, and we had no jobs lined up. My parents thought we were completely crazy. But we went anyway.

We rented a furnished house in County Sligo for the first few months while we were hunting around for a cottage to buy. Our daughter, Maggie, was dispatched to the local convent school—and if you have teenage girls yourself, you can probably imagine her reaction to a mud-brown uniform with mud-brown socks to match.

It's hard to believe now, but we went to Ireland with the idea of buying a home for less than $15,000. It took some months of searching, but we did eventually hit gold. We found a cozy cottage overlooking Lough Key in County Roscommon. This was just how I'd pictured country living: a huge garden where we could grow all our own vegetables, room enough to have a dog and three cats, a shop, and a couple of excellent pubs—all within a mile's walk. Plus we were surrounded by lovely neighbors—and, by the way, I can assure you that all those things you may have heard about Irish warmth and hospitality are true. (You'd better start developing a taste for strong tea and idle chit-chat now.)

Apart from the fact that we had to learn how to light fires and sweep chimneys (I was sure nobody had done this in England since Victorian times), the only fly in the ointment was our job situation. Michael had found work, but nobody seemed to want me. What could I do besides hiring myself out as a chimney sweep? My new enthusiasm for gardening seemed unlikely to pay dividends either. For some reason there didn't seem to be a market for tons of organically grown radishes, not in this corner of County Roscommon. Take it from one who knows: Do not sow four packets of radish seeds all at once.

Fortunately, I'd read one of those daft "You too can have a career as a writer" advertisements, and as luck would have it, the previous owner of our house had left behind an antique manual typewriter in the shed. Plus a collection of rubber Wellington boots with whiskey bottles buried inside them. I got really excited—until I discovered the bottles were all empty—but I did make use of the typewriter.

I decided to bash out a humorous article about our own search for the perfect Irish country cottage. I rambled on about real-estate agents taking us to see hovels with tin roofs and no bathroom facilities—mere shacks with no front doors. In fact, we even saw one where cows were using the kitchen as a barnyard. This was the first thing I'd ever written, and believe it or not, the property editor of a daily newspaper published it. She was kind enough to ask me for a follow-up, a factual piece outlining the kind of homes that were on sale in this forgotten corner of western Ireland.

Seventeen years on, we're still living in the same little cottage. Our daughter has married an Irishman, and we've acquired a bunch of grandkids—six in total. ("What are you trying to do?" I ask her. "Repopulate the west of Ireland all by yourself?") And my writing career has soared. . . .

Not only have I had books published, I also spend a fair bit of time traveling around Europe on behalf of an American magazine, writing about real estate. Would this have happened if I hadn't moved to Ireland? Don't think so. Chances are I'd still be on the other end of a telephone, explaining to irate customers why their printing orders weren't ready.

But here's the thing: I've never been tempted to move on again. Flying back from Portugal a week ago, the same tremendous thrill swept through me that I felt the first time I ever visited Ireland. My heart always lifts as the plane swoops over Dublin Bay, and once again I see my adopted homeland emerging from the mist.

I think what I'm trying to say is this: I love this country, and I can't imagine any reason why I'd want to say goodbye. After you've read this book, I very much hope that you too will come and experience the magic. It may be just for a visit, but then again, Ireland and its enchantments may keep you here forever. You have been warned!

—Steenie Harvey

© Steenie Harvey

Introduction

IRELAND

IRELAND

North Sea

Irish Sea

UK

ATLANTIC OCEAN

FRANCE

North Channel

Tory Island
Malin Head
Fanad Head
Rathlin Island
Aran Island
Lough Foyle
Londonderry
A26
Ballymena

ATLANTIC OCEAN

Rossan Point
Donegal
Donegal
NORTHERN IRELAND (UK)
Belfast
Strangford Lough

Donegal Bay
N15
Lough Erne
Lough Neagh

Erris Head
Sligo Bay
Sligo
Dundrum Bay

Belmullet
Achill Island
Sligo
N4
Leitrim
Monaghan
Cavan
Dundalk
Dundalk Bay

Mayo
N26
Castlebar
Roscommon
N61
Longford
N55
Louth
M1
Drogheda

Clare Island
Clew Bay
Lough Mask
N17
Lough Ree
Irish Sea

Inishturk
Inishbofin
Connemara
Lough Corrib
Tuam
N63
Galway
Athlone
Westmeath
N6
Meath
N4
N1

Galway
N6
Shannon
N62
Offaly
R. Liffey
Dublin
Dublin
N7
Wicklow

Galway Bay

Aran Islands
Clare
N18
Lough Derg
N7
Kildare
Laois
N9
Wicklow Mountains
Wicklow
Wicklow

Hag's Head
Ennis
River
N8
Carlow
N11

Loop Head
Limerick
Tipperary
Kilkenny
Wexford
St. George's Channel

Tralee Bay
N24
Limerick
N9
Rosslare Bay

Tralee
N21
N20
Carrick-on-Suir
Wexford

Killarney
Mallow
Waterford
Waterford
Ballyteige Bay

Kerry
Cork
N8
Dungarvan
N25

Kenmare River
Caha Mountains
River Lee
N22
Cork
Cork
Youghal Bay

Bantry
Galley Head
Cork Harbour

Mizen Head
Cape Clear
Old Head of Kinsale

Celtic Sea

N
W E
S

0 50 mi
0 50 km

© AVALON TRAVEL PUBLISHING, INC.

© Steenie Harvey

Welcome to Ireland

Wrapped in a soft green cloak of ancient memories, Ireland is one of the most beautiful and fascinating small countries in the world. Cast adrift in the Atlantic Ocean to the west of Britain, this jewel of an island has become one of Europe's most desirable addresses for those wishing to swap the stresses of city life for old-fashioned rural bliss.

Whether you hope to rent or buy a property, it's easy to acquire residency here. The renowned Irish welcome has never depended on the size of a person's bank balance. Maybe your idea of heaven is a little whitewashed cottage, maybe it's a thatched farmhouse, or maybe even an ivy-clad Georgian mansion. A pretty bungalow with ocean views? A centuries-old castle? A city apartment? Somewhere in Ireland you'll find your dream home waiting.

IS IRELAND RIGHT FOR YOU?

But why does Ireland exert such a pull on the imagination? What makes it so special? After all, anywhere that goes by the name of "the Emerald Isle"

3

certainly didn't get all its lush green meadows through having cloudless blue skies and unlimited sunshine. It has to be said that we can't boast of having the world's most glorious weather.

But constant sunshine isn't everything—most expatriates are enticed here for many of the same reasons vacationers are. Ireland lures expats and visitors alike with its unique amalgam of storybook scenery coupled with space, safe streets, and a far more gentle way of life. Along with an absorbing tangle of history, it also offers colorful festivals and curious traditions. What's more, its vibrant culture of music, dance, and poetry remains wonderfully intact and accessible to everybody. The country is so proud of its literary and cultural heritage that resident writers, artists, and musicians are allowed generous tax breaks. Here you're never considered too young or too old to learn to play the fiddle, take up painting, or write a masterpiece.

Here you're never considered too young or too old to learn to play the fiddle, take up painting, or write a masterpiece.

In our polluted world, the notion of a clean, green environment is hard to resist. Europe's industrial revolution hardly touched provincial Ireland. Between the bright lights of Dublin and the Atlantic's fossil shores, much of the country remains pleasingly rural, a pastoral haven of small farmsteads, quiet lanes, and rolling pasturelands. Particularly in the wilder reaches of the west, old-fashioned ways stubbornly survive with many communities clinging like limpets to the patterns of the seasons that departed from neighboring European countries generations ago.

Tradition is part and parcel of everyday life, not a tourist sideshow laid on by the heritage industry. Turf, the brown slabs of winter fuel, is still hand-cut from the bogs in many parts of Connemara. Some fishermen continue to put to sea in currachs, fragile hidebound rowing boats that have been used since Celtic times. Visit a horse fair such as Ballinasloe and you'll see deals conducted in old-fashioned style—with spits, handshakes, and the return of "luck money."

Yet the great paradox is that Ireland is also part of the new Europe, a modern country with good hospitals and top-class restaurants. Its capital, Dublin, is no stuffy museum-piece city but a place where you'll find cybercafés and a club scene as well as all that renowned Georgian architecture, traditional theater, and legendary pub crawls. And if you enjoy outdoor pursuits, there's plenty to keep you busy. The enviable array of activities includes sailing, hill walking, fishing, and riding to hounds (foxhunting), not to mention more than 350 superb golf courses. And although many of you may take a dim view of blasting our furry and feathered friends to kingdom come, shooting is also a tremendously popular country pursuit. Sunday afternoons are a favorite time for gun clubs to go rough shooting, something that remains an almost exclusively male activity. Even under deluge conditions, members of the unfairer sex will happily slosh their way through bog and ditch, potting whatever small game or wildfowl they and their gundogs can flush out: partridge, snipe, teal, rabbits, and so on.

Most Irish people enjoy good living standards and the economy is in great shape, combining steady growth with low inflation. Rather than laboring in smokestack industries, many of the country's young and highly educated workforce are employed in pharmaceuticals, telecommunications, and computers. Your new Irish neighbors are just as likely to be working at the cutting edge of technology as tending sheep and cattle.

The Lay of the Land

In contrast to many Irish home-buyers, the cityscape world of the workplace is what a lot of foreigners usually wish to escape. The majority of newcomers have a craving for nostalgia, preferring to seek out the quintessential Ireland of small towns and villages where everybody knows his or her neighbors. What they yearn for is a kind of Gaelic version of Paradise Lost, a picture-postcard country where the traffic is only a faint hum in the distance and timeless villages huddle below a backdrop of misty blue mountains. Thankfully that paradise is still pretty much intact.

Of course, that's not to say that you should write off Irish city life. For students and young professionals who need the cosmopolitan adrenaline rush, country life may perhaps prove a little too sleepy. So you may want to consider Dublin, Cork (Ireland's second city), or Galway—the country's self-styled Arts Capital.

Dublin, Ireland's political and financial capital, is a world-class city with ample opportunities for theatergoing, dining out, clubbing, and shopping. The country's most prestigious colleges, Trinity and UCD, are found here. Like all European capitals, it's a shining magnet for school-leavers from the provinces, constantly drawing new blood into its orbit.

Quiz—20 Teasers

1. The Republic of Ireland's flag is:
a) A gold harp on a green background.
b) A gold shamrock on a green background.
c) A tricolor of green, white and orange bands.

2. What should you do with a *crubeen*?
a) Eat it.
b) Wear it.
c) Show it to your doctor.

3. What's the name of Ireland's national airline?
a) Aer Fungus.
b) Aer Lingus.
c) Irlandia.

4. What's a *pishogue*?
a) A month-old piglet.
b) A spade for digging turf.
c) A fairy spell.

5. Sizewise, which is Ireland's largest county?
a) Dublin.
b) Cork.
c) Galway.

6. What can be heard in Dáil Éireann?

a) Political debate.
b) Opera music.
c) Silence.

7. Roddy Doyle and Maeve Binchy are?
a) Novelists.
b) Musicians.
c) Politicians.

8. What's a *sheila-na-gig*?
a) A spinning wheel.
b) A pagan fertility symbol.
c) A pony and trap.

9. Which film director made *The Quiet Man*?
a) Steven Spielberg.
b) Francis Ford Coppola.
c) John Ford.

10. Who is Ireland's president?
a) Mary McAleese.
b) Mary Robinson.
c) Bertie Ahern.

11. What color are Irish mailboxes?
a) Red.
b) Yellow.
c) Green.

12. What's a *Ban Garda*?
a) A sticky tea-bread.

b) A female police officer.
c) A blanket ban on immoral publications.

13. Who wrote Ulysses?
a) W. B.Yeats.
b) James Joyce.
c) Samuel Beckett.

14. Where are the Cliffs of Moher?
a) Clare.
b) Kerry.
c) Donegal.

15. In an Irish place-name the word *cnoc* means:
a) Fortress.
b) Church.
c) Hill.

16. How do you pronounce "lough," the usual word for an Irish lake?
a) Luff.
b) Low.
c) Lock.

17. Why would you go into a turf accountant's office?
a) To buy turf.
b) To place a bet.
c) To buy a horse.

18. When was the Battle of the Boyne?
a) 1690.
b) 1916.
c) 1140.

19) The Romans called Ireland "Hibernia." It means:
a) Land of Winter.
b) Land of Water.
c) Land of Dreams.

20. In Irish, what's an "Mei riceánach"?
a) A mercenary.
b) An American.
c) A missionary.

Answers: 1-c; 2-a; 3-b; 4-c; 5-b; 6-a; 7-a; 8-b; 9-c; 10-a; 11-c; 12-b; 13-b; 14-a; 15-c; 16-c; 17-b; 18-a; 19-a; 20-b.
Score: 16–20. Clever clogs! You've been here before, haven't you?
10–16. Well done! You obviously have a love for all things Irish.
5–10. Ah well, everyone admires a trier!
Under 5. Hmm. I'd like to be in the doctor's surgery when you show him your *crubeen*. (It's a pig's trotter!)

While this creates an exciting buzz, the downside of Dublin living is that it goes hand in hand with the country's highest house prices and rents.

With stunning seascapes on the doorstep, Cork and Galway are more affordable—and they're also top-class cities in their own right. In 2005, the title of European Capital of Culture passed to Cork—a good excuse for this City of Festivals to indulge in a yearlong festival. The Cork Jazz Festival, the International Choral Festival, and the International Film Festival are regular annual events.

Waterford in the southeast is another attractive option if you're seeking city life on a smaller scale. But by American standards it is a very small city, numbering fewer than 50,000 people. A working port, Waterford holds the distinction of being Ireland's oldest urban settlement. Vikings built a trading settlement here back in A.D. 850.

Dublin and Galway especially have long been a popular choice for foreign students wishing to brush up their English in language schools. Once school is out, the city streets become a hubbub of Italian, Spanish, and Portuguese. You can sometimes find yourself wondering what country you're in.

I realize I haven't really answered the "where should you live" question, but it's impossible to pinpoint any one county as being the place to head for. The entire western seaboard is a rugged patchwork of loughs, mountains, and offshore islands that's just as spine-tingling and heart-wrenchingly beautiful as imagination always promised. Alternatively, you may prefer the less well-known coastal villages of Ireland's sunnier southeast corner or the lush river valleys of an inland county such as Kilkenny. But even if you choose to live inland or in the middle of a buzzy city you'll never be too far away from the sea and the delights of crescent moon coves, craggy cliffs, and golden-sand beaches.

MYTH VS. REALITY

Complementing all the attractions for the eye is balm for the soul. The rich layer cake of Irish myth and tradition is just one awaiting feast. The call of the past is another. Laced with pilgrim paths, waymarked with countless historical remains, Ireland once shimmered at the very edge of medieval Christendom. This remote island outpost of saints and scholars was where the maps ran out and the known world ended.

For anyone with even a smidgen of romance in his or her soul, the allure of long ago is irresistible. The early Irish bequeathed an incomparably rich legacy—not just of ornately carved crosses and high round towers, but a huge trove of folklore, manuscript illumination, and gold and silver craftsmanship. Celtic metalsmiths produced sumptuous treasures, often decorated with enamel-work stylized animals and studded with amber and rock crystal. Masterpieces such as the Tara Brooch and Ardagh Chalice have never been equaled, let alone surpassed.

Ever yearned to slip through a crack in time and connect with the long-gone world of myth and magic? Countless localities resonate with even older messages than those left by the scholarly Celtic monks who darkened the druidic balefires with the beacon of Christianity. Ireland is a land with a thoroughly pagan past, a twilight realm of mysterious stone circles, hollow hills, and prehistoric earthen burial mounds known as "fairy raths." Every mirror-bright lough and green-cloaked mountain seems spellbound by enchantments: Listen hard and the westerly winds still carry the fading whisper of otherworldly voices.

A cliché it may be, but Ireland really is one of the friendliest, safest and most relaxing countries in which to live.

The midsummer bonfires of Saint John's Eve are but a continuation of the ancient fires lit in honor of the goddess Danu. Halloween originates from the great feast of Samhain, when the door to the Celtic otherworld was said to creak fully open. The Garland Sunday pilgrimage to Croagh Patrick (now a holy mountain but once a pagan sun sanctuary) takes place around Lughnasa, a Celtic feast that celebrated the onset of harvesttime. So does Kerry's Puck Fair, an age-old festival where a goat is hoisted aloft on a platform to oversee the shenanigans. You never have to scratch very hard below the surface to touch the pulse beat of Ireland's ever-present Celtic past.

The famous (or infamous) laid-back lifestyle of the Irish people is another good reason to bid farewell to the rat race. A cliché it may be, but Ireland really is one of the friendliest, safest, and most relaxing countries in which to live. It's a caring society where people are still more important than profits. Hospital treatment is free and if you need medical attention, you'll find family doctors make house calls—even if it's the middle of the night.

Whether you're looking for a retirement destination, a holiday home, or a place to raise a young family, Ireland is easy to fall in love with. Yes, the clouds do sometimes leak but contrary to wicked rumors, we often enjoy dry days and sunshine too.

The drawbacks? Well, Ireland isn't an especially inexpensive place to live and you'll certainly find the cost of running a car is higher than at home. And although it's still possible to buy cottages for under $150,000, nowadays much depends upon location. A fairly substantial prosperity gap exists between Ireland's eastern seaboard and many western communities. For anything resembling a bargain-priced home, it's necessary to look to rural areas where the Celtic tiger is yet to roar. Dublin and its surrounding counties have benefited most from the booming economy and this translates into property values. House prices in these pockets of affluence have now surpassed many other major European cities. To experience the Dublin lifestyle, you may have to consider renting rather than buying.

But wherever you choose to live, you won't pay property taxes. And many of you will be able to travel around for absolutely nothing—all qualified retirees travel free on the country's public transport systems. Seniors entitled to Irish citizenship or who are receiving Social Security pensions may also be able to benefit from an additional number of free health and welfare plans for older people. Who says that age doesn't have its advantages?

Although relocating to another country is always going to be a bold move, it's a blessing to know that here you won't have the constant frustration of trying to communicate in a foreign language. Well, not unless you go to live in one of the Gaeltacht areas where the ancient

© Steenie Harvey

Schull, County Cork

Irish language is still spoken. OK, it may take you a while to decipher the different Irish accents but folks here do speak English. Some Americans come here to enjoy new adventures. For others it often feels more like coming home. It's estimated that around 70 million people throughout the world have what you might call emerald-green blood coursing through their veins, largely because of the tragic famine years and the resulting Irish diaspora. But that doesn't mean you need Irish ancestry to make new friends and fully appreciate the quality of life here. Whatever your own ancestral background, you'll certainly find the phrase *Céad Míle Fáilte* (a hundred thousand welcomes) applies to you too.

COUNTRY DIVISIONS

Comprising a total area of 84,421 square kilometers (52,456 square miles), Ireland lies in the Atlantic Ocean at the extreme edge of northwestern Europe. If numbers mean nothing to you, imagine the island as being a little larger than West Virginia.

In 1920, Britain's Government of Ireland Act partitioned Ireland into north and south. Understanding how to refer to the two different parts of the island can sometimes baffle foreigners. More than 75 percent—70,282 square kilometers (43,671 square miles)—of the land mass forms the Republic of Ireland (southern Ireland). Official documents often refer to the Republic as "the State." You've probably also seen the word Éire. This, the Irish-language title for the island of Ireland, is rarely used in everyday speech. Éire is normally restricted to texts in the Irish language.

Living Abroad in Ireland deals only with the Republic of Ireland— effectively southern Ireland. Northern Ireland has a separate identity—it's a different political jurisdiction with different laws, money, residency rules, and property-buying procedures.

To further muddy the waters, the island of Ireland is divided into the same four provinces as before partition. Roughly corresponding to north, south, east, and west, these provinces are called Ulster, Munster, Leinster, and Connacht. Although Ulster is often used as a synonym for Northern Ireland, three counties within this province actually lie within the republic's territory.

The four provinces are subdivided into 32 counties: 26 in the Republic of Ireland and six in Northern Ireland. The republic's largest county is Cork, the smallest is Louth. The capital of the Irish Republic

Climate Chart for Dublin

Month	Temperature °F average max	°F average min	Rainfall average inches
Jan	46	37	3
Feb	46	38	2
Mar	49	39	2
April	52	41	2
May	57	45	2
June	62	50	2
July	66	54	2
Aug	65	53	3
Sept	61	50	3
Oct	55	46	3
Nov	50	41	3
Dec	47	39	3

is Dublin, which is also the country's main commercial port; Northern Ireland's principal city is Belfast.

Leinster Province takes in the counties of Carlow, Dublin, Kildare, Kilkenny, Laois, Longford, Louth, Meath, Offaly, Westmeath, Wexford, and Wicklow.

Munster Province is made up of Clare, Cork, Kerry, Limerick, Tipperary, and Waterford.

Connacht Province is counties Galway, Leitrim, Mayo, Roscommon, and Sligo.

Ulster Province includes the southern Irish counties of Cavan, Donegal, and Monaghan. The six countries of Northern Ireland that belong to Ulster Province are Antrim, Fermanagh, Tyrone, Armagh, Londonderry, and Down.

A highland fringe of hills and mountains hems the island's interior

Climate Chart for Valentia (County Kerry)

Month	Temperature °F average max	°F average min	Rainfall average inches
Jan	48	41	6.6
Feb	48	39	4.3
Mar	52	41	4.1
April	55	43	3
May	59	46	3.4
June	63	52	3.2
July	64	54	4.3
Aug	64	55	3.8
Sept	63	52	4.9
Oct	57	48	5.6
Nov	54	45	6
Dec	50	43	6.7

of fertile rolling plains, loughs, and river valleys: The western Atlantic coast is especially inviting with sandy coves tucked away between cliffs and rocky headlands. Hills march in an almost continuous chain from Donegal to west Cork, with the highest pinnacles clustering in the southwest. County Kerry's dramatic landscapes include Carrantuohill, at 1,038 meters (3,406 feet) Ireland's highest mountain.

Ireland's longest river is the Shannon, a 259-kilometer (161-mile) water highway that forms a glittering necklace of loughs as it meanders in a southwesterly direction from its source (the Shannon Pot) in County Cavan. Other notable rivers include the Liffey, which runs through Dublin, and Cork's River Lee. In the northeast, the banks of the Boyne River witnessed a bloody battle between Catholic and Protestant forces in 1690.

Almost 17 percent of the country is covered by peat bogs. Mainly found in the west and midlands, peat bogs are made up of water and decayed vegetation and were formed around 8,000–10,000 years ago. Two types of bogs—raised bogs and blanket bogs—provide fuel for domestic and industrial usage. Peat (or turf as it is usually called in Ireland) is mostly harvested by machine nowadays, but in some communities it continues to be cut by hand.

WEATHER

As far as the weather is concerned, Ireland knows little about typhoons, ice storms, or killer heat waves. Influenced by the Gulf Stream, the mild maritime climate is remarkably consistent with few extremes. Seasonal temperatures hardly vary throughout the entire country and April in Dublin feels much the same as April in Galway. Although it occasionally gets hot, it's never too hot. Winter sometimes results in a few chilly days but heavy snowfalls are rare except in mountainous areas.

The coldest months are usually January and February with mean daily air temperatures hovering in the upper 40s Fahrenheit. July and August tend to be warmest: in the mid-60s Fahrenheit on average, though the mercury has risen to 80°F on rare occasions. May and June usually produce the most sunshine, averaging 5–7 hours per day.

The driest months are April, May, and June but rainfall levels shouldn't be underestimated. The west's picture-postcard landscapes get it in bucketfuls and you may find yourself opening an umbrella on as many as 270 days of the year. A couple of years ago, the small town of Crossmolina in County Mayo endured 3.5 months of continuous rainfall. The likeliest place to escape a drenching is the southeast, where cloudbursts may produce only an annual 750 millimeters (30 inches). In low-lying midland areas, average rainfall usually amounts to between 800 millimeters and 1,200 millimeters (31–47 inches). Parts of the west regularly receive an annual 1,500 millimeters (59 inches), while the mountainous southwest often experiences a monsoonlike 2,000 millimeters (79 inches) or more.

FLORA AND FAUNA

From its limpid loughs to its encircling seas, Ireland is a world of water. Rivers and loughs are the habitats of wild salmon, brown trout, char, eel, pike, and bream—and also the haunt of the reclusive otter that feasts upon them. Seals bask along rocky coasts and Dingle has a famous resident wild dolphin. Of Ireland's 31 species of mammals, the ones you're most likely to spot are rabbits, foxes, and badgers. Hares, stoats, and squirrels are also common; smaller species include hedgehogs, field mice, and shrews. Elusive pine martens are found in forests and the country also supports herds of red deer, notably in Kerry and Donegal. And the legend is true—there are no snakes. Ireland's only amphibians are a solitary species each of toad, frog, and newt and a single reptile, the common lizard.

About 380 species of wild birds have been recorded with 135 breeding here. Year-round residents that feed in gardens include various types of finches and tits, blackbirds, song thrushes, and red-breasted robins. Walk by a lough and you'll often glimpse the turquoise flash of a kingfisher or a solitary gray heron flapping towards its reedbed hideaway. Summer migrants include swallows, swifts, and various kinds of woodland warblers; winter visitors include fieldfares from Scandinavia and white-fronted geese from Greenland—around half the world's population overwinters around Wexford. The thousands of miles of unspoiled coastline offer excellent opportunities for viewing seabirds such as cormorants, stormy petrels, and puffins.

Flowers refuse to be confined tidily to gardens and the seasonal colorfest explodes in spring with a blaze of wild pink rhododendrons, bluebells, and lacy May blossom. In summertime, hedgerows glow with crimson fuchsia flowers, charmingly known in the old Irish language as *Deora Dé* (the tears of God). You don't need a botany degree to appreciate a stroll along the crooked trackways of Clare's Burren region, a stony wilderness that blooms into a rock garden of orchids, gentians, and other rare wildflowers throughout spring and early summer.

During fall, woods are scented with the earthy smells of wild mushrooms; the hedgerows provide feasts of wild blackberries, hazelnuts, and elderberries—still often used in home winemaking.

Social Climate

When I tell any non-Irish person where I live, for some reason "the pub" is always mentioned. For many Americans, it may be a shock to see the joys of alcohol so keenly promoted—and so enthusiastically enjoyed.

Even visiting dignitaries usually get photographed in a pub with a pint of creamy-topped black stout. However, some campaigners believe this is not the kind of image Ireland should encourage. Although it isn't suggested we should stop foreign visitors from having a few drinks (or more than a few drinks), a tide of moralistic hysteria seems to have swept across the country recently. In 2004, politicians forced us to stop smoking in pubs, restaurants, and all public places. Now we're being pressured to sober up too.

Health professionals believe the country is paying dearly for its drinking culture. With higher incomes, people are spending more money than ever on drink. Since 1989, alcohol consumption has risen by nearly 50 percent. Alcohol abuse is estimated to cost the country 2.4 billion euros per year. A hospital accident and emergency department on a Saturday night is no place for the weak-kneed or fainthearted.

When President Mary McAleese spoke to Irish Americans in the United States last year, she mentioned Ireland's "dark side." She said the nation had a ridiculously unhealthy attitude toward alcohol. Binge drinking is becoming a major problem among teenagers and young adults. (If you're unfamiliar with the phrase, binge drinking is consuming lots of alcohol in a short time simply to get drunk.) One recent survey indicated that more than half of Ireland's youngsters experiment with alcohol before the age of 12. Once they reach the 15–16 age group, 50 percent of girls and 66 percent of boys are drinkers. The identity cards now demanded by publicans have had little effect. Older brothers or sisters willingly visit the supermarket to buy supplies for their siblings. If you have youngsters, the message is to keep a close eye on what they're up to.

As Ireland is such a small country, there is no distinct regional variation regarding social attitudes and lifestyles—regarding drink or anything else. However, there is something of an urban/rural divide. People tend to be more conservative on the so-called "moral issues" outside the cities and well-known tourist areas. 1995's referendum to allow divorce was passed by a mere 9,000 votes and a majority of voters in six of Ireland's rural constituencies actually voted "No" by margins of more than 25 percent. There was no obvious regional pattern to this—the six constituencies registering the strongest opposition were scattered throughout the entire country: Cork Northwest, Limerick West, Galway East, Mayo East, Cavan-Monaghan, and Longford-Roscommon. If the undiluted family values of "holy Ireland" appeal to you, you'll be cheered to know they still hold sway in these deeply traditional rural strongholds.

In both city and countryside, favorite conversation topics include house prices and vacations. In years gone by, only wealthy Irish people vacationed abroad. Most families had little extra cash for luxuries. It took months of hard saving to manage a week away at traditional Irish seaside resorts such as Bundoran or Tramore. But with increasing incomes and cheap airfares,

© Steenie Harvey

Galway's Connemara region

foreign travel is booming. It's now quite common for many Irish families to have two or three overseas vacations a year.

With flights on budget airlines often being cheaper than a train ticket, you'll find that many Irish people have become almost blasé about travel. The most popular destination is Spain and its islands—and not just for holidays. After cashing in on savvy investments in the home market, sizable numbers of Irish families now own homes in Spain too. My last conversation with a Dublin cabby was about his property investments on the Costa del Sol!

Make no mistake, wealth has brought tremendous changes to Ireland in the past decade or so. For example, I can't think of anybody who doesn't own a cellular phone—even most 10-year-olds now have one. (Plus their own TV, computer, and Playstation.) There are many more cars on the roads—more than a million households own at least one vehicle. From my own experience, I'd have to say motorists have become more aggressive and driving is no longer the pleasure it used to be. Driving under the influence of alcohol is an offense, but it is widespread—and also socially condoned.

As an incomer myself, one thing that still surprises me is how willingly Irish people accept what can often be fairly shoddy standards and services. Long queues in banks, even longer queues in post offices—but nobody murmurs a word of complaint. None either about waiting in the doctor's or dentist's office for more than an hour after your allotted appointment time. And with a booming economy, it's baffling why travelers are still forced to stand in the rain getting soaked at Dublin airport's taxi rank. As for Dublin's central bus terminal, Busaras, it's no exaggeration to say it resembles a tramp's night shelter. For a capital city, it's an utter disgrace.

IRELAND AND FOREIGNERS

As an American, maybe you're wondering how your countrymen are regarded in Ireland. In general, pretty favorably but you'll have to get used to being known as "the Yanks," even if you hail from deepest Alabama.

Although there are occasional grouses about the creeping Americanization of Irish life (the march of McDonald's, TV schedules crammed with idiotic soaps and chat shows), it's almost impossible for the Irish to think too harshly of a country that acted so generously to their ancestors. Centuries of emigration means many Irish families have American relatives somewhere in the background.

Whereas in many countries it may be unwise to air a particular political viewpoint, Ireland thrives on argument and debate. The debate may often get heated, but things never come to blows.

That said, Ireland is a highly politicized society. Don't expect everyone you meet to agree with American foreign policy. When it comes to global affairs, Ireland instinctively sympathizes with the perceived underdog and invariably advocates diplomacy rather than military action. But whereas in many countries it may be unwise to air a particular political viewpoint, Ireland thrives on argument and debate. The debate may often get heated, but things never come to blows.

Despite the Irish reputation for friendliness, racial prejudice occasionally surfaces. In recent years, certain marginalized peoples from throughout the world have targeted Ireland as a country with fairly lax asylum laws.

This has led to resentments, particularly against Romanian gypsies, who are regarded as economic migrants rather than genuine refugees. Some commentators (and many Dublin taxi drivers freely comment on the subject) think it's wrong that such migrants are readily found accommodation while little is done for homeless Irish people. African refugees have also reported incidents of racial abuse, especially in inner-city Dublin. For refugees who do encounter racism, it must seem ironic that so many past generations of Irish people emigrated to create better lives overseas.

Ireland also has its own marginalized section of society—the tinkers, or traveling people as they prefer to be called. There are around 10,800 travelers within the country and very few "settled" Irish people have a good word to say about them. Prejudice runs high, and whether justified or not, any outbreak of petty crime is invariably put down to tinkers. Journeying between halting sites and litter-strewn roadside rest stops, few tinkers wander the roads in horse-drawn caravans any longer. The barrel-shaped Romany *vado* wagons have long since been replaced by unromantic modern trailer-homes.

Some say the tinkers are descended from orphans cast out on the roads during the famine, others that they share distant kinship with European gypsies. Close-knit communities who still produce large families, their average lifespan is shockingly low: Census figures suggest that only 1 percent of travelers can expect to live longer than the age of 65. Tinkers once made a living by tinsmithing and horse-dealing but although they still congregate at horse fairs, no housewife requires her pots and pans to be mended by nomads these days. Most menfolk now deal in scrap metal and used car parts and it's not uncommon to see traveler children begging. At festivals, some women make money by telling fortunes.

© Steenie Harvey

History, Government, and Economy

Ireland's history has been shaped by invasions. Can any other country have been battled over so fiercely or so long? Head-hunting Celts were later followed by marauding Vikings, land-hungry Anglo-Norman knights by armies of the British Crown. For good or ill, each successive wave of invaders left its mark.

History

CELTIC IRELAND
One of Ireland's most fascinating historical chapters is that of those early invaders: the Celts. Evoking dreams of a glorious heritage, their legacy never fails to kindle the imagination. Yet much of what we *think*

Prehistory

Ireland's turbulent tale begins soon after the Ice Age, 10,000 years ago. The first inhabitants, who may have came via Scotland, were hunter-gatherers who left little evidence of their lifestyle. Small communties developed only with the arrival of Neolithic tribes around 5000 B.C. Raising cattle in stone-walled fields, building hill forts, Ireland's Stone Age farmers also practiced elaborate funerary rites. The island's thousands of Neolithic sites include the chambered passage tombs at Newgrange (County Meath), mysteriously decorated with cosmic symbols.

One of Europe's most famous prehistoric centers, Newgrange existed long before the Celts invaded. When dawn breaks on the morning of the winter solstice (December 21), a pencil-thin ray of sunlight creeps along the passageway and illuminates the lightless inner chamber. On the shortest day of the northern year, was this perhaps a symbol of rebirth? Nobody knows the real explanation for why Newgrange was built but it remains a remarkable feat of Stone Age engineering.

we know about the Celts is based on guesswork. Theirs was an oral tradition and they left no written records.

It's generally presumed they were Iron Age warrior tribes from central Europe who migrated northwest, reaching Ireland around 500 B.C. However, folklore clouds the issue with some tales having the Celts originating from Spain. Wackier myths moot the theory that Ireland's Celtic forebears sprang from doomed Atlantis, whose people had migrated to Mediterranean and Middle Eastern regions several millennia before.

Like their origins, the customs of Ireland's early Celts are also shrouded in historical mist. Their stories weren't recorded until centuries later, when Christianity had eclipsed the old pagan beliefs. What is indisputable is that they brought with them a new language, a tremendous appetite for feasting and drinking, and an ability to fashion native gold into highly decorative jewelry and weapons. Their bloodthirsty Earth gods took their places in the existing pantheon of Irish deities, becoming part of the mysterious "Otherworld."

Tantalizing glimpses of that Otherworld appear in folklore, place-names, and symbolic carvings such as the lasciviously grinning fertility figures known as *sheila-na-gigs*. The Celts had a great veneration for the forces of nature and other stone figures may portray the guardian spirits of wells, rivers, and sacred trees. One winter's afternoon, in an overgrown graveyard on Fermanagh's Boa Island, I gazed upon the

The Celtic Calendar

The Celts dated the beginning of their year from **Samhain** (SOW-an). This was the most important of the annual festivals. Not only did it mark the passing of the old year and the end of the grazing season, but it was also a symbolic occasion of death and rebirth. Surplus livestock were brought down from mountain pastures to be slaughtered; hearth fires died and didn't blaze again until the great ritual balefires of the Druids had been lit. Samhain wasn't a time to be far from home for this was when the invisible veil between the mortal world and the Otherworld got torn asunder. Who could say what supernatural dangers lurked in the lengthening shadows? The Christian church rechristened the feast as All Hallows, and All Hallows' Eve (October 31) lives on today as Hallowe'en.

Imbolc corresponds to February 1, Saint Brigid's Day. A pastoral festival, it marked the start of the lambing season and the first lactation of the ewes. It was dedicated to the pagan fire-goddess Brigid, who was associated with fertility and crafts. Made from straw, the Saint Brigid's crosses often seen in Irish homes may have more of a heathen than a Christian origin.

Beltane (Beltanny) fell on May Day. May 1 heralded the advent of summer in the Celtic lands and was a frolicsome festival of regeneration. May bushes were decorated with spring flowers to appease the spirits of the land; cattle were driven through the charmed smoke of the Beltane bonfires to give them protection in their summer pastures.

August 1 was **Lughnasa** (Loonasa) and harvest-home. It was dedicated to the god Lugh and a symbolic loaf was baked for him from the first corn. The Christian calendar transformed Lughnasa into Lammas but it remains an auspicious day for digging up the first potatoes. On Ulster's north Antrim coast, the Ould Lammas Fair at Ballycastle is one of Ireland's oldest-known harvest gatherings.

implacable features of a two-faced January God. Definitely no Christian figure, his exaggerated eyes stared both forward into the realm of men and backward into some unknown twilight. It was an uncanny sensation, realizing that this cross-limbed idol had watched the sun go down long before Saint Patrick ever reached these shores.

Although the observations of classical writers relate only to mainland Europe, Ireland's Celts probably had similar customs to their continental cousins. According to Julius Caesar, their Druid priests taught that souls were immortal and passed after death into another body. They also believed that all men were descended from the god of the underworld. To Irish Celts this was Donn, "the Dark One."

Common to the entire Celtic world was the Cult of the Head. Much as crucifixes represent Christianity, the Celts' foremost religious symbol was the human head. Even when parted from the body, heads possessed numerous mystical powers. In myths, severed heads sing, prophesy, tell stories, and preside over warriors' banquets. Most important of all, these grisly trophies also protected against the unbenign forces of the Otherworld. It's not only literature that suggests Celtic Ireland enthusiastically collected human heads; skulls excavated from hill forts have shown the marks of nails where they were suspended from gateways.

CHRISTIANS AND VIKINGS

Ireland's Celts escaped the acquisitive clutches of the Roman Empire but their animistic world began to disintegrate once Christianity arrived. This was a bloodless invasion and conversion came slowly. By the time Saint Patrick was brought to Ireland as a slave (circa A.D. 405), most inhabitants remained under the sway of pagan religions. To help foster the new faith, the early monks of what became known as the Celtic Church built places of worship on sites sacred to the Druids: in woodland groves or beside healing springs and wells. One pagan goddess, Brigid, even found herself Christianized and elevated to sainthood.

By A.D. 563, monastic settlements had grown sufficiently in size and numbers to export missionaries. Columba's Hebridean foundation on Iona is well known, but other Irish monks also established centers in mainland Europe. Within Ireland itself, monastic communities at sites such as Clonmacnoise, Kildare, and Clonard became major seats of learning in a period tagged "the Golden Age." It was in such monasteries that gospels were elaborately illuminated and tales about the old heroes and gods recorded.

Along with European trade, Ireland inherited its first coinage from the Vikings. Who knows—one day you may dig up a 1,000-year-old King Sitric silver penny.

Despite Christian teachings, Celtic magic and mystery hadn't fled Ireland's landscape. News from the annals has showers of honey and blood raining down in the year A.D. 717. In A.D. 752, a whale came ashore bearing three teeth of solid gold, each weighing 50 ounces. And the fiery ships seen in the air in A.D. 784 were perhaps a dire portent of a new invasion force. Many of the fledgling abbeys and churches were soon to be rededicated into temples to Odin; prayers and plainsong replaced by lusty drinking bouts and sagas about Valhalla and its shieldmaidens.

"The wind is fierce tonight, it tosses the sea's white hair. I fear no wild Vikings sailing the main," penned one optimistic monk. But come the

Faces from the Celtic Past

mighty dragon ships did. From A.D. 795, Ireland was subjected to sporadic Viking attacks and by A.D. 823 the Norsemen had rounded the coastline. Vikings craved booty like vampires crave blood and Ireland's great rivers served as watery highways to fabulous prizes: the wealthy inland monasteries. In A.D. 842, Clonmacnoise was burnt and pillaged by a Viking named Turgesius. His wife apparently used one of the altars to give out oracles.

The Viking Age lasted until the 11th century. Early raiders returned to Scandinavia with their treasures but they quickly began settling in Ireland, first in winter quarters and then more permanently. Alliances with local chiefs and intermarriages gave the invaders a secure footing to establish trading posts: Dublin, Limerick, Waterford, and Wexford all have Viking origins.

Along with European trade, Ireland inherited its first coinage from the Vikings. Who knows—one day you may dig up a 1,000-year-old King Sitric silver penny. And although the Celtic Church was never to recapture its glory days, many of the invaders eventually embraced Christianity. The ancient cathedral in the Shannonside town of Killaloe repays a visit as it's home to Thorgrim's cross, which carries a blessing in Norse runic script.

THE MIDDLE AGES

For centuries Ireland's petty kingdoms (80–100) had battled over territory, cattle, and women. Now control of trade meant control of wealth. A powerful dynasty under the kingship of Brian Boru emerged. Brian set out to win high kingship and by 1011 had achieved his goal. However, "the Emperor of the Irish" didn't enjoy his position for long. A Viking-aided revolt against the king ended with the Battle of Clontarf in 1014. Brian's side won, but he himself was killed.

With Brian's death, Ireland returned to tribal squabblings. In 1166, control of Dublin was wrested from a very aggrieved Dermot MacMurrough. Dermot fled to Britain in search of mercenaries to help gain back his kingdom—a move that had far-reaching consequences.

Saint Patrick

Ireland's patron saint is popularly credited with copper-fastening Christianity in 5th-century Ireland. But although Saint Patrick is a worldwide symbol of Irish identity, you may be surprised to learn that he wasn't Irish at all. In his own *Confessio* (a type of spiritual biography), the saint tells us he was born in Britain, in a Roman settlement called Bannavem Taburniae. Where exactly this village was is a bit of an unsolved mystery—guesses vary from Wales up to the Scottish borders. What is clear is that Patrick came from a wealthy family of priests and minor officials; his father, the deacon Calpurnius, owned a villa.

Imagine coming from such a background and then finding yourself kidnapped and sold to an uncouth Irish chieftain. That's what happened to the 16-year-old Patrick. Instead of continuing his studies, he was forced to tend his new master's pigs and sheep in the bitter winds of a northern winter. Snatched from his home by marauding pirates, the youth lived as a slave in Ireland until escaping to France, and thence home, on another pagan ship. He later returned to France and entered the priesthood. Believed to have been ordained as a bishop by the pope, he returned to Ireland as a missionary in A.D. 432, landing at Saul in Northern Ireland's County Down. There he made his first convert—a local chieftain named Díchú.

Numerous places, north and south, have links with Saint Patrick. Legend tells that he lit a Paschal (Easter) fire on the Hill of Slane in County Meath as a challenge to the pagan king of Tara. He also apparently visited the Rock of Cashel in County Tipperary for a conversion ceremony in which he accidentally pierced the local king's foot with his crosier. Thinking this was an important part of Christian ritual, the king suffered his pain in silence!

Both Slane and Cashel claim to be the place where Saint Patrick plucked a shamrock leaf to explain the concept of the Holy Trinity. As most people know, Saint Patrick's Day is March 17th.

Ireland's next invaders entered with the clink of chain mail and clash of broadswords. The first Anglo-Norman knights arrived in 1169 and after recapturing Dermot's territories they began invading adjoining kingdoms. This was Ireland's first taste of English rule. Although nobody could have guessed it at the time, it was to endure for more than seven centuries.

As the 13th century progressed, the Anglo-Normans imposed themselves on about three-quarters of the land, building castles and fortified towns such as those at Limerick, Trim, and Waterford. Like the Vikings before them, many secured their position by marrying into Irish clans. But by the mid-1300s, both natives and newcomers were terrorized by a new and sinister invasion: bubonic plague. Carried by rats, the "Black Death" killed around half the population, some 750,000 people. England's writ of authority shrank to a small area around Dublin known as "the Pale." In case you've ever wondered, that's how the term "beyond the pale" originated.

EARLY MODERN PERIOD

Ireland's fortunes plummeted when England's Henry VIII (the one with the six wives) broke with the Catholic Church. He also declared himself king of Ireland, a title successive monarchs resolutely hung on to. Under the Tudor and Stuart dynasties of the 16th and 17th centuries, Ireland was subjected to a new kind of "invasion": colonization. These were confusing times with a dizzy array of Protestant monarchs succeeding Catholic monarchs and vice versa. Religion became a major factor in Ireland's colonization process and previous generations of English settlers were often uprooted to make way for new royal favorites.

The seeds of Ulster's troubles were sown in 1607, when it was opened for expansion by England's new Protestant king, James I. In an episode known as the Plantation of Ulster, it was decreed that settlers should outnumber the Irish, who mostly remained loyal to the Roman Catholic religion.

"Undertakers," new arrivals from England and Scotland who guaranteed to bring 10 Protestant families with them, were given land completely cleared of natives. "Servitors," who had served the crown in some fashion, were allowed to retain some native labor for an increase of 50 percent on rent. Finally, any "deserving Irish" were allowed to rent land for double the normal rate. Areas remained segregated: Scots here, English there, Irish somewhere else. Around 100,000 Protestant settlers arrived between 1610 and 1640. Unlike the Celts, Vikings, and Normans, this new batch of invaders rarely integrated.

In 1641, as the English Parliament vied with its monarchy for absolute power, Ulster's native Irish took up arms. Around 2,000 Protestant settlers were murdered but civil war raging in England prevented any large-scale measures against the rebels. It was 1649 before action was taken against Ireland's unruly dispossessed.

CROMWELL AND THE PENAL TIMES

Retribution came courtesy of England's "Lord Protector," Oliver Cromwell, the villainous bogeyman of Irish history. With England's civil war over, his victorious Parliamentary Army set sail for Ireland. Heading a 20,000-strong invasion force, Cromwell quickly crushed the rebellion, butchering the citizens of Drogheda and Wexford in the process. Widespread confiscation of estates was accompanied by the banishment of thousands of Irish citizens to the country's poorest lands. Like Cromwell himself, the infamous diktat of "To hell or Connacht" still arouses bitterness.

Catholicism in the form of public worship became illegal as Cromwell considered demands for the right to celebrate Mass as "abominable." Yet the Mass continued in secret, often being held in places sacred to the old Celtic religion: remote woodland glades or mountain areas where large boulders made for improvised altars. In memory of those times, an annual outdoor Mass is still celebrated at many such sites today.

In 1685, after more than a century of unbroken Protestant rule, Britain and Ireland found themselves with a new Catholic king, James II. Although the contrary-minded James had quite lawfully succeeded his brother (Charles II) who died without legitimate offspring, the English establishment was staunchly opposed to "popery." It decided the best way to keep the Protestant flag flying was by deposing James and depriving his son of any succession rights.

The throne was offered to a Dutchman, William of Orange. Backing his claim with force, William's troops inflicted rapid defeats on the king's loyal forces in England. The conflict moved to Ireland, where the deposed monarch again lost crucial battles, including the decisive Battle of the Boyne in 1690. That victory by Protestant King Billy (William of Orange) over Catholic James Stuart is still celebrated by many Ulstermen every July 12th.

Even though he died nigh on 300 years ago, William of Orange's name still echoes down the centuries. An icon within Northern Ireland's Unionist culture, Dutch William appears on countless banners during the Easter to July marching season. It explains why Ulster Protestants are known as Orangemen and their meeting places as Orange Lodges.

Penal laws for the governance of Ireland were quickly enacted. Catholics couldn't enter Parliament, buy land, nor own a horse worth more than £5. Nor could they marry Protestants without first converting. The purpose of the draconian legislation was to ensure a Protestant ascendancy within Ireland. It succeeded, but the Irish Parliament remained subordinate to its English counterpart at Westminster: Any bill of law for the governance of Ireland had to first receive approval from English politicians. This was much to the chagrin of Ireland's new ruling class, who were mostly descended from Norman knights and Protestant settlers who had arrived in Tudor and Cromwellian times.

Toward the end of the 18th century, rebellion simmered once again. America's War of Independence and the French Revolution had engendered radical ideas of establishing an Irish republic. In 1791, two years after the storming of the Bastille, the Society of United Irishmen was formed. The society's most illustrious member was Wolfe Tone, but

© Steenie Harvey

Stone circle, Drombeg, County Cork

(somewhat ironically) the founding fathers were predominately Belfast Presbyterians—today probably the staunchest opponents of a united Ireland and Republican aims.

Wolfe Tone managed to enlist French support for his fellow republicans and an invasion force was sent to Ireland in 1796. Yet despite all the patriot games, Ireland never experienced any glorious revolution and no aristocratic necks bowed to Madame Guillotine's kiss. Ireland's weather conspired against the plotters: Severe storms broke up the French fleet, preventing the landing.

When rebellion finally erupted in 1798, it was badly organized and speedily suppressed. After this latest revolt, the London government decided the troublesome Irish were best dealt with through the union of both Parliaments. Although many of Dublin's ruling class trenchantly opposed the idea, bribery won the day. Ireland's Parliament voted itself out of existence and the union came into force on January 1, 1801.

IRELAND IN THE UNION

Few towns don't have a street named after Daniel O'Connell, a Kerry lawyer and an important figure in Ireland's long struggle against sectarianism. In the opening decades of the 19th century, Irish Catholics remained in a political wilderness. Attempts to introduce Catholic Emancipation were continuously blocked in London's Westminster Parliament, where all Irish matters were now decided. However, the arrival on the scene of O'Connell gave Catholics hope of gaining some form of political representation.

O'Connell began the Catholic Association in 1823 "to further the interests of Catholics in all areas of life." Fearing a mass political party had been born, the authorities unsuccessfully attempted to indict him for incitement to rebellion. Despite the association's suppression, O'Connell was elected member of Parliament for Clare in 1828.

Because of his Catholicism, the law forbade O'Connell from taking his Westminster seat. However, the government was alarmed at the possibility of numerous democratically elected Irish Catholics seceding. To counter this, a Catholic Emancipation Act was passed in 1829. The victory wasn't without cost. Freehold property ownership was the deciding factor as to whether citizens were entitled to a vote. Known as "the franchise qualification," the entry level of property value was immediately increased fivefold from 40 shillings to £10. As most Irish Catholics were impoverished tenant farmers who didn't own property, ordinary people were consequently still denied voting rights. It was only the Catholic owners of grander properties who retained the franchise.

Even so, O'Connell was hailed as "the Liberator" and began campaigning for the repeal of the Act of Union. Huge crowds attended his rallies, often held on famous Irish sites. In 1843 a vast gathering took place on the Hill of Tara, the centuries-old seat of Ireland's high kings. The satirical magazine *Punch* nicknamed O'Connell "King of the Beggars," but an agitated British government made it plain the union would be defended. When another "monster rally" was planned for Clontarf (site of Brian Boru's famous victory in 1014), the government banned the meeting, threatening to send in troops if it proceeded. Not wanting to subject his countrymen to a full-scale military invasion, O'Connell accepted the ban and the Repeal Association's campaign petered out.

FAMINE AND THE PUSH FOR HOME RULE

In 1845, an old invader returned to haunt Ireland: famine. Throughout the centuries the country had experienced disastrous harvests and widespread starvation. Crop failure in the 1740s may have killed an equivalent proportion of Ireland's populace but the Great Hunger of the 1840s was better documented and thus had a greater historical impact.

The potato crop failed again in 1846, 1847, and 1848 with horrific and devastating consequences: one million people died from hunger. Another million people were lost to disease or by emigration on the coffin ships that carried them away from their homeland forever. By 1851, Ireland's population had fallen from more than eight million (1841) to a little more than six million.

The crazy thing is that Ireland continued to export food during the famine years, which may have given rise to rumours that mass starvation never happened or was greatly exaggerated. Certainly there were abundant harvests of wheat and oats, but grain crops do not thrive in Ireland's rock-strewn west, the part of the country that suffered an almost apocalyptic devastation. Here the potato really was the staple foodstuff—if the poor wanted grain, somehow they had to find the wherewithal to pay the market price for it. Very few could. Nor was there much in the way of charitable handouts, though some landlords did set up soup kitchens. However, for the people of Mayo's Achill Island, accepting famine aid brought with it the risk of excommunication and thus eternal damnation. Under the supervision of the Reverend Edward Nangle, a kind of missionary outpost was established on the island. Catholic families were indeed fed and clothed—providing they worshipped at the Church Mission Society's newly founded Protestant church and the island children attended its school.

Proindependence activists decided the time for rhetoric alone was past. Despite the very real threat of transportation to Australia's Botany Bay, secret societies proliferated and sectarian violence became commonplace. In 1858, the Irish Republican Brotherhood was established, followed the next year in America by the "Fenian Brotherhood." Both aimed to achieve an independent republic by means of violent revolution.

A Home Government Association, founded in 1870, again signaled that the majority of Irish people yearned to follow a more peaceful route to self-determination. In Britain's (and thus Ireland's) first secret ballot election, an Alliance of Home Rule candidates won 60 percent of the Irish seats in 1874. The alliance's leader was Charles Stewart Parnell, whose name is also honored by numerous streets within the republic. A skillful politician, he even persuaded the Fenians to travel the parliamentary road to reform with him.

But Ireland still wasn't about to witness an invasion of democratic ideals. The passing of the Victorian Age saw Ulster's politicians uncompromisingly saying "No" to the notion of autonomy and a Dublin government. However, British Prime Minister Gladstone indicated his awareness of Ulster's opposition and that an amendment to exclude the province from any Irish Home Rule bill was a possibility. For the first time, the specter of partition beckoned.

Scandal erupted in 1890 when it became public knowledge that Parnell was living with Kitty O'Shea, a colleague's wife. Gladstone refused to continue negotiations with someone who was "morally tainted" and the disgraced Parnell died the following year. 1893 saw Gladstone successfully steer an Irish Home Rule bill through Parliament, but the nonelected aristocrats of the House of Lords rejected it. Not entirely surprising, considering that many of them owned Irish estates.

THE 20TH CENTURY

After 1910's general election, the Irish National Party's 84 members held the balance of power at Westminster. However, the Ulster Unionist Party and its leader, Sir Edward Carson, still fiercely opposed any change in the status quo. When a new Irish Home Rule bill was passed by Westminster's Parliament, Carson formed what was effectively a private army, the Ulster Volunteer Force (UVF).

Although the Lords again rejected the bill, delaying its implementation, Ulster sensed the times they were a-changing. And from a Unionist standpoint, not for the better. Determined to remain British at all costs, the UVF's early paramilitaries quickly acquired arms from Germany and began drilling. On the Nationalist side, the Irish Republican Brotherhood formed the Irish Volunteers.

Ireland's Home Rule bill received royal assent in 1914 but the outbreak of World War I resulted in the knotty Irish problem's being put on the governmental back burner once again. Continually thwarted in their attempts to achieve any form of autonomy by parliamentary methods, a number of Nationalists weren't prepared to wait for British agreement any longer.

Why was Britain so reluctant to let Ireland go? Well, it has been suggested that Ireland was seen as the linchpin of that empire on which the sun proverbially never set. Remember, in those days Dublin was the "second city" of the British Empire, Britain a major power, and more than a fifth of the global map was colored red. To British eyes, removing the linchpin opened the horrendous possibility of other colonies' demanding independent status.

On Easter Monday 1916, the Irish Volunteers and the smaller Irish Citizen Army finally rebelled against British rule. With a force of under 2,000, they occupied the General Post Office and other buildings in central Dublin. Patrick Pearse, elected by the IRB as "president," emerged from the post office to declare a republic.

But the Easter Rising generated little public support and after six days of holding out against superior numbers and heavy artillery, the Volunteers surrendered. However, the British government's response soon changed popular opinion when martial law was declared and rebel leaders were court-martialed. Fourteen faced the firing squad in May that year and many others would be shot before American pressure stopped the executions.

By now the public's general mood had changed and a small group formed in 1905 by Arthur Griffith called "Sinn Féin" began attracting support. In 1918's general election, Sinn Féin swept the boards. Pledging not to go to Westminster, they formed the first Dáil, or independent parliament, under Eamon De Valera as president. Britain's attempt to suppress the new Parliament led to more conflict. The Irish Volunteers became the Irish Republican Army (IRA) and fought a guerrilla war against British troops and police.

In today's Ireland most people shun terrorism. Yet the fact remains that violence and bloodshed served as midwives to the birth of what became known as the Irish Free State. Were the original IRA bad guys or good guys? Terrorists or patriotic freedom fighters? It's still hotly debated whether the people of southern Ireland would have cast off the shackles of imperialism without the gunmen.

But if nationalist Ireland were to be given autonomy, what was to be done about Ulster, whose majority Protestant community insisted on remaining part of the union? In agreement with Ulster Unionists, British Prime Minister Lloyd George came up with new legislation—Ireland was to be divided. The 1920 Government of Ireland Act partitioned the island the following year.

Negotiations to end the war of independence in the south took place later in 1921 with Arthur Griffith and Michael Collins representing the Dáil. Offered much less than hoped for, they nevertheless signed the Anglo-Irish Treaty. An Irish Free State of 26 counties was given dominion status with six Ulster counties remaining British and outside the new state authority.

The British Parliament's satisfaction with the deal wasn't mirrored in Dublin: Bitter divisions arose. Having to swear allegiance to the British monarch was an especially contentious issue but in January 1922, the Dáil voted to accept the treaty. De Valera, trenchantly opposed, resigned. Civil war followed within months, with the country splitting into pro and anti-treaty factions. Friends and neighbors who had fought as comrades-in-arms against the British now started slaughtering each other. The brutal conflict finally ended with a truce in May 1923.

Slowly, and by degrees, southern Ireland continued to break with Britain and the monarchy. In 1937 the Irish Free State declared complete independence and changed its name to Éire. Finally, on Easter Monday 1949, Éire became the newly inaugurated Irish Republic and said farewell to the British Commonwealth.

In 1972, the country elected to join the European Community, which effectively resulted in an influx of financial help from wealthier neighbors such as Germany. Not only did this set the scene for today's economic success, it gave Ireland newfound confidence. As a member state on equal terms with its European neighbors, there has been a transformation of the national psyche. Most Irish people fully embrace the European ideal and it could be that the country has at last emerged from the shadows of its ancient struggle with Britain.

THE RELATIONSHIP WITH NORTHERN IRELAND

Often referred to by its citizens as "the Province," Northern Ireland is part of the United Kingdom (U.K.) of Great Britain and Northern Ireland. Although many people regard its problems as solely sectarian, recent struggles have been about political power. The majority of Northern Ireland Protestants vote the Unionist ticket and both David Trimble's Ulster Unionist Party (UUP) and Ian Paisley's Democratic Unionist Party (DUP) want to maintain strong links with Britain and its monarchy. Most Catholics vote for Nationalist or Republican parties such as the SDLP or Sinn Féin, which both support the concept of a united Ireland.

Although Northern Ireland's "Troubles" never really affected the economy or day-to-day lives of Irish people in the south, happenings across the border have always been headline news. When the Irish Republic's Constitution was drawn up, it laid claim to the entire island of Ireland, which didn't help to foster good relations with the North's Unionist majority. However, in a referendum after 1998's Good Friday Agreement between Northern Ireland's Unionists and Nationalists, the Republic's citizens voted by an overwhelming majority to rescind constitutional claims to their neighbors' territory.

Formed in 1998, the new Northern Ireland Assembly devolved greater power to local politicians. However, at the time of writing, the province is back under Westminster's jurisdiction. Political wrangling and arguments about the IRA's decommissioning of weapons have left the Good Friday Agreement in what can only be described as a mess. The DUP, the majority Unionist party, refuses to work with Sinn Féin.

Government

With a legal system based on the Constitution of 1937, the Republic of Ireland is a parliamentary democracy. The Oireachtas, or national Parliament, consists of the office of the president along with a House of Representatives (Dáil Éireann) and Senate (Seanad Éireann). The main political power rests with Dáil Éireann, whose 166 members are elected by the people for a maximum term of five years. Elected members to the Dáil are called Teachtaí Dála (TDs). The prime minister holds the title An Taoiseach.

The republic's 26 counties are divided into 41 Dáil constituencies, each returning between three and five TDs. Known as proportional representation by single transferable vote, the voting method (PRSTV) is fairly complicated and based on a quota system.

The electoral system invariably returns coalition governments. Under Taoiseach Bertie Ahern, the present government is a power-sharing arrangement between the centrist Fianna Fáil party, the smaller but more right-wing Progressive Democrats, and various Independents. The previous administration (the Rainbow Coalition) consisted of some curious bedfellows: the right-of-center Fine Gael party, the soft-left Labour Party, and the solidly socialistic Democratic Left. As Fianna Fáil or Fine Gael always make up the largest party in whatever coalition is formed, the governance of the country remains on a fairly even keel with few major policy swings. Other political parties attracting limited amounts of support within the Republic include Sinn Féin, the Workers' Party, and the Green Party.

The Seanad's 60 senators are either nominated directly by the Taoiseach or indirectly elected from within five panels with particular expertise. More a talking shop than a body with political clout, the Seanad can, however, petition the president to refuse to sign a bill until the matter is put before the people in a referendum. No bill can become law without the president's signature.

Like TDs, the president (an Uachtarán) is elected by popular vote. The current incumbent is Mary McAleese, who followed Mary Robinson. The president's term of office is seven years and he or she can stand for re-election only once. Although the office is largely ceremonial, the president takes on the role of guardian of the Constitution, which lays down the fundamental rights of citizens.

Guaranteeing a swath of rights, the Constitution covers personal rights, the family, education, private property, and religion. Amendments can take place only if the people give their say-so in a referendum. Social change recently resulted in one important amendment: that of allowing divorce through the Irish courts. And while the rights of the unborn child were designed to be protected by the Constitution, abortion remains a thorny issue.

In the early 1990s, a case in which a young rape victim was prevented by the courts from traveling to Britain for an abortion resulted in a hotly contested public debate. Were Irish women to be subjected to pregnancy tests at ports and airports before being given leave to travel? In the subsequent 1992 referendum, the people voted to clarify the matter by allowing all citizens freedom of movement. Even so, abortion for any reason whatsoever (including rape, incest, or the mother's carrying a severely malformed fetus) remains outlawed.

Economy

Despite a backdrop of rising oil prices and uncertainties in the global economy, the most recent check on the Irish economy indicates that it is "strong and in good health."

The prospects for the next few years appear positive. Indeed some analysts are already using the label "Celtic Tiger 2." The so-called original "Celtic Tiger" saw growth rates of more than 9 percent per year between 1994 and 2000. The forecast for the next few years is growth of around 6.5 percent with inflation at 2.5 percent.

The Irish economy is in remarkable shape when compared to the other countries in the Eurozone. The rate of growth and public investment is more than twice the European average. The unemployment rate is less than half the average, and Ireland's debt burden is one of the lowest in Europe.

The balance of trade figures are just as impressive. For 14 consecutive years, the country has had a trade surplus. Exports have risen from €18,200 million in 1990 to reach €82,200 million in 2003.

The low rate of corporation tax has ensured that Ireland still enjoys a high level of foreign investment, with an inflow estimated at $25 billion in 2003. The United States accounts for almost half of the 1,050 foreign companies that have set up operations in the country, with one leading U.S. tax journal rating Ireland as the No. 1 global location for U.S. profits.

It is a long way removed from the situation in Ireland 30 years ago. When Ireland first joined the European Union in 1973, it was a fairly impoverished, high-taxation country that imported more goods than it exported. But by 2003, the value of exports from Ireland was 73 percent higher than the value of imports.

The Irish economy is in remarkable shape when compared to the other countries in the Eurozone. The rate of growth and public investment is more than twice the European average.

Perhaps the main benefit of membership in the European Union has been the free access to the large European market. Before 1973, Ireland was largely dependent on the United Kingdom for trade. At that time almost 55 percent of exports went to the United Kingdom, with less than 24 percent going to the rest of the world and the United States combined. By 2003, the situation has almost completely reversed. The United Kingdom now accounts for only around 18 percent of Irish exports, while the United States now takes over 20 percent. Indeed, the United States is now Ireland's most important trading partner.

The changing fortunes in the economy have been mirrored in the various exporting sectors. Thirty years ago, the production of food, drink, and tobacco accounted for 43 percent of exports and employed around 24 percent of the working population. Since then Ireland has seen a massive rise in chemical production, which now accounts for almost 45 percent of all exports. Machinery and transport (including computers) makes up around 30 percent. However, the production of food, drink, and tobacco, although still an important aspect of the Irish economy, now accounts for only 7 percent of those in employment.

The immediate prospects for the economy seem fairly positive. However, as in all economies, there are risks. Ireland's continued success depends on future international growth. How will oil prices influence world trade? No one could have predicted in 2003 that oil prices would reach $50 a barrel in 2004. How will international exchange rates pan out? These are just a few of the unanswered questions that will influence Ireland's prospects.

© Steenie Harvey

People and Culture

S omeone once said that the Irish are really a Mediterranean people who got stranded much farther north than they should have been. It's true that most people are extremely convivial with an unflagging appetite for music and chat but where does the blarney end and reality start? Not every Irishwoman is a red-haired beauty, wrapped in a long green cloak, wandering the hillsides with an Irish wolfhound. Nor is every Irishman a silver-tongued charmer. Remember movies such as *The Quiet Man* were made for a mostly American audience and those Hollywood images often still color foreign ideas about Irish identity.

Ethnicity and Class

You'll certainly not encounter the kind of stage Irishman who spends his days making moonshine and gazing out at the ocean muttering "Ah, Begorrah, the shores of Americay… " And you'll get some strange

Sports

With more horses per head of population than anywhere else in Europe, Ireland is the Equine Isle. Thanks to generous tax concessions, many top European racehorses are at stud here and there are pony-trekking facilities and riding stables in every part of the country. Even if you don't ride yourself, one of the most enjoyable events is a day at the races, whether it be at a little local course or one of the major classic meetings at the Curragh in County Kildare.

Leaving aside skiing, baseball, and American football, most sporting interests are catered for. Ireland's 350-plus golf courses are world-renowned and vary from parkland courses to breezy seaside links where the hazards often include dry-stone walls and mad-eyed sheep who've gone walkabout. There are sailing clubs in many maritime counties, loughs and rivers provide tremendous fishing, and almost every community has a gun club. The traditional rural pursuits of foxhunting and beagling are particularly strong in counties Limerick, Tipperary, and Cork. As regards spectator sports, Ireland's soccer team reached the World Cup Finals in 1990 and 1994 and the rugby team takes part in the annual Six Nations Championship along with England, Scotland, Wales, Italy,

looks if you insist on greeting people with "Top o' the morning to ye." Within Ireland itself, such phrases are mockingly dismissed as "Oirish-isms" or "Paddywhackery" so please don't use them unless you want to be laughed at behind your back.

It's difficult to package the Irish lifestyle into a neat little box but it's safe to say that most people abhor pretentiousness. Delusions of grandeur and classism do not go down well. The Republic of Ireland's rebirth as a nation state sounded the death knell for its former masters, the Anglo-Irish ascendancy. With their demise went any notions of forelock-tugging or perceived inferiority—most people have peasant forebears in their background and don't feel any need to apologize for it. Unlike in neighboring Britain, Irish people aren't categorized into that ludicrous system of working class, lower middle class, upper middle class, and so on.

Nowadays the aristocratic "Big Houses" with their courtyards, coach houses, and servants' quarters belong to wealthy business people and rock stars rather than lordlings with obscure titles. As regards the other end of the lifestyle scale, the country's fairly recent history of high un-employment means no real social stigma is attached to the jobless or those receiving social-welfare payments.

Not everybody you'll meet will be university-educated, but never presume that just because somebody has a modest job, he or she has a and France. And although rugby can often be violent and bloody, it seems like a game for namby-pambies once you've encountered Gaelic Games.

Gaelic Games are almost exclusive to Ireland and both Gaelic football and hurling have huge followings. Gaelic football is a field game of 15 players who use a round ball that can be played with either hands or feet and a goal similar to that on a rugby pitch. Depending on whether the ball goes over or under the bar, scoring is a mix of points and goals. Dating to Celtic times and mentioned in epic sagas, hurling has a simi-lar scoring system but in this case the game involves a hurley stick and a smaller ball. And regardless of what you'll see, hurley sticks are intended to whack the ball-- they're not supposed to be used as clubs for whacking opponents' heads. Teams from the 32 counties, north and south, annually compete in the All-Ireland Championships and fans have the county flag fluttering from windows, gateposts, and anywhere else they can proclaim their allegiance. Watched by enthusiastic crowds of around 70,000, hurling and Gaelic football finals take place at Croke Park in Dublin.

stunted intellect. In no other country have I encountered such a thirst for knowledge or interest in the wider world. I once met a housepainter whose favorite author was Dostoevsky—and he was teaching himself to read it in the original Russian.

Of course, people are people the world over and money always creates its own kind of social gulf. For example, you'll rarely come across professionals such as doctors, lawyers, and accountants socializing with the hoi polloi who live in rented accommodation on local authority council estates. Nor are the unemployed likely to be found at prestigious golf clubs such as Mount Juliet and Druids' Glen.

In the cities it's patently obvious which are the "posh" sections of suburbia but in rural areas the neighborhood mix is usually far more diverse. My neighbors include a telephone engineer, a plumber, a schoolteacher, a retired civil servant, a 90-year-old bachelor, three farming families, an Englishwoman involved in flowercraft designs, and a wildlife warden. Until fairly recently the former Church of Ireland rectory was owned by a German artist, but it has since been bought by two Dublin families as a weekend holiday home.

As mentioned earlier, the country was only very recently offered the option for divorce. The liberal agenda has its strongest support in the Dublin area but when it comes to the abortion issue, even Dublin

The Shamrock

Anybody can be Irish on Saint Patrick's Day—all you need to do is wear a sprig of shamrock. But although many people imagine that this unofficial symbol of Irishness must be something really unique and special, the truth is rather mundane. Shamrock is nothing other than young clover.

Seamróg in the Irish language, it derives its name from *seamair* (clover) and *óg* (young). The expression "drowning the shamrock" comes from the custom of dropping a sprig of clover into the last pint you swallow on Saint Patrick's Day. Once the glass is drained, toss the soggy shamrock over your shoulder. This should ensure a full year's good luck!

lobbyists come up against a brick wall in the shape of the church-backed Society for the Protection of the Unborn Child (SPUC). Abortion remains outlawed. Even on vital medical grounds, pregnant women still have to travel to England for surgery.

Although social change has been slow in coming, attitudes to marriage have altered considerably. According to a report published by the Economic and Social Research Institute, almost 33 percent of births are now to single mothers. In 1991, the figure was only 15 percent.

Traditional Culture

Ireland's symbol is the harp, a wonderful motif for a land of music, dance, and storytelling. Nowhere else in Europe does the folk tradition carry quite as much impact, burst with quite so much dynamism. Wherever you settle, you won't be very far away from the tinkle of the pennywhistle, the droning lament of the *uillean* pipes, or the unmistakable thump of the *bodhrán,* the Irish drum.

Music and dance have overlapped and woven themselves into the very fabric of society. More than just cultural pastimes, these are art forms that are accessible to everyone. The fellow who comes to fix your plumbing or dig your garden may well be an accomplished fiddle player or flautist who learned his skills in a farmhouse kitchen. And all over the country you'll notice little girls skipping along in what seem to be Celtic party frocks, intricately embroidered with the kind of patterns usually associated with the Book of Kells and other illuminated manuscripts. The youngsters are off to their Irish dancing class, heads filled with dreams of traveling the world as part of the Riverdance troupe.

The bastion of the traditional music scene is, of course, the pub. Inns in tourist towns such as Killarney have *seisiúns* (sessions) of music scheduled on a nightly basis, usually at regular times. Much of the instrumental music that's played is actually dance music and includes everything from jigs to reels to the hornpipe. Sessions also often include ballads, rebel songs, and the lone voice of a *sean-nós* singer. Unaccompanied by any instrument and usually sung in Irish, their throbbing songs are the stories of thwarted love, sad farewells, and a heart-wrenching yearning for a faraway homeland.

In quieter areas where tourists rarely go, *seisiúns* are more impromptu. Someone whips out a fiddle, an accordion appears, and before you know it the entire bar is tapping its feet and raising the rafters with a rousing rendition of *The Fields of Athenry*. Once under way, the entertainment can roister on until way past pub closing time.

The fellow who comes to fix your plumbing or dig your garden may well be an accomplished fiddle player or flautist who learned his skills in a farmhouse kitchen.

County Clare is especially good for tuning into traditional melodies that have been passed on like heirlooms through the generations. Folk-music enthusiasts from all over the world embark on a kind of pilgrimage to the fishing village of Doolin and its three "singing pubs": McGann's, O'Connor's, and McDermott's. Some come to listen, others to join in. Another Clare village, Miltown Malbay, is the venue for the Willie Clancy Summer School, Ireland's largest musical summer school that attracts beginners and local masters every year. As much social event as musical academy, there are classes for most instruments, as well as set-dancing and singing, too.

The Irish word for a traditional music festival is *feis* (FESH). There are dozens of them—the biggest is the *Fleadh Cheoil* (pronounced flah-kol, it means "feast of music') which takes place in a different Irish town each year at the end of August. Ten days of nonstop competition and entertainment, it's an unmissable chance to see the country's top step, set, and *ceili* dancers.

In step dancing, the dancers' arms and upper bodies stay rigid while the feet perform the mazy magic of slip jigs, triple jigs, and the hornpipe. Step dancing is as rigorous as it looks and you really need to learn it as a child to reach competition standard. *Feis* rules require "authentic Gaelic dress" to be worn but although today's costumes look fabulous, they're hardly authentic. Not when you consider that these dances used to take place at country crossroads and were performed by peasant villagers dressed in shawls, petticoats, and homespun breeches!

Like *ceili* dancing, which developed from the French quadrille, set dancing is a form of social dancing bearing some resemblance to English and Scottish country dancing. It generally involves four couples who follow the intricate turns, steps, and patterns of a series of figures—the set. It often takes 15–20 minutes to dance an entire set, so participants need plenty of stamina.

Competitively danced sets at a *feis* come from an approved repertoire of dances with evocative names such as the Siege of Ennis, the Blackthorn Stick, the King of the Fairies, and Hurry the Jug. Some dances are more than 250 years old—a dance known as the Blackbird actually doubled as a secret code for Irish supporters of the ill-fated Bonnie Prince Charlie, who tried to wrest back the Scottish throne for the Catholic Stuart dynasty.

Many set dances originated during the 18th century, the heyday of the Irish dance master. Circuiting a county's villages, he passed on his latest stock of dances to local people, devising new steps and sets with each visit. It was considered a great honor to have a dance master boarding with you, even though he was likely to be eating you out of house and home for a period of anything up to six weeks.

Another mainstay of the *feis* is the *seannachie,* or storyteller. The art of storytelling is as old as man himself and was a revered profession during Celtic times. Journeying from fireside to fireside, the ancient bards and poets thrilled their audiences with elaborate creation myths and stories of heroic victories achieved with the aid of magical weapons. They told of doomed love affairs, of lone warriors battling against the shadowy forces of the supernatural, of severed heads that could prophesy and provide wondrous entertainment. Like his or her poetic forebears, the *seannachie* too relies on memory alone. Some of the best hail from the Kingdom of Kerry, a county where stories are apt to grow very long legs indeed.

The name Comhaltas Ceoltoiri Éireann loosely translates as "a gathering of Irish musicians," though it exists to promote all aspects of traditional culture. Pronounced Coal-tis Kyol-tory Air-in, the organization has branches all over Ireland and you don't have to be Irish-born or Irish-speaking to join.

Throughout the country, CCE branches usually meet for a weekly

Home ground: the gravestone of the famous poet W. B. Yeats carries an epitaph he penned himself

musical *seisiún* in a bar. Other nights are given over to teaching *ceili* and set-dancing—fees are generally less than $5 per person per night. And, if you have a basic level of competence in your chosen instrument, they'll teach you traditional tunes and how to play with other musicians. Concerts are regular events with performances given in local churches at Epiphany and on Saint Patrick's Day.

In Carrigaline, County Cork, another big day in the social calendar is Saint Stephen's Day, December 26th. As part of the celebrations, musicians and dancers dress up as Wren Boys and roam Carrigaline's streets and pubs, collecting money for local charities. It's always a colorful occasion with the Wren Boys giving a cheery send-off to the horses and hounds of the South Union Hunt, its riders dressed in hunting pink. Preparations actually start around August, when oats are cut to make the straw skirts worn by the Wren Boys. (There are craft workshops in how to make these "skirts," by the way.)

"Hunting the Wran" (the wren) was more common in previous years than it is today, but groups of colorfully disguised revelers still appear on Saint Stephen's Day as part of Christmastime's festivities. Although costumes sometimes differ from county to county, most Wren Boys wear white tunics, conical straw hats, and paint their faces black and red. A century ago, they would have rambled across open fields to call on neighbors. In return for a money donation and some food and drink, the odd-looking visitors entertained the household with music, dancing, poetry, and drama.

Mean householders often got more than they bargained for. Along with their musical instruments, the Wren Boys carried a holly bush or pole decorated with the slain bodies of harmless little birds called wrens. Any house or farm making an inadequate donation could later expect to find a wren buried near the doorstep. As well as being a dire insult, this unneighborly act supposedly ensured that the stingy family suffered a full year's bad luck.

Today it's illegal to hunt wrens so revelers top their poles with a papier-mâché effigy. And instead of making house calls, most Wren Boys center their activities on pubs and clubs. Besides Carrigaline, two other places where you're certain to see Wren Boys are Woodford in County Galway and Dingle in County Kerry.

Customs and Etiquette

The Irish love to talk. Every possible subject is open to discussion and debate, including religion and politics. Your views are always likely to be welcome, though it's probably best not to introduce a confrontational topic yourself.

One warning. Although the Irish thoroughly enjoy criticizing themselves and their country, they do not look kindly on "outsiders" doing the same thing. Banter is one thing, but should you start berating Ireland, the Irish, or the Irish way of doing things—and doing it in an arrogant way—you may find yourself drowning in a torrent of abuse.

Whether you choose to live in urban or rural Ireland, you'll find there's much less urgency regarding timekeeping than you're probably used to. Tradesmen promise to do work on a certain day and then don't appear until a fortnight later. Letters sometimes stay unanswered, phone calls go unreturned. You may even make an appointment with a real estate agent and then find he's neglected to inform you that he'll be out of the office all afternoon. Of course, it's possible that you'll experience no problems whatsoever but it's as well to be forewarned.

People still count and maybe the real estate agent didn't show because he was at a neighbor's funeral. Provincial Ireland's strong sense of community means that it's not uncommon for hundreds (and sometimes thousands) of people to pay their respects to the surviving family by attending the graveyard ceremony. It doesn't matter if you knew the person only slightly or even if it was a neighbor's mother whom you had never met. Being part of a village community means attending neighborhood funerals, even if it means closing down your business for an hour or two. What faith you belong to doesn't matter. Most of my own neighbors are Catholic, but almost 3,000 people attended the funeral of a young local Protestant boy who tragically died in a house fire.

Although money is important, when it comes to the idea of the work ethic, Ireland has more in common with the Mediterranean than its northern European neighbors. Want to do business on Saturday? Tough. Few businesspeople will work weekends for something that can wait until Mondays. Nor are employees prepared to give up their social life to work long hours of overtime, let alone take a second job.

The pub undoubtedly plays a major part in Ireland's social life but it's a complete fallacy that the entire country is drink-mad. (Though if you visit Dublin's Temple Bar on a Saturday night it can seem that way!) Many people are teetotalers but the pub is where they'll gather to play cards, trade gossip, and often meet with their local political representative. A number of Western Ireland TDs (members of Parliament) actually hold "surgeries" for their electoral constituents in the pub! Not to be confused with doctors' offices (which are also called "surgeries"), these are a forum where you can ask what he—and it's usually "he"—plans to do about the state of the roads or improving farm incomes.

Another curiosity is that it's still common in the west of Ireland to give up drink for Lent. Again neighbors will still meet friends in the pub, but conversation will be oiled with glasses of lemonade rather than pints of the black stuff.

Central to Irish society is "the family." Older people are treated with tremendous respect and there isn't the same emphasis on youth culture that exists in many other western countries. Visitors often comment on how Irish youngsters seem so polite and good-mannered. It's not unusual to find three generations of an Irish family sharing the same house, especially if "Mammy" or "Daddy" has been left bereaved.

Gender Roles

Mary Robinson's appointment as Ireland's first woman president (since succeeded by Mary McAleese) gave women's self-esteem a big boost. Although there aren't many women who've achieved top positions in day-to-day politics, 72 percent of Ireland's small and medium-sized enterprises have at least one woman on the management team.

However, there's still a tendency for women to gravitate toward the "caring" professions such as nursing, teaching, and the social services. Until the early 1970s, women had to give up civil service jobs on marriage and even today there's a commonplace attitude within rural Ireland that a woman's place is in the home. Only 47 percent of women have outside jobs compared to 71 percent of men. For career-minded Irishwomen, "tradition" sometimes has negative aspects.

GAY AND LESBIAN CULTURE

The Republic of Ireland didn't decriminalize homosexuality until 1993. Since the 1970s, campaigners had been calling for reform of 1861's archaic Offences Against the Person law. Although this law didn't outlaw homosexuality as such, the committing of homosexual acts was illegal.

In 1983, a gay senator called David Norris challenged the constitutionality of the law in Ireland's Supreme Court. Citing "the Christian and democratic nature of the Irish State," the judges ruled against him. They maintained criminalization served both public health and the institution of marriage.

In 1988, the indefatigable Norris sought a ruling from the European Court of Human Rights. The court ruled that Ireland's criminalization of homosexuality breached the Human Rights Convention. Although Ireland dragged its heels for another five years, it was eventually forced to change the law.

Compared to those in London and large American cities, Ireland's gay and lesbian community remains fairly low profile. As you might expect, the best place to meet gay men or lesbians is in the capital. Along with the Outhouse Community and Resource Center on Capel Street, Dublin has a number of gay clubs, pubs, and saunas. There are also gay and lesbian pubs in Cork, Galway, and Waterford, though don't expect to find as wide a choice of venues as in the capital.

When gay men or lesbians want to socialize, they usually head for the big city. Although there are a few support groups, you rarely hear the sound of the proverbial "closet" door opening in the Irish countryside. Within small-town Ireland, the older generation prefers to hang on to its traditional belief that children, friends, and neighbors are 100 percent heterosexual.

To find out what's happening in Ireland's gay and lesbian community, one of the best sources of information is the online magazine *Gay Community News* (www.gcn.ie).

Religion

The 2002 census recorded that approximately 88 percent of the republic's population is Roman Catholic, though this figure rises to 93 percent for those born in Ireland. Steeped in ancient values, this truly is a land of holy wells, visions, moving statues, and pilgrim paths. Thousands of people annually climb to the summit of Croagh Patrick, Ireland's "holy mountain" on the shores of County Mayo. Another famous pilgrimage is to Saint Patrick's Purgatory in County Donegal, where the ritual involves fasting, sleeplessness, and going barefoot.

Ireland's spiritual power plant: Knock shrine, County Mayo

Ireland's Flag

Sent as a gift by French revolutionaries in 1848, the Republic of Ireland's flag is a tricolor of vertical bands: green, white, and orange. The green and the orange represent the island's Catholic and Protestant traditions. White, the color of peace, symbolizes what should be the unity between them.

But although most people describe themselves as Catholic, church attendance has been falling. Weekly Mass attendance in rural areas is around 60 percent, in urban areas around 43 percent. A report in Ireland's *Sunday Business Post* in 2004 stated that in some Dublin parishes, Mass attendance had slumped to below 10 percent.

Steeped in ancient values, this truly is a land of holy wells, visions, moving statues, and pilgrim paths.

Recent scandals have meant that the Catholic hierarchy no longer commands the same unquestioning respect and political influence as in past decades. And while the church remains closely involved in the health and education services, Ireland's new generation is less awed by authority.

Of Ireland's minority faiths, the largest grouping is the Protestant religion, which numbers around 3 percent (mostly Church of Ireland, Presbyterian, and Methodists). There are also 19,000 Muslims, 10,000 Orthodox adherents, and small communities of Jehovah's Witnesses and Jews. The census also recorded that the number of people who indicated they had no religion increased from 66,000 in 1991 to 138,000 in 2002. In Northern Ireland, the religious breakdown is approximately 60 percent Protestant and 40 percent Catholic.

The Arts

Although Ireland's cultural reputation is founded on its Celtic traditions and huge body of literature, many people in today's arts world have achieved a high international standing. Irish playwrights such as Brian Friel *(Dancing at Lughnasa)* are well known on Broadway and the Druid Theater Company's production of Martin McDonagh's *The Beauty Queen of Leenane* garnered four Tony awards. Irish-made movies go from strength to strength and even if you haven't heard of home-grown directors such as Neil Jordan and Jim Sheridan, you'll undoubtedly be familiar with silver screen celebrities such as Liam Neeson, Gabriel Byrne, Brenda Fricker, and Pierce Brosnan. Irish films that successfully transferred to an international audience include *The Field, The Crying Game, The Snapper, In the Name of the Father, and Circle of Friends.*

Contemporary Irish music encompasses everything from rock giants U2 to teen heartthrobs Westlife and the granny's favorite crooner, Daniel O'Donnell. Country and western bands attract a big following, especially in the midlands. If you're a jazz fan, make for the annual fall festival in Cork; if you're an Enya fan get yourself to Leo Brennan's Tavern near Crolly in County Donegal—Enya is Leo's daughter and customers are occasionally treated to a free performance when she's back home. By now a musical institution, the Eurovision Song Contest has been won by Ireland more times than anyone cares to remember.

Dublin is where to hear the widest range of live music, with both local and international acts regularly packing out venues. Whether it's jazz, folk, traditional, soul, reggae, or rock, you're guaranteed to find a gig to suit in Dublin's event pages.

To get an insight into both traditional and contemporary Irish painting, two good places to start are the National Gallery and IMMA (Irish Museum of Modern Art). Both are in Dublin—the former on Merrion Square, the latter in the old Royal Hospital in the Kilmainham neighborhood.

In the National Gallery, Irish painting is charted from its rebirth in the 17th century to Jack B. Yeats and Paul Henry, Ireland's best-known 20th century artists. There are also Italian, French, British, and Dutch collections. The National Portrait Collection of 50 Irish people who have made significant contributions to the country's cultural and political life includes a commissioned portrait of rock singer Bono by Louis le Brocquy.

Including special exhibitions and on-loan collections, IMMA's current collection of modern and contemporary international and Irish art comprises about 4,500 works. Highlights include lens-based work by Gilbert and George, installations by Rebecca Horn, and sculpture by Kathy Prendergast, Damien Hirst, and Stephan Balkenhol; paintings by Sean Scully, a large sculpture by Barry Flanagan, and a film by Neil Jordan.

Another interesting place to feel the pulse-beat of contemporary Irish art is in Dublin's Temple Bar, at Temple Bar Gallery and Studios. With two exhibition spaces and 30 studios, it's one of the country's largest art complexes. If you prefer art-house movies to Hollywood blockbusters, the Irish Film Center is also in the Temple Bar quarter.

Of course, the arts aren't confined to Dublin. Along with being home to a sizable number of performing arts companies, Cork and Galway in particular are also highly creative cities of workshops, galleries, writers' circles, and artists' collectives. Smaller provincial towns also usually have writers' groups and artist/craft-worker collectives. If you're interested in joining, a good place to get contact details is from the local library.

ARCHITECTURE

From the prehistoric chambers of Newgrange to Dublin's much-derided Millennium Spike, architecture is another highly visible art form. Certainly in Dublin, the Georgian heyday lives on in the form of imposing public buildings created by James Gandon, the country's foremost architect of the 18th century. Masterpieces include the Four Courts (the law courts), the Custom House, and the old parliament building, which is now the Bank of Ireland. Laid out around grassy gardens, Merrion Square and Fitzwilliam Square are also a favorite with photographers for their red-brick Georgian houses with fan-lights and colorful front doors.

Like Ireland's multitude of abbeys and monasteries, castles always seem to invoke romance. Not that they were designed for romance— they were generally built as bases from which to subdue local chieftains. The favorite place to construct them was at strategic locations such as river crossings.

The countryside is studded with ivy-clad tower castles in various states of ruination, but to see the very best example of an early medieval fortification, visit Trim in County Meath. The largest Anglo-Norman stronghold in Ireland, Trim Castle still looks much as it did back in A.D. 1200. Another great example of a Norman stronghold is Cahir Castle at Cahir in County Tipperary. On an island in the river, it was built to control the crossing of the River Suir.

Although a number of the grand mansions of the Anglo-Irish ascendancy were razed to the ground during Ireland's struggle for independence, enough remain to give an insight into the aristocratic lifestyle. Near Blessington (County Wicklow), one of the most interesting is Russborough House. Constructed between 1741 and 1751, this stately Palladian mansion of local silver-gray granite has an entrance front extending to 700 feet. Monumental chimneypieces of black Kilkenny marble; rococo plasterwork featuring flowers, garlands, and cherubs; walls covered with crimson Genoese velvet—this really was living on the grand scale.

Russborough's collection of art treasures is rather better guarded than in days gone by. In 1974, an IRA gang stole 19 paintings including a Vermeer, a Goya, two Gainsboroughs, and three Rubenses. Like most houses open to the public, Russborough has a magnificent garden—don't get lost in its maze.

Near Maynooth (County Kildare) Castletown House is Ireland's largest "Big House." Also a Palladian-style mansion, it was built in 1722 for William Conolly, speaker of the Irish Parliament. Designed by an Italian architect, Alessandro Galilei, it's believed to have provided the model for the White House in Washington, D.C. Castletown's Print Room is the only one in Ireland to have survived. Originating in England in the 18th century, print rooms were once highly fashionable. Basically the style was to paste engravings and mezzotints onto the wall and then frame them with decorative borders.

In Georgian and Victorian times, many wealthy landowners embellished their gardens with numerous architectural curiosities. Ireland has a treasure trove of these oddities, collectively known as follies. They include pyramids, obelisks, Greco/Roman temples, gothic towers, Chinese pagodas, fake ruins—and at Dromana (County Waterford) there's even a Hindu gateway in the Mogul style of northern India.

Naturally Castletown House also has a couple of follies. The first is an obelisk mounted on arches and adorned with stone eagles and pineapples. It was once described as a "140 foot high monument to chimney-sweeping." The Irish Georgian Society uses a logo of this folly as its emblem.

Castletown's second folly is the Wonderful Barn. Standing 73 feet high, this conical building has 94 stone steps corkscrewing around its exterior. It is flanked by two smaller dovecote towers. In Georgian times, doves were often served as a delicacy. Both follies provided work for estate workers hit by 1739's famine.

LITERATURE

Ireland always seems to have had more writers, poets, and playwrights than there are sheep in the fields and when you consider the country's size, its literary achievements are tremendous. You could say that it all began with the unknown monks of the Celtic Church. Not only did they create illuminated gospels such as the *Book of Kells* and *Book of Durrow,* they recorded the ancient myths and heroic sagas that had been thrilling listeners since pagan times. It is these early Irish monks you can thank for timeless stories such as *The Children of Lir* in which four children were bewitched into swans by a jealous step-mother. The most famous ancient epic is *The Cattle Raid of Cooley (Táin Bó Cuailnge),* whose hero Cúchulainn uses a frightening array of otherworldly powers to aid the warriors of Ulster in battle against Queen Maeve of Connacht.

Dublin's streets alone have spawned an incredible number of literary greats—not only James Joyce, but also George Bernard Shaw, William Butler Yeats, and Samuel Beckett, who all won the Nobel prize for literature. Sean O'Casey told of a tenement world of poverty and revolution in dramas such as *The Plough and the Stars, Juno and the Paycock,* and *Shadow of a Gunman,* classics that are still performed today. Jonathan Swift, who became dean of Saint Patrick's Cathedral, has delighted generations of youngsters with *Gulliver's Travels.* Then there is the witty Oscar Wilde, who once informed customs officials "I have nothing to declare but my genius." Add Brendan Behan, author of *The Borstal Boy,* and Bram Stoker, master of gothic macabre and author of *Dracula,* and the litany is staggering.

Other acclaimed names include the Wicklow wordsmith John Millington Synge, who wrote of the vagrants who tramped the empty white lanes of County Wicklow and told of village humor and cruelties in the islands of the west. One of Synge's best-known works is *The Playboy of the Western World,* which had the distinction of being greeted with riots when first performed at Dublin's Abbey Theater in 1907. The entire country brims with literary associations: The bleak hills of Monaghan provided Patrick Kavanagh with poetic inspiration; the now empty Blasket Islands are brought back to life in works such as Maurice O'Sullivan's *Twenty Years A-Growing* and Peig Sayers's *Peig.* Sligo will forever be linked to W. B.Yeats; Edgeworthstown in County Longford was the home of Georgian novelist Maria Edgeworth of *Castle Rackrent* fame; County Westmeath is associated with Oliver Goldsmith, who lived here during the 1740s.

Dublin now has a Writers' Museum on Parnell Square to go with its literary pub crawls, James Joyce Trail and Bloomsday (June 16th), when Joyce's admirers don Edwardian dress and retrace the odyssey of *Ulysses's* Leopold Bloom around the city's landmarks. Yet Irish literature isn't solely devoted to past glories—the country continues to produce an endless stream of talented writers and poets. John McGahern, John Banville, and Edna O'Brien are only a few contemporary novelists whose books are well regarded by critics.

For an inkling into the trials of working-class life on Dublin's sprawling council estates, read Roddy Doyle—memorable books include *The Van, The Snapper, Paddy Clarke Ha Ha Ha,* and *The Woman Who Walked into Doors.* If you like romantic weepies, Maeve Binchy never disappoints—of her numerous novels three of my own favorites are *Light a Penny Candle, Circle of Friends,* and *Tara Road.* One of the most unlikely recent best-sellers was *Angela's Ashes* by retired New York schoolteacher Frank McCourt, a grim autobiography about his impoverished Limerick childhood that won 1997's Pulitzer Prize.

The poet Seamus Heaney scooped another Nobel Prize for Ireland in 1995. His 1997 collection of poems, *The Spirit Level,* encompasses both the hopes and disappointments of the peace process. If you enjoy poetry, I can promise you Ireland still has plenty of it. Éigse Éireann is the national poetry organization. As well as prizes and competitions, it arranges a program of readings and festivals throughout the 32 counties, north and south, by Irish and international poets. To find out what's on where, check its site at www.poetryireland.ie.

© Steenie Harvey

Prime Living
Locations

PRIME LIVING LOCATIONS

ATLANTIC OCEAN

North Channel

Tory Island

Fanad Head

Malin Head

Rathlin Island

Aran Island

Lough Foyle

Londonderry

Ballymena

NORTHERN IRELAND (UK)

Belfast

Rossan Point

Donegal

Donegal

Donegal Bay

Lough Erne

Lough Neagh

Strangford Lough

Erris Head

Belmullet

Sligo Bay

Sligo

THE NORTHWEST AND LAKELANDS

Monaghan

Dundrum Bay

Achill Island

Mayo

Sligo

Leitrim

Cavan

Dundalk

Dundalk Bay

Clare Island

Castlebar

Roscommon

Longford

Louth

Drogheda

Irish Sea

Inishturk

Clew Bay

Lough Ree

Westmeath

River Boyne

Meath

Inishbofin

Connemara

Lough Mask

Tuam

Galway

Athlone

DUBLIN

THE WESTERN SEABOARD

Lough Corrib

Galway

Offaly

R. Liffey

Dublin

Dublin

Galway Bay

Kildare

Wicklow Mountains

Wicklow

Aran Islands

Clare

Laois

Wicklow

Hag's Head

Ennis

Lough Derg

St. George's Channel

Loop Head

River Shannon

Limerick

Tipperary

Carlow

Tralee Bay

Tralee

Limerick

Carrick-on-Suir

Kilkenny

Wexford

Wexford

Killarney

Mallow

Cork

Waterford

Rosslare Bay

THE SOUTHWEST

Waterford

THE SOUTHEAST

Kerry

Dungarvan

Caha Mountains

River Lee

Cork

Kenmare River

Bantry

Youghal Bay

Old Head of Kinsale

Cork Harbour

Mizen Head

Cape Clear

Galley Head

Celtic Sea

N
W E
S

0   50 mi
0   50 km

© AVALON TRAVEL PUBLISHING, INC.

Overview

Although the next chapters on Prime Living Locations don't detail all of the republic's 26 counties, they will give you a good indication of price levels in the places that most foreign buyers are drawn to.

Of the unmentioned counties, some have become sought after with Dublin commuters—and high prices reflect this. Other counties, particularly in the midlands, don't offer a great deal in the way of scenic splendor. Well, not unless you have a peculiar yearning for endless vistas of sugar beet fields or flat brown boglands being plowed up by industrial machines.

The buzz of the big city? Those looking to indulge in a nonstop social whirl—or who are planning to insert themselves at the very heart of the country's arts, political, business, music, and student scenes—will undoubtedly be tempted by Dublin's siren song. But don't write off Ireland's other two main cities, Cork and Galway. Certainly on the arts and educational fronts, both have much to offer.

Grafton Street, Dublin

The cities and regions highlighted have properties in all price ranges. Yet although it's an important consideration, cost shouldn't be the only factor when it comes to choosing where to live. So, what makes these particular places so special?

To be honest, choice has been influenced by my own particular interests: folklore, walking, and wildlife. While I've included some urban options, many people who dream of a home in Ireland often seem to want the kind of environment that attracted me. Maybe to live in a village with wild seascapes all around, or one where the view is of green fields, golden gorse, and distant mountains. I'm also drawn to anywhere that sends out murmurs of long ago—pilgrim paths, prehistoric forts, holy wells—and you don't find those kind of places in cities.

Although I'm happy with where I've settled, it's always fun to imagine what it would be like to live somewhere else. One of my favorite memories is walking down a deserted lane in west Cork on a hot summer's day, through tunnel-like hedgerows of wild blood-red fuchsias, and coming across a perfect circle of standing stones dating to before the

Celts. Beyond this incredibly ancient place I could glimpse the sapphire shimmer of the sea and little whitewashed homes nestled in the folds of the hills. If anywhere could be described as a perfect location, this one came close.

DUBLIN

Sprawling either side of the River Liffey, Ireland's capital is an eclectic mix of the old, the new, the brash, and the genteel. It's no longer considered a second-string European capital, and prosperity has resulted in bringing the city right to the forefront of fashionability.

But although Dublin and its handsome Georgian squares are now firmly on the traveler's radar screen, most of the people you'll encounter here are local residents enjoying their city. The pubs and coffee shops of the Rathmines neighborhood teem with students. Families are out feeding the ducks in Herbert Park, shopping down Henry Street and Grafton Street, walking and taking bike rides along the seafront at nearby seaside villages such as Dalkey and Howth.

A third of Ireland's population now lives in and around the capital. An expanding city with limited housing inevitably means an escalation in prices.

And, of course, chatting—in pubs, in cafés, on buses, on street corners. One thing you'll very quickly discover is that Dubliners are noted for their irreverent wit. And one favorite pastime is to immediately rechristen any new monument or sculpture that appears with a new name.

For example, the Anna Livia monument on O'Connell Street is better known as the Floozy in the Jacuzzi. The statue depicting Molly Malone at the bottom of Grafton Street is the Tart with the Cart. The women at the Ha'Penny Bridge are the Hags with the Bags. And American scholars who revere James Joyce may be somewhat upset to realize that Dubliners have renamed his statue the Prick with the Stick.

Is Dublin affordable? Well, just as in London, Paris, or Rome, it's hard to find anything nowadays that can remotely be described as a housing bargain. But if you think about it, that's not altogether surprising. Capital cities everywhere always tend to command far higher prices than in the provinces—and Dublin is also the country's fastest-growing area. A third of Ireland's population now lives in and around the capital. An expanding city with limited housing inevitably means an escalation in prices.

Neolithic Ireland—the PoulnaBrone Dolmen, County Clare

Yet although the cost of buying houses and apartments may make you swallow hard, rents don't seem too outrageous when compared to those in major American cities. Spacious two-bedroom apartments in classy Dublin neighborhoods can still be had for less than $1,500 per month. If you're happy to share with housemates, rooms in houses and apartments often go for less than $500 monthly.

THE WESTERN SEABOARD

Strung with offshore islands, the western seaboard counties of Galway, Mayo, and Clare have a wildness about them, and it's no exaggeration to say the changing lightscapes of the mountainous Connemara area are an artist's delight.

Renowned for its music and folklore, this is another region that has given me immense pleasure through the years: searching for rare spring orchids in Clare's Burren; climbing the holy mountain of Croagh Patrick in Mayo; going to Galway to eat oysters; experiencing the fun of the Ballinasloe Horse Fair; taking the ferry to the Aran Islands.

It's a great place to live if you want to immerse yourself in traditional ways, but with Galway city within easy reach, you don't have to eschew any of the benefits of the 21st century.

THE SOUTHWEST

The southwest—which takes in the counties of Cork and Kerry—is one of the most sought-after areas with foreign buyers. Put it down to the tourism factor. Outside of Dublin, the southwest attracts more foreign visitors than anywhere else in the country. Some visitors are so smitten that they decide to extend their vacation into a lifelong commitment. Often it's a vacation home that's the target, but sometimes it's a decision to move here permanently.

It's not hard to understand why. The southwest region has some of the most varied and beautiful landscapes in the whole of Ireland—golden beaches and rugged peninsulas, mountains and lakes, colorful villages where houses are painted in a riot of rainbow colors.

As you drift down the coastline, there are just so many places that tug at the heartstrings: harbor town Kinsale, Clonakilty, Kenmare, Dingle—dozens of friendly little towns and villages that are very easy to fall head over heels in love with.

And unless you're especially seeking solitude, there's no need to live the life of a hermit. Skibbereen in County Cork and Tralee in County Kerry feel like real towns, not overgrown villages. When you need it, Cork city can provide you with the big-city, bright-lights factor. Culturewise it can give Dublin a good run for its money.

THE SOUTHEAST

In the southeastern section, you'll find details about the counties of Wexford, Waterford, Kilkenny, and Tipperary. Wexford, a former Viking stronghold, is renowned for its October opera festival and winter bird-watching. While most people tend to associate seaside counties with summer pleasures, the great swaths of golden beaches that extend around the corner into County Waterford are an absolute joy to walk during the late fall and on a clear crisp winter's day.

The southeast hinterland is pretty special too—one of the most enjoyable vacations I've had in Ireland was a walking holiday around Waterford's Nire Valley and Comeragh Mountains. Kilkenny, a town with a real medieval feel to it, is another favorite location. I came here to research an article on Irish witchcraft (see the sidebar on the *Witch of Kilkenny*), but I spent just as much time exploring the surrounding countryside of green river valleys and tumbledown monasteries. County Kilkenny acts like a magnet to craft workers and you'll find lovely villages here such as Inistioge and Graiguenamanagh.

In this southeastern section you'll also find details on one of the lesser-known counties—Tipperary. Although it doesn't have a sea coast, its gentle pastoral scenery is very appealing and full of historic interest, too. It's here you'll find the awe-inspiring Rock of Cashel as well as the Silvermines Mountains and the still waters of Lough Derg.

THE NORTHWEST AND LAKELANDS

If I had to sum up the northwest and Lakelands in three words, I'd use unspoilt, uncrowded, and undiscovered. This is my own home region and so far it has largely managed to escape the notice of the crowds. I can't understand why. County Sligo, named by the poet W. B. Yeats as "The Land of Heart's Desire," is beautiful—full of wistful landscapes and fascinating legends. Donegal has more than 200 miles of spectacular coastline and an intriguing Gaeltacht (Gaelic-speaking) area where the old music, songs, and dances are preserved and celebrated.

Delve into the Lakelands counties of Roscommon, Cavan, and Leitrim and you'll discover quintessential Ireland... country Ireland, if you like. These three counties of quiet laneways, sparkling loughs, and small villages are what I think of as the real Ireland: the kind of place where everybody knows everybody else's granny as well as every third cousin twice removed. And again—full of historical interest. The Tain, one of Ireland's oldest epic legends, begins at Cruachan—the present-day village of Rathcroghan in County Roscommon. According to the annals, this Neolithic site of earthen *raths,* standing pillars, and a circular bullring enclosure was the location of Queen Maeve's palace.

These three counties of quiet laneways, sparkling loughs, and small villages are what I think of as the real Ireland: the kind of place where everybody knows everybody else's granny as well as every third cousin twice removed.

I think the reason most people ignore Ireland's Lakelands is that there are no mountains or seascapes—in other words, the kind of picture-postcard landscapes you see in tourist brochures. Yet the scenery isn't boring—my own house overlooks a lough and on a clear day I've got distant views of the Sligo Mountains.

And there are lots of wonderful walks here too—across the low hills to glittery little loughs, out to holy wells, and through the bluebell woods. You do really have to live in the area to appreciate it, though—all the best places are out of sight, lost in the tangled maze of backroads. It was only last year that I discovered a mossy stone court cairn from Celtic times, buried in woodlands a couple of miles from my home.

Planning Your Fact-Finding Trip

Y ou shouldn't plan to cover all of Ireland in a two-week trip. Where's the joy in spending most of your precious time on the road, seeing nothing but snapshot views and fleeing like hunted refugees from one overnight stop to another?

How are you going to make time to feel the pulse of a strange town or absorb any local history and folklore? Or to walk along a silver strand to a little fishing village and watch the nets being mended? To talk to locals? And most important of all, where will you find opportunities to visit real estate agents' offices and get to see any properties?

Take your time and get to know one or two areas really well— everything else will still be here when you return.

Preparing to Leave

If you're planning to buy property, you'll generally need to make appointments with real estate agents ahead of time. Don't expect to walk into an office thinking that the agent will drop everything to take you on an inspection tour. It could be that he or she does have some free time—but it's for tomorrow, not today. Not much use if you've already arranged to move on.

Another reason why planning is important is that most Irish homeowners work. They too are unlikely to be waiting around for potential buyers to view their property. While many vendors will leave a spare key with the real estate agent, they appreciate some warning that a viewer is on the way. Others insist on being present when the agent is showing the property.

The first thing to decide is which region of Ireland appeals most. Then use the resources given in this book to contact agents with a good selection of suitable properties.

Indicate when you will be in the area and arrange a day to meet. Explain the type of property you seek and also your price range. Don't be vague. If you have a three-bedroom period cottage in mind, say so. Otherwise the unsuspecting agent may arrange to take you to see homes on suburban estates, modern bungalows, or apartments in new developments.

WHAT TO BRING

As Ireland's weather is so unpredictable, packing is no easy feat. Even in summer, you may need thick jumpers (sweaters) and a jacket. Then again, you could be wearing shorts. You may be doing a fair amount of walking, so comfy shoes are essential.

Hiking boots aren't necessary—not unless you aim to go hiking. Whether you need rubber boots (wellingtons) depends on the type of properties you plan to view. If your idea of the perfect Irish home is a farmhouse, then yes, rubber boots are handy. Farmyards tend to be muddy places, especially in winter and early spring.

Whether it's winter or summer, always prepare for rain. A light pac-a-mac to keep you dry when the summertime clouds burst won't take up much suitcase space. And if by chance you should forget your umbrella, be assured they are readily available in Ireland.

Will you be bringing a laptop computer or any kind of electrical ap-

Travelers' Tips

• Passport in order? You'll need it to enter Ireland and, just in case of accident, ensure it's valid for longer than your intended stay.

• If you take vital medication, carry a doctor's letter detailing why you need it and any generic brand that could be substituted.

• Take advantage of duty-free shopping. Despite the European Union's single market, visitors from North America can still avail themselves of duty-free allowances. Current regulations let you import 200 cigarettes, 1 liter of spirits, 2 liters of wine, 60 milliliters of perfume, and 250 milliliters of *eau de toilette*.

• Try planning your visit outside of July and August. Transatlantic fares are lower and driving around Ireland will be much more leisurely.

• Change currency and travelers checks in banks, normally open on weekdays 10 A.M.–4 P.M. Hotels, *bureaux de change*, and post offices offer less favorable rates.

• When buying gifts, watch for stores displaying "Tax Free Shopping" signs. Non-EU citizens can claim back VAT (sales tax) on purchases. You'll be given a voucher that can then be encashed at Dublin or Shannon airports.

• Guard against pickpockets, particularly at Dublin's bus and railway stations.

pliance? Then make sure you have the correct adapters and transformers. Your appliances will not work without them—and in the worst-case scenario, they could get ruined. Ireland's voltage system is different from that in the United States: We use 230 volt AC current and flat three-pin plugs. Although you can buy Irish-to-U.S. adapters in Ireland, it's difficult getting hold of ones that work the other way around. If your U.S. supplier has never heard of special adapters/transformers for Ireland, explain that it's the same electrical system as used in Britain.

If you're receiving special medication prescribed by a doctor, ensure you have enough supplies to last throughout your trip. But don't bring remedies for general aches and pains, coughs and colds, or headaches. All Irish pharmacies stock a wide range of over-the-counter medications.

It's important to check if your medical insurance covers you for foreign travel. If not, you will need to take out a policy providing cover for any possible treatment or hospitalization when you are out of the United States.

Currency

Ireland's currency is the euro. At the time of writing the exchange rate was one euro to $1.24. The symbol for the euro is €. Once you've decided to buy a property, the way to make payment is through a bank transfer—not by returning to Ireland with suitcases full of cash. Nor is it necessary to arrive with bulging wallets or purses for your fact-finding trip.

Hotels, restaurants, garages—they all accept major credit cards. For cash for day-to-day needs, simply use your Visa or MasterCard check cards. These let you get cash from home directly. You can insert your card into an ATM cash machine anywhere in Ireland. Depending on which bank operates the ATM, the normal amount you can draw in any one day is between €200 and €300.

To obtain larger amounts of euros in a single day, you'll need to go to a bank's foreign-currency counter and exchange travelers checks or dollars. But for everyday money, ATMs are the sensible way to go.

WHEN TO GO

If you're serious about house-hunting, avoid Christmas, New Year, and Easter. Real estate agencies are often closed for longer than the official public holidays. Other than those times, though, the choice is yours. Unlike in continental Europe, businesses rarely close for a monthlong summer vacation. Certainly the larger agencies employ a number of real estate agents.

Spring, summer, and fall are all appealing times to visit. Although winter isn't the time to see Ireland looking its best, at least you'll immediately realize if a house has dampness problems or is difficult to heat.

Arriving in Ireland

Compared to going through U.S. immigration and customs, arriving in Ireland is a breeze for most North American visitors.

At Dublin and Shannon airports, there are sometimes separate booths for EU passport holders and non-EU passport holders. At other times everybody passes through the same booths. Just watch the lit-up signs above to see which line is applicable to you on arrival.

It has to be said that immigration officials seem to operate a policy of quizzing certain black or Asian visitors about their purpose for being in Ireland. In the main, however, North American visitors are rubber-stamped straight through.

You go through Customs after collecting your luggage. If you have nothing to declare, arrivals from non-EU destinations should pass through what's called the Green Channel rather than the Blue Channel (which is for passengers who started their journey in an EU country). Unless you somehow give the impression you've just emerged from an opium den, it's very unlikely you'll be stopped by Customs officials. If you do have goods to declare, then use the Red Channel.

VISAS AND PASSPORTS

Holders of U.S. or Canadian passports don't need a visa for a short fact-finding mission. With a valid passport, round-trip ticket, and funds to support yourself, you can stay in Ireland for three months. (Information on the type of visa or residency permit you'll need for a longer stay is covered in the *Making the Move* chapter.)

TRANSPORTATION

Although a car isn't essential to get about Ireland's cities, the country-side is another matter. Trains and buses can be infrequent and travel only along main routes. Some counties are not served by trains at all.

Unless they're on main roads between sizable towns, villages are very ill-served by public transport. While you could take a taxi to places you want to see, this will be very expensive.

Dublin and Shannon airports have a slew of major car-hire (rental) firms. You'll also find a good choice within cities and most major towns. Rates depend on the firm you choose, type of vehicle, and also the time of year. Typically, a week's rental of a two-door economy car in March costs around €150 ($186). But hire the same car for a week in July and the rate jumps to more like €320 ($397).

Sample Itineraries

Most property-hunters will need two weeks to get a proper feel for any of Ireland's regions. If you have a rural home in mind, this is a minimum time frame.

Constantly changing your accommodation can be time-consuming. One option is to base yourself in a central location and then explore the surrounding areas on day trips. Yes, you'll be spending quite lengthy times in the car, but you will get to cover a lot of ground.

This won't work everywhere, of course. To make the most of Cork and Kerry, for example, plan for at least four separate stopovers. And if a County Donegal home appeals to you, you can't realistically expect to see much of any other county in the space of a single week.

But do also try and spend at least a couple of days of your trip in Dublin. Even if you're not interested in buying or renting here, it makes an excellent jumping-off point for Ireland's other regions. Besides which, you'll have had a long plane journey. It makes sense to spend some time relaxing before beginning house-hunting.

Where you start your journey may depend on where your flight touches down. Ireland has two airports with flights to the United States: Dublin on the east coast and Shannon on the west.

You may choose to hire a car when setting out from Dublin. Alternatively, you can easily leave it until you reach your first destination. Take the plane, take the train, take the bus—the capital is Ireland's transport hub.

DEVISING AN ITINERARY

Ireland is a small country, but clocking up the distances takes much longer than almost every first-time visitor imagines. And you're not visiting as a tourist—you're here to check out property too.

The first thing to determine is what is enticing you across the Atlantic in the first place. Ireland's scenery and historical heritage? The quirky pubs, colorful festivals, and traditional music culture? Golf? The bright lights of Dublin? Maybe it's even the chance to trace your roots and get to know local people in the area your ancestors came from. With preliminary planning, it won't be difficult to devise an itinerary to cover your own particular interests—and do some house-hunting too.

EXPLORING DUBLIN AND SURROUNDING COUNTIES

Suggested seasons: spring, summer, early fall.

Dublin Airport is on the city outskirts with buses leaving every 20 minutes for the center, the Central Bus Station (Busaras) and Connolly Railway Station which serves the midlands, northwest, and north—for example, Carrick-on-Shannon, Boyle, Sligo, and Belfast. Some buses continue to Heuston Railway Station, for trains to Kilkenny, Galway, Waterford, Cork, Westport (County Mayo), and Tralee in County Kerry. You can also take a taxi from the airport to the city center.

From the Liffey Quays to its elegant Georgian squares, Dublin is compact enough to explore on foot. There's more than those legendary pubs to keep you busy: Visit Trinity College and see the Book of Kells, spend some time in the galleries and museums, plunge into the stores around Grafton Street, and wander the cobbled laneways of bohemian Temple Bar.

Be sure to take the DART suburban rail to Dublin's seaside suburbs. Northbound trains go to Howth with its spectacular cliff paths rambling around the Howth Head peninsula. Alternatively, head south to Dalkey, where the affluent have grand villas overlooking the beaches and Killiney Bay.

If you're in Dublin longer than a couple of days, you may want to explore some of its surrounding counties too.

County Kildare

Dublin is bordered on its west by Kildare. Lush meadows and limestone plains have helped to make the county classic horse-breeding country. This is where you'll find the National Stud and many thoroughbred racehorses are bred, trained, and also raced around the Curragh, a grassy plain that stretches unfenced for more than 5,000 acres. Top-class golf courses include the K Club. Frequent trains make the 30-minute journey from Dublin's Connolly Station to the neat town of Maynooth, noted for its ecclesiastical colleges.

County Meath

Once the seat of the high kings of Ireland, County Meath has some important archeological sites: Newgrange, Knowth, and Dowth. Unless you take a day excursion, these sites are best explored by car. Trim is a sleepy little town with a mighty Anglo-Norman castle, one of the country's best preserved.

County Wicklow

South of Dublin, County Wicklow is known as the Garden of Ireland. Its coast, the walking trails of the Wicklow Hills, and the ancient monastic settlement of Glendalough make for a grand day out. Suburban trains from Dublin serve the Wicklow towns of Bray and Greystones.

EXPLORING THE WEST COAST

Suggested seasons: spring, summer, early fall. Arrive in Galway via Dublin Airport or Shannon Airport.

Galway city is around 135 miles from Dublin Airport; 55 miles from Shannon Airport. Trains run from Dublin's Heuston Station with a journey time of three hours. Leaving from the Central Bus Station, buses take an hour longer. Some private operators also run scheduled buses from Dublin Airport directly to Galway. The information desk at the airport will have details. Taking around 90 minutes, buses also go between Shannon Airport and Galway. There are also flights between Dublin and Galway.

On the River Corrib, Galway city brims with history—it's also filled with shopping precincts, theaters, pubs, and restaurants. The city's cultural calendar includes a Festival of Literature at Easter, the Arts Festival and Galway Race Week in July, and the International Oyster Festival in September.

With a car and an early start, you can reach many parts of counties Mayo and Clare as well as Connemara from Galway city. However, to make the most of this region, allow at least three stopovers. Good bases would be Galway city, somewhere around the Westport/Castlebar area in County Mayo, and the Ennis vicinity of County Clare.

Connemara

Connemara is County Galway's northernmost part. Its craggy coastline, sparkling lakes, mauve-tinged mountains, and sandy beaches continue to inspire artists, writers, and dreamers. With frequent stops to drink in the scenery, it's around a 90-minute drive from Galway city to Clifden, Connemara's main town.

The Aran Islands

The three Aran Islands—Inishmore, Inisheer, and Inishmaan—are rocky bastions of Gaelic civilization where Irish is the day-to-day language. The largest island is Inishmore. You can fly there from Galway's small airport or take a ferry from Rossaveal, 23 miles from Galway city. There are also direct ferries from the city during the summer. Reaching Inishmore takes 90 minutes.

Lough Corrib

Pleasure-cruisers sail across Galway's island-studded Lough Corrib to Ashford Castle in County Mayo. Walks through the castle's woods lead to Cong village with its ruined abbey, market cross, and stone bridges.

North County Clare

Although it's a full-day trip from Galway by car, you can easily sample some of the best that northern County Clare offers. First make for the coastal village of Ballyvaughan. From here, tracks join with the Burren Way, where you can look for rare wildflowers among the Neolithic stone settlements and abandoned famine villages. Then continue to the Cliffs of Moher and Doolin village, renowned for traditional music.

County Mayo

Its bays peppered with little islands, the western seaboard county of Mayo shares similar seascapes and mountain scenery with neighboring Galway. Visible from most of the county, conical Croagh Patrick is a pilgrimage mountain that thousands of people climb every year.

House-hunters could choose to base themselves in or around either the coastal town of Westport or the inland county town of Castlebar. It's less than an hour's drive between the two; both are served by trains from Dublin's Heuston Station.

Southern County Clare

The southern reaches of County Clare are best explored from Ennis, the county town. Seaside towns within easy striking distance include Lahinch and Liscannor. Small towns and villages dot the shores of Lough Derg, a popular place in summer for water sports. The south Clare countryside is home to a host of abbeys, castles, and ancient monuments and a very good hunting ground for reasonably priced cottages.

EXPLORING CORK AND KERRY

Suggested seasons: spring, summer, early fall. Arrive in Cork via Dublin Airport or Shannon Airport.

If you decide to bring North Kerry into the equation, add a stop in the Tralee area. It doesn't boast Kerry's most enticing scenery, but you'll find some of the county's best-value properties here.

Internal flights link Dublin with Cork, and you can also take buses or trains from Heuston Station. Buses and trains also serve Kerry's two main towns of Killarney and Tralee. There are also bus links to both Cork and Kerry from Shannon Airport.

Spare 12 days at least for this spectacular region—and hire a car. From a base in Cork city, first explore the nearby harbor towns of Youghal to the east and Kinsale to the west. Then drift slowly westward through Clonakilty toward the Skibbereen area. This market town makes a good stopover for exploring around Bantry Bay, the pretty fishing villages of Glandore, Baltimore, and Schull, and the Mizen Head, Sheep's Head, and Beara peninsulas.

Then onto Kerry. Known as "the Kingdom," its stunning scenery has long attracted visitors. There are also many lovely coastal resorts, excellent fishing, a plethora of golf courses, and the fabulous Dingle Peninsula. Two likely bases here would be Kenmare and Dingle town. If you decide to bring North Kerry into the equation, add a stop in the Tralee area. It doesn't boast Kerry's most enticing scenery, but you'll find some of the county's best-value properties here.

During summer, the colors are delectable in both counties. Purple heather blankets mountains, gardens overflow with pink and blue hydrangea bushes, and hedgerows blaze with blood-red fuchsias, lacy white cow parsley, and the mauve foxglove spires.

Cork City

On the River Lee, Cork city is Ireland's second-largest city. A city of spires and bridges, it has its own university and a thriving arts scene. 2005 saw it granted the title of European Capital of Culture.

Youghal and Cobh

East of Cork city, Youghal is a 13th-century walled harbor town. Sir

Barleycove, West Cork

© Steenie Harvey

Walter Raleigh was once its mayor. Cobh has an immense natural harbor: This was where 2.5 million of Ireland's 19th-century emigrants had their last glimpse of Ireland before embarking for the New World. In those days the town was called Queenstown after Britain's Queen Victoria.

Kinsale

Kinsale lies west of Cork city. A harbor town, it has a marina, cliff-top fortresses and higgledy-piggledy laneways. Its shops and restaurants are bright as paint and laden with flower-filled window boxes.

Clonakilty

West again along the coast road, Clonakilty is a pretty heritage town of color-washed houses and shops with hand-painted wooden signs. Distractions from house-hunting include hiking along shady laneways to discover the mysterious druidic stone circle at Drombeg.

Skibbereen and Baltimore

A prosperous farmers' town, Skibbereen has a plethora of attractive seaside villages within a short drive. With its ruined castle and a lookout over Roaringwater Bay and Carberry's Hundred Islands, Baltimore is a particular gem.

The Mizen and Sheep's Head Peninsulas

For one of west Cork's best beaches, continue west from Skibbereen through Schull and along the Mizen Peninsula to Barleycove. The sea here is an entrancing swirl of sapphire, jade, and turquoise. More fine sandy coves decorate the adjoining Sheep's Head Peninsula, which has Dunmanus Bay on one side and Bantry Bay on the other.

Kenmare

Kenmare, a stopping point on the Ring of Kerry, is a bustling town of brightly painted houses. Many date to the 17th century. One of its crafts is lace-making, a business originally set up by nuns to create employment after 1845's famine.

The Ring of Kerry

Whizzing around the 112-mile length of the Ring of Kerry drive takes a minimum of six hours and that's allowing for only cursory stops at main highlights. Summer traffic over the mountain passes linking

Killarney, County Kerry

© Steenie Harvey

Kenmare to Killarney town moves at the speed of molasses—you've been warned!

Killarney Town
Vying with Blarney Castle for the title of Ireland's biggest tourist trap, Killarney is overburdened with tourist coach-loads. The major draw is the wooded shores and glens of the Lakes of Killarney: island-studded lakes guarded by Ireland's highest mountains.

The Dingle Peninsula
Kerry's Dingle Peninsula has more than 2,000 archaeological sites—everything from monastic beehive huts to prehistoric forts. A drive around the peninsula delivers magical views across to the deserted Blasket Islands. Dingle town's music pubs provide lively entertainment and many serve evening meals.

North Kerry
Fringing fertile green pastures, north Kerry also has beaches and secluded

coves. With its miles of silver strands and golf course, Ballybunion is very popular with Irish vacationers. The major towns in north Kerry are Tralee and Listowel.

EXPLORING SOUTHEAST IRELAND

Suggested seasons: spring, summer, early fall. Arrive in the southeast via Dublin Airport.

Away from the house-hunting trail, Ireland's southeast offers much to waylay you. Highlights include the thatched-cottage coastal villages of counties Wexford and Waterford, walking in the Nire Valley or Comeragh Mountains, and exploring Kilkenny's peaceful river valleys and craft villages. County Tipperary's historic showpieces include the Rock of Cashel and Cahir Castle.

Wexford town is a little more than 2.5 hours by train from Dublin's Connolly Station. Trains also call at Gorey, Enniscorthy, and Rosslare, three other towns within County Wexford. Along with buses, the other three counties have services from Dublin's Heuston Station. Trains also run between the ferry port in Rosslare and Limerick, and these pass through Waterford city and also Clonmel and Cahir in County Tipperary. But to make the most of the region, hire a car.

My own choice of places to stay in this region would be Wexford town, Kilkenny city, Waterford city, and also Clonmel in County Tipperary. But if you want to explore without changing your accommodation too often, Kilkenny is ideally placed for forays into County Waterford—Waterford city is only an hour's drive. Alternatively you could use Waterford city as a base for exploring County Kilkenny.

Clonmel in County Tipperary is also handy for dipping into County Waterford and across into Kilkenny; an added bonus is that you're an easy drive from both Cahir and Cashel. Although one definite stopover should be Wexford town, wherever else you choose to stay, much of the southeast is within fairly easy driving distance. That's if you make an early start.

Kilkenny City

Complete with a castle, an abbey, and ancient laneways, Kilkenny is Ireland's finest example of a medieval city.

The Nore Valley

Usually with a ruined abbey or castle on the doorstep, villages along County Kilkenny's Nore River Valley are noted centers for arts and crafts. Villages to particularly look out for are Thomastown, Bennets-bridge, Graiguenamanagh, and Inistioge.

Waterford City

Renowned for its exquisite crystal, Waterford is Ireland's oldest city. Vikings built a trading settlement here in A.D. 850. The Spraoi Festival, Waterford's big summer event, is a riot of musicians, street theater, parades, and fireworks. For three days (usually at the end of July), the city's quays become a huge outdoor stage.

Dunmore East

Dunmore East is a County Waterford fishing village with thatched cottages, lighthouse. and 12th-century castle. Nearby beaches include Ladies' Cove, Badger's Cove, and Counsellor's Strand. Go sea-angling from Dunmore's harbor or relax in the Strand Inn, once a smugglers' meeting place.

Wexford Town

Another old Viking settlement with a harbor, Wexford town's ribbon-thin streets are full of character. There's a great choice of pubs and restaurants, a summer Viking festival, and an October opera festival. The Irish National Heritage Park is just outside the town boundary. Seven miles away, Curracloe provides an example of the great beaches found in this county.

Kilmore Quay

On Wexford's south coast, Kilmore Quay is a village of lobster pots and thatched houses. Out to sea the Saltee Islands were once nicknamed "the Graveyard of a Thousand Ships." You can take boat trips to these uninhabited islands, one of Europe's most important bird sanctuaries.

Clonmel

On the River Suir, Clonmel still has something of the air of an old-fashioned Georgian coaching town. Although in County Tipperary, it's the ideal base for exploring Waterford's Nire Valley.

Cashel

Deep in County Tipperary, the Rock of Cashel is Ireland's Acropolis. Rising above Cashel town, this spectacular medieval settlement includes a 12th-century round tower, a 13th-century Gothic cathedral, and a 15th-century castle. Not far from here is Cahir, site of one of Ireland's best-preserved Anglo-Norman castles.

EXPLORING THE NORTHWEST AND LAKELANDS

Suggested seasons: spring, summer, early fall. Arrive in The Northwest and Lakelands.

County Sligo is synonymous with the poet W. B. Yeats—you can visit many sites mentioned in his poems. Like County Roscommon, it's a place of quiet country roads and unspoiled scenery dotted with archaeological sites. Loughs and rivers make Leitrim and Cavan a paradise for anglers and boaters.

County Sligo is synonymous with the poet W. B. Yeats—you can visit many sites mentioned in his poems. Like County Roscommon, it's a place of quiet country roads and unspoiled scenery dotted with archaeological sites.

If it's beaches that attract you, it has to be Donegal. The county possesses some of Ireland's very best. Unfortunately it isn't really practical to visit the wildest and most wonderful parts of Donegal from outside the county. However, almost any base in counties Sligo, Roscommon, and Leitrim will allow you to cover a good deal of those three counties. Leitrim is best-placed for forays into County Cavan.

Trains from Dublin's Connolly Station to Sligo pass through Boyle (County Roscommon) and Carrick-on-Shannon (County Leitrim). Buses also serve this route. Without a car, bus is the only way to reach County Donegal's main towns. The county isn't served by trains.

Sligo Town

Sligo town's spires are overshadowed by the tabletop mountain of Benbulben. The youthful stamping ground of W. B. Yeats, many localities around the town have Yeatsian associations. The best known is Lough Gill and the Lake Isle of Inisfree. Here the poet imagined building a little cabin made of clay and wattles, planting nine rows of beans, and living alone in a bee-loud glade.

Strandhill

On the Sligo coast, Strandhill is a seaside resort with fine sandy beaches overlooked by a high cairn-topped hill called Knocknarea. According to legends, it's the burial place of the warrior-queen Maeve.

Lough Key

Near the County Roscommon town of Boyle, Lough Key and its islands are surrounded by a Forest Park where herons nest in reed beds, goldcrests flit through treetops, and deer scamper along the trails. One walk takes you across a Fairy Bridge, others lead to ring forts and a Wishing Chair.

Carrick-on-Shannon

In Leitrim, the marina town of Carrick-on-Shannon is a busy base for River Shannon cruising.

Ardara and Glencolumbcille

With wide golden beaches and sea caves close by, the town of Ardara is a good place to seek out locally made knitwear at prices far lower than in the cities. Also in southwest Donegal, Glencolumbcille is an Irish-speaking village of thatched cottages where Saint Columba was reputedly born.

Inishowen Peninsula

Girdled with small coastal towns, Donegal's Inishowen Peninsula is where you'll find Malin Head, Ireland's most northerly point.

Practicalities

ACCOMMODATIONS

Dublin
Buswells Hotel
In the heart of Georgian Dublin, Buswells Hotel is an 18th-century town house. Just across the road from the Parliament buildings, it offers a special midweek rate of €130 ($161) for doubles, €100 ($124) for singles, including breakfast.
Molesworth Street, Dublin 2; tel. 01/614-6500; buswells-reservations @quinn-hotels.com; www.quinnhotels.com.

O'Neills
If you want to spend all night in a pub, O'Neills is the place for you. Including breakfast, twin rooms in this city-center Victorian pub—established in 1885—cost €35–65 ($43.50–81) per person sharing.

36/37 Pearse Street, Dublin 2; tel. 01/671-4074; oneilpub@iol.ie; www.
oneillsdublin.com.

Auburn Bed-and-Breakfast
Auburn is a family-run bed-and-breakfast in Drumcondra, close to the
city center and airport. Price per person sharing a double room is €36
($45). Singles cost €55 ($68).
61 Grace Park Terrace, Drumcondra 9; tel. 01/837-8389; enquiries@auburn
.ie; www.auburn.ie.

Dublin Tourism
If you arrive without accommodation, tourist offices at the airport
and within the city offer a booking service. You can also book accommodation through the official website. If you're staying for more
than one night, many hotels offer special weekend and midweek rates.
These are worth inquiring about as they're a lot more advantageous
than rack rates.
Suffolk Street, Dublin 2; tel. 01/605-7700; fax: 01/605-7757; inform
ation@dublintourism.ie; www.visitdublin.com.

The Western Seaboard
Glenlo Abbey Hotel
Five minutes' drive from Galway city center, one of the best places to
stay is the five-star Glenlo Abbey Hotel. A charmingly restored 18th-
century manor house, it has its own golf course beside Lough Corrib
and an excellent restaurant. Rack rates are from €195 ($242) for a
double room; from €145 ($180) for a single. Breakfast is extra at €18
($22.50) per person. However, during winter, you can get midweek
bed-and-breakfast specials for €75 ($93) per person sharing.
Bushy Park, Galway; tel. 091/526666; fax: 091/527800; info@glen
loabbey.ie; www.glenlo.com.

Great Southern Hotel
Eyre Square is only a short stroll from the countless stores, pubs, and
restaurants around Shop Street and Quay Street. Looking over the
square, the Great Southern Hotel offers a raft of special deals: the current web deal for a standard double is €89 ($110.50).
Eyre Square, Galway; tel. 091/564041; res@galway.gsh.ie; www.gs
hotels.com.

Maple House
Mostly charging around €30 per person per night, there's a plethora of bed-and-breakfast establishments in Galway's seaside suburb, Salthill. It's only a 10-minute bus ride to the heart of the city and you can watch the sun going down over Galway Bay.
Doctor Mannix Road, Salthill; tel. 091/526136; maplehouse@eircom.net.

Pontoon Bridge Hotel
A well-known fishing hotel, the Pontoon Bridge in County Mayo offers bed-and-breakfast for €75–85 ($93–105.50) per person per night depending on season. Dinner is €23–40 ($28.50–50).
Pontoon, County Mayo; tel. 094/925-6120; fax: 094/925-6688; sales@pontoonbridge.com; www.pontoon.mayo-ireland.ie.

Ireland West Regional Tourism Authority
You'll find plenty more accommodation options on the website of Ireland West Regional Tourism Authority.
Eyre Square, Galway; tel. 091/563081; fax: 091/565201; www.ireland west.ie.

The Southwest
The Blue Horizon
Overlooking the Old Head Golf Links and the ocean, the Blue Horizon in Kinsale is a cozy bar offering bed-and-breakfast accommodation. Price per person sharing ensuite, €45 ($56).
Garrettstown, Kinsale, County Cork; tel./fax: 021/477-8217; blueh @indigo.ie.

Actons Hotel
Also in Kinsale, Actons Hotel has a gourmet restaurant on the premises. Rack rates are €70–100 ($87–124) per person sharing for bed-and-breakfast, but check the website for special deals. At the time of writing, midweek breaks are available between Sunday and Thursday night. The rate of €250 ($310) per person includes three nights' accommodation with full Irish breakfast, and dinner on two evenings.
Pier Road, Kinsale, County Cork; tel. 021/477-9900; fax: 021/477-2231; information@actonshotelkinsale.com; www.actonshotelkinsale.com.

Springfield House
Just outside Clonakilty, Springfield House offers bed-and-breakfast on a dairy farm with a panoramic view of the Atlantic Ocean. The owners will make you a packed lunch if you're touring. Price per person sharing ensuite, €33 ($41).
Kilkern, Castlefreke, Clonakilty, County Cork; tel./fax: 023/40622; jandmccallanan@eircom.net.

The Townhouse Bed and Breakfast
The Townhouse Bed and Breakfast in Dingle has a sandy beach nearby and the owners also speak Irish if you want to practice your Gaeilige. Price per person sharing is €35 ($43.50). All rooms are ensuite with tea-making facilities.
Main Street, Dingle, County Kerry; tel. 066/915-1147; fax: 066/915-2044.

Park Hotel
If you intend on treating yourself to a top-class hotel, do it in Kenmare and contemplate the splendor of Kerry from your window. The Park Hotel has its own golf course, tennis courts, and spa, and boating, horseback-riding, and angling are nearby. Rack rates for standard rooms with breakfast are €158–217 ($196–269) per person sharing, but check the website for special offers.
Kenmare, County Kerry; tel. 064/41200; fax: 064/41402; info@park kenmare.com; www.parkkenmare.com.

Cork Kerry Tourism
Cork Kerry Tourism has plenty more options on its website.
Áras Fáilte, Grand Parade, Cork city; tel. 021/425-5100; fax: 021/425-5199; www.corkkerry.ie.

The Southeast
Foxmount Country House
Ten minutes' drive from Waterford City, Foxmount is a 17th-century country house on a dairy farm. Breakfast-time breads and jams are all homemade and this bed-and-breakfast is a past winner of the "Galtee Best Breakfast" award, a meal that will set you up for a day's sightseeing or house-hunting. Price per person for bed-and-breakfast is €55 ($68).

Passage East Road, Waterford; tel. 051/874308; fax: 051/854906; info @foxmountcountryhouse.com.

Carraig Rua
Close to Kilkenny town center, with a golf club, restaurants, and the bus and rail stations within a short walk, Carraig Rua is a two-story bed-and-breakfast residence on the main road to Dublin. Price per person is €33 ($41) sharing ensuite.
Dublin Road, Kilkenny, County Kilkenny; tel./fax: 056/772-2929.

The Blue Door
The Blue Door is a beautifully decorated Georgian town house in Wexford town center, just a stroll to charming shops, traditional music pubs, and excellent restaurants. All rooms are ensuite with television, tea, and coffee. Bed-and-breakfast is €40 ($50) per person, sharing.
18 Lower George Street, Wexford town, County Wexford; tel. 053/21047; bluedoor@indigo.ie.

South East Tourism
More accommodation options are to be had from South East Tourism. 41 The Quay, Waterford; tel. 051/875823; fax: 051/877388; www.southeastireland.com.

The Northwest and Lakelands
The Sandhouse Hotel
Overlooking the Atlantic, beside one of County Donegal's best beaches, the Sandhouse Hotel is open February to December. Per person rates for bed-and-breakfast in standard rooms go from €85 ($105.50) low season to €95 ($118) high season. If you want to have dinner in its Seashell Restaurant, house specialties include Donegal Bay salmon, sea trout, scallops, crab, and lobster, as well as prime beef, lamb, veal, and game in season. Rossnowlagh, County Donegal; tel. 071/985-1777; fax: 071/985-2100; info@sandhouse-hotel.ie; www.sandhouse-hotel.ie.

Drumraine House
Budget bed-and-breakfast options include Drumraine House in Donegal town. Prices per person sharing are €27 ($33.50).
Upper Main Street, Donegal, County Donegal; tel. 074/972-1516; shanec@iol.ie.

Gratuities

When eating out, it's customary to leave around 10 percent of the bill, though this doesn't apply in fast-food places or eateries with counter service where patrons help themselves. Some restaurants add a "service charge" to your bill so check it carefully. It's not necessary to tip again and if you've received bad service, stand up for your rights and refuse to pay the service charge.

Don't tip bartenders unless drinks are brought to a table. As few establishments offer table service anyway, it's not something you'll encounter much. However, if you get into conversation with a friendly bartender, you may want to ask them to join you in a drink.

It's not obligatory to tip porters but most people give a small amount of coinage to avoid feeling uncomfortable. Nor is it obligatory to tip taxi drivers, but few enjoy being deprived of their expected 10 percent--some Dublin cabbies aren't slow in treating ungrateful customers to rather colorful language. As regards hairdressers, women customarily tip around 10 percent. Barbers and unisex salons don't really expect a man to leave anything.

Cromleach Lodge Country House

On the border between counties Sligo and Roscommon, Cromleach Lodge comes into the splurge category. Standard room bed-and-breakfast rates per person sharing are €126–166 ($156–206) depending on season. A double room let as a single is an extra €50 ($62) per night. Half-board rates per person include a seven-course gourmet dinner. For a five-night stay the per person sharing price is €854–1,039 ($1059–1288). Castlebaldwin, County Sligo; tel. 071/916-5155; fax: 071/916-5455; www.cromleach.com.

Meadow Vale

A mile from Carrick-on-Shannon and within walking distance of the River Shannon, Meadow Vale is a modern farm bungalow offering bed-and-breakfast accommodation. Rates are €35 ($43.50) per person sharing. Dublin Road, Carrick-on-Shannon, County Leitrim; tel. 071/962-0521.

North West Tourism

You can get more accommodation ideas from North West Tourism. Temple Street, Sligo; tel. 071/916-1201; fax: 071/916-0360; www.irelandnorthwest.ie.

FOOD

Dublin
The Cedar Tree
Dublin has a fantastic choice of ethnic eateries. A personal favorite is the Cedar Tree's Lebanese cuisine—a tempting range of vegetarian *mezze* including tabbouleh (tomato, onion, parsley, and bulgur wheat salad), tender lamb dishes, and traditional desserts such as baklava.
11 Saint Andrews Street, Dublin 2; tel. 01/677-2121.

The Trocadero
In business since the 1950s, the Trocadero is Dublin's best-known theater restaurant. Decorated with red velvet drapes and autographed photos of stars, it attracts both pre-theater diners and posttheater performers. Complete with over-the-top theatrical behavior, more than a few after-show parties have been held here. The restaurant food is best described as Irish with French overtones. Deep-fried brie might not be for everyone, but the steaks and fish are generally superb. Reservations advised.
3 Saint Andrews Street, Dublin 2; tel. 01/677-5545.

Patrick Guilbaud
Awarded two Michelin stars, Patrick Guilbaud is top of the range. However, there is a special *table d'hote* lunch menu for €30 ($37) for two courses, €45 ($56) for three. Mains include pan-fried breast of wood pigeon and wild salmon marinated in maple syrup. Reservations essential for both lunch and dinner.
21 Merrion Street, Dublin 2; tel. 01/676-4192.

The Western Seaboard
Pierres
In Galway city, Pierre's is a French-style brasserie. Just as in France you can choose from a set-price menu with a range of choices. A three-course dinner costs €22.90 ($28.50) with wine extra. Starters include mussels steamed in white wine and garlic cream, farmhouse pâté, and roulade of salmon and spinach. Mains vary from caramelized fillet of pork to sole filled with a spinach and prawn mousse.
8 Quay Street, Galway city; tel. 091/566066.

Tulsi

Curries, tandooris, and a fabulous range of vegetarian dishes. A favorite with Galway fans of Indian cuisine, Tulsi won the Restaurant Association of Ireland's "Best Ethnic Restaurant" award last year.
3 Buttermilk Walk, Middle Street, Galway city; tel. 091/564831.

Moran's

Not far from the west coast village of Clarinbridge, Moran's is a 250-year-old thatched pub and seafood restaurant serving smoked salmon, crab, prawns, crab claws, and lobster all day. The Galway Bay oysters come from Willie Moran's own oyster beds.
The Weir, Kilcolgan, County Galway; tel. 091/796113.

Quay Cottage

Creamy seafood chowder followed by corn-crusted monkfish, pan-fried in garlic butter and served with a julienne of vegetables and pink peppercorn sauce? Or maybe a crispy spring roll, then honey-roasted duck in an orange liqueur sauce?
The Harbour, Westport, County Mayo; tel. 098/26412.

The Southwest
The Captain's Table

Tian of smoked duck and bacon with avocado and raspberry vinaigrette... *canon* of lamb on a black pudding *rösti with thyme and rosemary jus*... carrageen moss *mousse* in a chocolate cup followed by a west Cork cheese board. In Kinsale, the Captain's Table is a member of the gourmet Good Food Circle. The waterfront bar features music every Thursday, Friday, and Saturday night during the summer. Cork City Jazz Band plays every Sunday lunchtime.
Actons Hotel, Pier Road, Kinsale, County Cork; tel. 021/477-9900.

An Sugan

Dating to 1902, An Sugan is a popular seafood restaurant and bar with fish and shellfish delivered fresh daily from local suppliers. Depending on the catch, the menu changes daily, but there's usually seafood pie, salmon and potato cakes, and chowder.
Wolfe Tone Street, Clonakilty, County Cork; tel. 023/33719 or 023/33498.

Wild Banks Restaurant
In the center of Dingle Town, Wild Banks takes its name from a legendary fishing ground near West Kerry's Blasket Sound. It opens at lunchtime between July and September; evenings March to early January. Mondays are its closing day.
Main Street, Dingle, County Kerry; tel. 066/915-2888.

The Southeast
The Wine Vault Restaurant
The Wine Vault Restaurant is a beautifully restored 18th-century bonded warehouse and wine vault in the old quarter of Waterford city. Quality meat and vegetarian dishes as well as freshly caught seafood are offered daily. Reservations usually essential.
High Street, Waterford city; tel. 051/853444.

The Strand Inn
In the seaside village of Dunmore East, the family-run Strand Inn restaurant specializes in freshly caught seafood and always tries to use organic vegetables and fruits in season.
Dunmore East, County Waterford; tel. 051/383174.

Kilkenny Design Centre
The Kilkenny Design Centre has its own coffee shop and restaurant overlooking the cobbled courtyard of Kilkenny Castle. Savor a snack of smoked salmon with brown bread and a glass of wine, or indulge in piping-hot Irish stew with a glass of locally brewed ale.
Castle Yard, Kilkenny Town; tel. 056/772-2118.

The Northwest and Lakelands
Hargadons
For a lunchtime sandwich and a pint in Sligo, you won't go wrong in Hargadons—an amazingly old-fashioned pub with a "must-photograph" interior. In winter, head for one of the backroom snugs or grab a seat beside the pot-bellied stove. During summer, the beer garden is open.
4 O'Connell Street, Sligo; tel. 071/917-0933.

Seaview Tavern
At Malin Head, the Seaview is Ireland's most northerly restaurant. It

overlooks the harbor, beautiful beaches, and on a clear day the hills of Scotland are clearly visible. The extensive lunch and dinner menu specializes in local seafood and homegrown produce.
Ballygorman, Malin Head, Inishowen, County Donegal; tel. 074 /937-0117.

Woodhill House
In Ardara, Woodhill House offers a menu that's French-based but uses fresh Irish produce. The specialty is seafood from nearby Killybegs, Ireland's principal fishing port.
Ardara, County Donegal; tel. 074/954-1112.

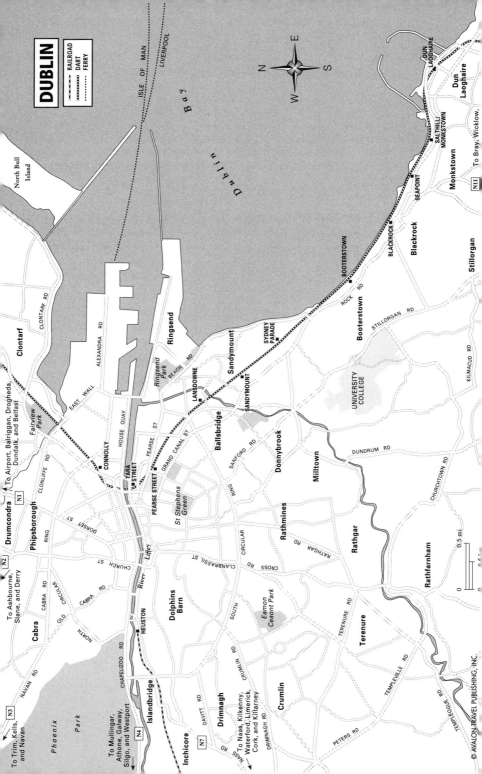

Dublin

To some people, it's the crock of gold at the end of the Irish rainbow. To others, it's a dirty congested city with major traffic problems. You'll love it or hate it, but there's nothing parochial about Dublin. Home to more than one million residents, bursting at its seams, Ireland's capital is also its most vibrant and cosmopolitan city. Street markets, Georgian doors, Viking excavations, and traditional pubs, yes—but also shopping malls, shiny office buildings, and pulsating night clubs.

Because it gazes out over the Irish Sea, Dublin's growth from an 8th-century Norse trading post into a major city has been restricted by both the sea and a collar of green mountains. But, as its center is fairly compact, this means it's easy to explore on foot.

Beguilements come thick and fast. Some are historical, some are downright fantastical (what other cathedral other than Dublin's Christchurch displays the mummified bodies of a cat and a rat?), but there's lots of enticing shopping, eating, and entertainment beguilements too.

Unusually for a European capital city, Dublin can boast that it still has the wilderness right on its doorstep. Mountain walks, castles, sandy beaches, grandiose gardens, and fishing ports are within 30 to 50 minutes' distance from the center. Easily accessible by public transport, they act as the perfect foil to the uproar of the metropolis.

The passing centuries have left Dublin with distinctive overlays of character and architecture. What strikes many visitors is the city's peculiar mix of affluence and deprivation. Often steps away from Georgian splendor, you come across litter-strewn streets and inner-city blight. The majority of Dublin's residents have done extremely well out of the Celtic Tiger, but not everybody heard its roar. Unlike 20 years ago, the city now has many immigrants who came here seeking their fortunes.

You have only to stroll down Grafton Street, Dame Street, South Great George's Street, or around the laneways of Temple Bar to realize that Dublin has become a multicultural city with an exotic melange of music, dance, cuisine, and fashion. Conversely, if you explore some of the more run-down areas north of the River Liffey, it's all too obvious that not all of these recent immigrants have struck lucky.

On a more upbeat note, Dubliners can boast of being the happiest people in Europe. Dublin topped the list of European capitals surveyed in 2004's Pfizer Healthy Neighborhood Survey. Respondents had a 68 percent satisfaction rating with their neighborhood.

The Lay of the Land

On a crescent-shaped bay of the Irish Sea, Dublin spreads out from its port to the plains of Kildare, the farming fields of Meath, and down into the Wicklow Hills. With the population explosion, the city has now almost filled up all the spaces within the old County Dublin boundaries. It is now divided into four administrative units. These are Dublin City, Fingal, Dun Laoghaire/Rathdown, and South Dublin.

The River Liffey divides central Dublin into two distinct sectors: South Side and North Side. All South Side districts carry even-numbered postal codes: Dublin 2, Dublin 4, Dublin 6, and so on. All the North Side districts carry odd-numbered postal codes: Dublin 1, Dublin 3, Dublin 5, and so on.

Although it can only be a generalization, the districts of South

Side Dublin are considered more middle-class and affluent than their North Side counterparts. However, when it comes to the city center, you'll find luxurious new apartment developments on both sides of the River Liffey.

Some visitors worry about safety, but Dublin is no more dangerous than any other European capital. It can't be denied that the growing gap between rich and poor has brought with it a rise in crime but there's no need to be paranoid—just keep alert. Aside from the Phoenix Park at night—which can be dangerous—there are no real no-go areas. Some streets in the vicinity of Connolly Station (Dublin 1) are rather seedy and insalubrious, but there's no good reason for you to go wandering up places such as Upper Gardiner Street in the dead of night.

Housing

SAMPLE PROPERTIES

Here's an example of properties you might expect to find in Dublin and surrounding areas:

- Two-bedroom apartment (657 square feet) in the outer suburb of Swords: €215,000 ($266,600).
- In the shadow of Glasnevin's cemetery, a 323-square-foot apartment in a newly built residential block: €240,000 ($297,600).
- Within walking distance of St. Stephen's Green and Grafton Street, a one-bedroom apartment (344 square feet) in Dublin 2—as central as you can get: €229,000 ($284,000).
- A short stroll from the city center, a one-bedroom urban cottage (452 square feet) tucked away off Lower Clanbrassil Street, Dublin 8. These tiny cottages were once home to railway workers, dockers, and their families: €265,000 ($328,600).
- Bracing seaside walks and a two-bedroom apartment (743 square feet) in Howth: €320,000 ($396,800).
- Also in the seaside suburb of Howth, a two-bedroom cottage (527 square feet) close to schools, shops, restaurants, and the DART (Dublin Area Rapid Transport) station: €380,000 ($471,000).
- Single-story red-brick house (807 square feet) in Drumcondra (Dublin 9). To the rear is a 38-foot garden, paved and planted with shrubs and flowers. Close at hand are local shops, restaurants, and bus routes, Griffith Park, and the Botanical Gardens. It's being marketed as having plenty

to offer to any young couple moving up the property ladder: €440,000 ($545,600).
- Victorian period–style villa (1,948 square feet) with rear garden on Merrion Road (Dublin 4), one of the capital's most exclusive addresses: €1 .4 million ($1,736,000).

LONG-TERM RENTALS

The average monthly rent for a one-bedroom apartment in Dublin is now €850 ($1,054); €1,125 ($1,395) for a two-bedroom apartment. Here are some examples:
- In Applewood Village, Swords, a one-bedroom ground-floor apartment, furnished; close to shops, gym, and local amenities: €825 ($1,023) monthly.
- Furnished one-bedroom apartment overlooking Clarinda Park in the seaside suburb of Dun Laoghaire: €900 ($1,116) monthly.
- Overlooking the Liffey, a furnished two-bedroom apartment on Ellis Quay, Dublin 7: €1,100 ($1,364) monthly.
- Furnished two-bedroom cottage near Christchurch (Dublin 8), just 10 minutes' walk from Saint Stephen's Green: €1,400 ($1,736) monthly.
- Two-bedroom penthouse apartment, furnished, in a development at Clarion Quay (Dublin 1), close to the International Financial Services Center: €1,500 ($1,860) monthly.

HOUSE AND APARTMENT SHARES

A daily newspaper that comes out at lunchtime, the *Evening Herald* is the best newspaper for finding shared accommodation for both students and young professionals. The website www.daft.ie is another good source. In addition, every Students Union has a notice board with postings for accommodation offered as well as accommodation sought. And don't neglect one of the obvious ways in which accommodation sharers hook up together—by word of mouth. If your new housemates are cool, you'll have an instant invitation to Dublin's social scene.

How much you'll pay for a room obviously depends on location as well as the standard of accommodation. Realistically, it's likely to be in the region of €350–500 ($434–620) per month. Sometimes more. Advertisements don't always indicate if utility bills are included in the rent, so this is something you would need to ask before committing. In most cases, they're separate.

To give you an idea of what's out there, a couple of ads that were recently spotted said something like this:

Clontarf, Dublin 3. €400 ($496) monthly. Single room in luxury duplex apartment in beautiful area near Dart, shopping area, and opposite a major supermarket. The apartment consists of a huge living room, closed kitchen. Fully equipped and decorated to the highest and most modern standards. To be shared with a male and female in their 20s. Both tenants are tidy and friendly and expect the third to be the same. The apartment is near East Point business park and less than 15 minutes to the city center by bus. P.S. Tenants are smokers.

Beaumont, Dublin 9. Large double room available in spacious three-bedroom house with two easygoing females. House newly decorated with all mod cons. Room would suit single professional (€500/$620) or couple (€600/$744). Parking included. House five minutes from 27B bus stop, 20B stop to Saint Stephen's Green, and 103 feeder bus to Clontarf Dart Station. Seven minutes' walk to Artane Shopping Centre and 10 minutes to Beaumont Hospital. Sitting room includes cinema surround sound system. Must be seen!

WHERE TO LIVE

Buying a home in Dublin or its satellite counties (Meath, Kildare, and Wicklow) requires deep pockets. House values in the east of Ireland have rocketed in recent years—most young Irish buyers are saddling themselves with huge mortgages to get on the first rung of the housing ladder.

House values in the east of Ireland have rocketed in recent years—most young Irish buyers are saddling themselves with huge mortgages to get on the first rung of the housing ladder.

Leaf through the property sections in the *Irish Times*, the *Irish Independent*, and *Evening Herald* and you would think that the capital's streets must be paved with emeralds. The average price of a Dublin home is now €324,000 ($401,760). Of course, "the average" includes all kinds of properties. If you're considering Dublin as a place to live, you're probably not envisaging some cookie-cutter starter home in the outermost reaches of the capital's suburbs.

Even though the price for a one-bedroom apartment was €350,000 ($434,000), properties in a new waterfront development at Gallery Quay (Dublin 2) were snapped up the moment they were released. If your dream is of a Georgian town house, be

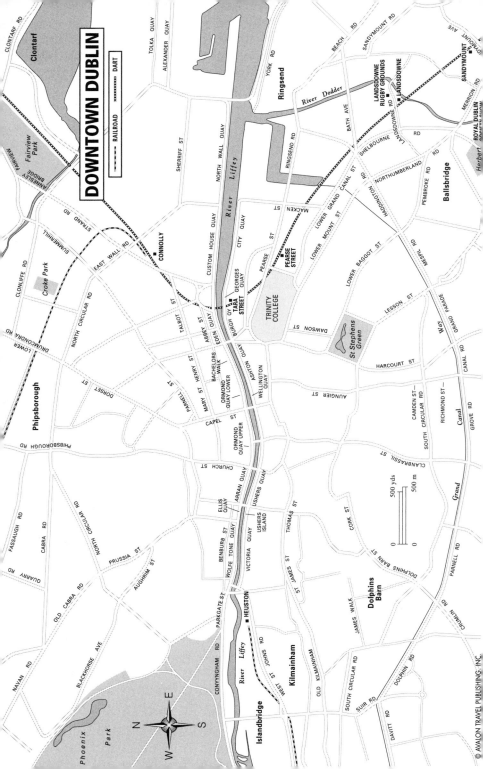

© Steenie Harvey

The IFSC is a tax haven, but not for Irish residents.

prepared to part with at least $2.5 million—some have sold for more than $5 million. Even a two-bedroom apartment in an exclusive area of the city such as leafy Ballsbridge can list for an incredible €574,000 ($711,760).

Most family residences in the more pleasant suburban areas easily achieve more than $400,000. Let me give you a typical example of an "ordinary" family home: in Dublin's Swords neighborhood, a three-bedroom house priced at €328,000 ($406,720). It's not even a detached property—it's semi-detached, which means it shares a partition wall with a neighbor.

South Side

The south side of the River Liffey takes in most of the city's visitor attractions. Surrounded by high mossy walls, the highlight for many is Trinity College and its famous library where the Book of Kells is kept. Dublin's oldest university, Trinity College was founded in 1592 by England's Queen Elizabeth I on the site of the Augustinian priory of All Hallows. Among its famous graduates are the writers Jonathan Swift,

Oscar Wilde, Bram Stoker, and Samuel Beckett. The Book of Kells, an illuminated 8th-century copy of the Gospels, is rightly considered one of Ireland's greatest treasures. Don't miss it.

Spanning the River Liffey, the Ha'penny Bridge links Lower Ormond Quay on the north side to Merchant's Arch and the narrow laneways of Temple Bar on the south side. The bridge takes its name from the toll—one halfpenny—that was levied on people right up until the 1900s. During the 18th century, the Temple Bar quarter was noted for its printers and bookbinders. Interspersed with numerous coffeehouses and taverns, many other craftsmen, such as mirror-makers, picture-framers, and wig-makers also plied their trade here.

Nowadays, Temple Bar is a trendy quarter with an impressive array of arts complexes and studios, restaurants, pubs, boutiques, and small shops selling everything from aromatherapy candles to second-hand books. In recent years, old buildings have been restored, lanes recobbled, and new street lighting installed. It's fascinating to explore, but there are a lot of tourist traps here. And it's not the ideal place to live if you're seeking even a smidgen of peace and quiet. This is one of Dublin's main nightlife areas and party night is every night, not just at weekends. Pubs get so crowded that revelers spill out of the pubs and carouse in the streets. It can get rowdy.

In the Steps of Leopold Bloom

Not all of Dublin's literary plaques commemorate real characters. James Joyce's *Ulysses* has spawned 14 bronze pavement plaques marking the fictional journey Leopold Bloom took around Dublin on June 16, 1904. Designated Bloomsday, this June day sees hundreds of Joycean scholars following Bloom's footsteps from one landmark to the next.

Joyce's works are peppered with real Dublin addresses—52 Upper Clanbrassil Street carries an official Dublin Tourism plaque saying: "Here, in Joyce's imagination was born in May 1866 Leopold Bloom—Citizen, husband, father, wanderer, reincarnation of Ulysses." The novel opens with Bloom's leaving 7 Eccles Street, but this house has disappeared: The street is now the site of the Mater Hospital.

Joyce himself had an unsettled childhood. Because of his father's habit of moving every few months, piling the household belongings onto one or two floats, it has been estimated that the family had at least 18 Dublin addresses. A number of those houses have been demolished and only two of the remaining ones are open to the public: the Martello Tower in Sandycove and 1 Martello Terrace in Bray, which opens one day per week.

Dublin 2 also takes in pedestrianized Grafton Street, where Bewley's Oriental Café is still the place of choice for shoppers to rest their weary feet; Dublin Castle, from where the British once ruled; the Guinness brewery and the antique shops of the Liberties; Saint Stephen's Green, where kids can have fun feeding the ducks; and many old pubs mentioned in Joyce's *Ulysses*.

From Saint Stephen's Green, it's only a short stroll to Merrion Square. Boasting some magnificent Georgian houses, the square also attracted more than its fair share of famous people. Look out for the wall plaques—they'll tell you who once lived here. The poet William Butler Yeats lived at No. 82; Joseph Sheridan Le Fanu, whose gothic horror novellas included the tale of a female vampire called *Carmilla* was resident at No. 70; Daniel O'Connell, "The Liberator" who strived for Catholic Emancipation, lived at No. 58.

Merrion Square's most controversial resident lived at No. 1, now part of the American College. This was Oscar Wilde, whose witticisms included telling U.S. customs officers that "I have nothing to declare but my genius." As well as seeing his former home, you can also admire a sculpture of the "genius" lounging in Merrion Square Gardens.

Particularly with writers, it's always interesting to speculate if their surroundings helped inspire them. Another writer on the Dublin roll call is Bram Stoker, author of *Dracula*. Rather disappointingly, he didn't live beside a creepy churchyard. His residence was at 30 Kildare Street, opposite the National Museum.

As Dublin 2 is the city's Georgian heartland, it's obviously prime city-center real estate. It commands high prices for both sales and rents. However, students have been known to find affordable apartment shares around Leeson Street and Aungier Street.

The south side of the River Liffey is also where you'll find Dublin's poshest residential neighborhood, leafy Ballsbridge (Dublin 4). Many foreign embassies and the more select hotels are here. Its houses mostly date from the Victorian and Edwardian eras, though a few streets can still boast some impressive Georgian mansions. Ballsbridge is also the site of the Royal Dublin Society, whose show grounds host numerous exhibitions as well as the Dublin Horse Show. Continuing on the sporty theme, Lansdowne Road is the venue for international soccer and rugby matches. It's peaceful during nonmatch days, but when a major event is on, Lansdowne Road is transformed from a sleepy tree-lined avenue to a heaving parade of bodies.

A favorite with both visitors and Ballsbridge residents, Herbert Park is a wonderful place to unwind after a hectic day. There are a duckpond, flower beds, and walkways, soccer pitches, bowling green, tennis courts, and children's playground. During summer, live jazz sessions are held on the park's old-fashioned Victorian bandstand. It also has a history. This was the venue for the Great Exhibition of 1907, where all the countries of the then-British Empire were represented.

Like Ballsbridge, Ringsend also comes under the Dublin 4 postal code. Instead of imposing Victorian mansions, though, here you'll find the streets are more likely to contain terraces of single-story urban cottages. Often with brightly painted facades, these were built in the 19th century to provide affordable housing for dockers, railway workers, and laborers. Many of these rowhouses seem impossibly small, but well-maintained ones can now fetch $250,000. The giant iron ring of the old Ringsend gasworks isn't exactly photogenic, but the quaint streets are often transformed into yesteryear by film crews and the producers of TV advertisements.

In the shadow of Christchurch Cathedral and the Guinness Brewery, the Liberties and Coombe neighborhoods that form part of Dublin 8 are some of the oldest sections of the city. In medieval times the Liberties was a quarter of tanneries and leather workers, and its name is derived from the fact that it was once outside the city's legal jurisdiction. Between 1650 and the early 18th century, 10,000 Protestant Huguenots escaping religious persecution in France took up residence here. They brought with them skills in tailoring and silk-weaving.

Although parts of the Liberties have a distinctly disadvantaged air, some brand-new apartment developments have sprouted in recent years. These are often favored by professionals who want to be within walking distance of their workplaces. Even if you wouldn't want to live here, don't miss taking a stroll down Francis Street, home to some of the capital's best antique shops. Don't be fooled by the small storefronts. The shops stretch back for yards and often have merchandise on a number of floors. Along with specialist antique dealers, there are outlets selling cast-iron fireplaces, garden statuary, enamel signs, old advertisements, and all kinds of bric-a-brac. If you're seeking someone to restore a marble fireplace, upholster an 18th-century chair, or repair and clean brasswork, it's a good hunting ground.

Less expensive than Ballsbridge, sought-after South Side districts include Rathmines and Rathgar, both in Dublin 6. Twenty minutes by bus or taxi from Saint Stephen's Green, Rathmines is practically a student suburb. A popular residential area since the turn of the last century, many of its Edwardian houses have now been turned into student apartment shares. It has a really lively atmosphere with many pubs, coffee shops, and restaurants as well as a busy shopping center and the wide expanse of Belgrave Park.

With five golf clubs on the doorstep, Rathfarnham is an outer southern suburb that manages to keep rural charm as part of the urban development plan. Here Marley Park offers 214 acres of woodland and parkland interspersed with water features and a sculpture trail. One of Ireland's best-known hiking routes, the Wicklow Way, begins within the park.

South Side Coastal Villages

If you travel south along the coast, past the bird sanctuary of Booterstown Marsh and the Victorian seaside suburb of Dun Laoghaire, a whole new world opens up. The capital's outer fringes are punctuated with small towns and seaside villages strung out along the strands of Dublin Bay. As they're all mostly connected to the city center by the DART (Dublin Area Rapid Transit), they're a good option if you prefer to wake up to the smell of ozone rather than traffic fumes.

Three such seaside villages are Sandycove, Dalkey, and Killiney. One of Sandycove's claims to fame are its links with James Joyce. The village was immortalized in *Ulysses,* and a Joyce museum is in the Martello Tower on the promenade, originally built as part of a series of watchtowers against any possible French invasion. Other literary figures have been drawn to Sandycove, including John Millington Synge and Samuel Beckett. In more recent times, the village has attracted a new wave of writers and playwrights. Its residents include the novelist Maeve Binchy and playwright Hugh Leonard.

On Christmas Day, the rocky natural swimming area known as the Forty Foot pool at Sandycove always makes an appearance on TV news bulletins. Most people would think it an act of insanity to plunge into the Irish Sea in winter, but the Christmas Day dip is a long-standing tradition for some hardy Dublin swimmers. The pool takes its name not from its size, but from the fact that it was once used by a detachment of the 40th Foot Regiment of the British Army. For many years, the pool was a male-only preserve, with nude bathing commonplace. Nowadays it's open to all, and a notice-board says Togs (swimming costumes) Required—By Order.

Made famous by residents such as George Bernard Shaw—and more recently musicians Bono and Enya—both Dalkey and neighboring Killiney have fine homes, narrow streets, and a great choice of pubs and restaurants. Plus walks that offer some magnificent sea views over Dalkey Island and Killinney Bay. Some people compare Killiney Bay to the Bay of Naples. While that's taking Irish hyperbole a bit too far, it is undeniably lovely. As elsewhere along this stretch of coast, plenty of good shore fishing is also available year-round. There are also opportunities for canoeing, sailboarding, waterskiing, and local diving.

Dalkey can trace its roots back to Viking times. After the Norman invasion, it became a busy port for trading vessels from the continent and England. Until the 17th century, it had the distinction of being Dublin's main port. Seven castlelike structures were built to store merchandise—Goat Castle, which houses the Heritage Center, and Archibold's Castle on the main street stand to this day. Killiney's 200-acre-park was laid out during Victorian times. The park takes in an old quarry where climbing enthusiasts practice their abseiling techniques.

North Side

Dublin's North Side feels more gritty and working-class. Immediately north of the river, O'Connell Street is where you'll find the General Post Office, the scene of violent fighting in the Easter Rising of 1916. Moore Street's fruit and vegetable market is off Henry Street, a pedestrianized thoroughfare. This is where locals shop—you're far more likely to find clothing bargains in Henry Street's stores than on Grafton Street. This area comes under the postal code Dublin 1.

One unmissable Dublin 1 stopping-off point if you're on the literary trail is the Writers Museum on Parnell Square.

One unmissable Dublin 1 stopping-off point if you're on the literary trail is the Writers Museum on Parnell Square. In a magnificent 18th-century mansion, the collection showcases the lives and works of Dublin's major literary figures through the last 100 years.

Taking in Fairview and Clontarf, Dublin 3 is fairly close to the city center and has the benefit that you can just about smell the sea air. Take the bus outside of rush hour and you'll be there in around 15 minutes; otherwise it's at least a 45-minute walk. It's a mix of family houses, apartments, and houses divided into apartment shares.

Falling under the Dublin 5 and Dublin 7 post codes, Phibsboro and Artane have their run-down grimy areas, but they are fairly popular with students and young professionals. Although they're within walking distance of the center, and well served by bus routes, many students seem to prefer to cycle in from here.

Closer to the center, also in Dublin 7, the urban renewal going on around Smithfield has resulted in its being cited as the new Temple Bar. This district is only 20 minutes from the Quays and O'Connell Street. Smithfield has long played an important role in Dublin's history as a lively hub of social and commercial activity. For hundreds of years, certainly back as far as the 1600s, markets and fairs drew crowds of people into its cobbled streets.

But decay set in and Smithfield declined into one of the city's poorest areas. Until the 1990s, it was pretty much a byword for inner-city decay. Now though, the 2.5-acre site of the old horse fairs and hay-sellers has become Ireland's largest urban civic square—a pedestrianized cobbled plaza with museums, bars, restaurants, shops, high-profile concerts, and high-priced apartment developments. Known as the Flue with the View, the old chimney of the Jameson distillery has been transformed into a 175-foot viewing tower offering a panoramic lookout over the city. One-bedroom apartments in a brand-new Smithfield Market development are selling off-plan (pre-construction) for €340,000 ($421,600). Two-bedroom apartments are €435,000 ($539,400).

One of the best of the traditional North Side neighborhoods is Drumcondra in Dublin 9. It's also just about within cycling distance of the city center, but it doesn't feel as edgy as the inner-city area that radiates north, east, and west of O'Connell Street. The multitude of local services means it's certainly not necessary to travel into the heart of the city center for day-to-day shopping needs. Indian and Chinese takeaways; dry cleaners, pharmacies, supermarkets; real estate agencies, opticians, pubs; launderettes, banks, and bookmakers where you can place a bet on the 3:30 horse race at Leopardstown—you'll find all these kind of outlets along Drumcondra Road. Dublin 9 also takes in Beaumont, where there's a major hospital, so the area is also quite popular with medical workers.

Neighboring Glasnevin in Dublin 11 is best described as family residential, but it attracts visitors for two main reasons: the National Botanic Gardens and the 124 acres of Prospect Cemetery. This is where many of Ireland's famous revolutionaries, leaders, poets, and scholars lie buried. The roll call of names among the 900,000 or so graves includes Charles Stewart Parnell, Michael Collins, Eamon DeValera, Brendan Behan, and Sir Roger Casement, who was executed as a traitor by the British in 1916. Dominating the Celtic crosses and other gravestones with their Celtic motifs is a 168-foot-high Round Tower in memory of Daniel O'Connell.

As far as North Side residential districts go, many areas that didn't used to be considered part of the city at all have been swallowed up by estates of small shopping malls and cookie-cutter houses. The farther away you get from central Dublin, the more the feeling is of suburbia. Thirty minutes' drive or bus ride from the center, near Dublin Airport, Swords village has a friendly buzz and is popular for families with children. Avid sportspeople have a variety of golf courses and sports clubs to choose from.

North Side Coastal Villages

North Side coastal suburbs include Malahide, Clontarf, Skerries, Portmarnock, Sutton, and Howth. Although fairly expensive for home buyers, these are all great residential areas where you can stroll along the seafront and enjoy good nightlife at weekends. Skerries in particular still has something of the feel of an old-fashioned fishing village.

Along with buses, the DART (Dublin Area Rapid Transit) travels up the coast as far as Howth, a seaside village of steep streets with both a battlemented castle and an abbey, the latter founded in A.D. 1042 by Sitric, the Norse king who laid claim to Dublin.

Howth also has a fishing harbor, marina, and cliff-top walks. From Howth Head, you can look right across Dublin Bay to the Wicklow Mountains. On the clearest of days, and if atmospheric conditions are right, it's reputedly possible to see the Mountains of Mourne in northern Ireland and also the mountain ranges of Wales. Just offshore from Howth is the tiny, rocky island of Ireland's Eye. Seabirds such as kittiwakes, fulmars, gannets, puffins, guillemots, and razorbills roost on its cliffs.

Getting Around

Certainly for visitors, life is likely to be a lot more enjoyable if you elect to use public transport rather than hiring a car. Once you're living here, and depending on how much travel you plan to do, you may decide

Hop aboard a Dublin bus

otherwise. But a car isn't necessary for getting around Dublin. Frequent buses serve even the outermost residential districts.

The DART (Dublin Area Rapid Transit) is a light urban rail system that runs between the North Dublin seaside village of Howth as far south as Greystones in County Wicklow. The three city-center stops are Connolly Station, Tara Street, and Pearse Street.

The DART is the best option for getting out to coastal districts. The Luas is the city's brand-new Light Rail Transit system, and it is designed to try to help relieve the traffic snarl-up resulting from people's coming into the city from noncoastal districts. Before it came into operation, commuters from far-out suburbs such as Tallaght had to undergo a lengthy bus journey into the city center. The most useful city-center stop on the Green Line is Saint Stephen's Green. On the Red Line, useful central stops are Heuston Railway Station, Smithfield, Four Courts, Jervis Shopping Center, Abbey Street, Busaras, and Connolly Railway Station.

Note that it's not yet possible to link from one Luas line to another. Getting from Abbey Street to Saint Stephen's Green involves a 15-minute walk. However, even if you need to change lines, tickets are still valid for your planned journey. You do not need to buy separate tickets.

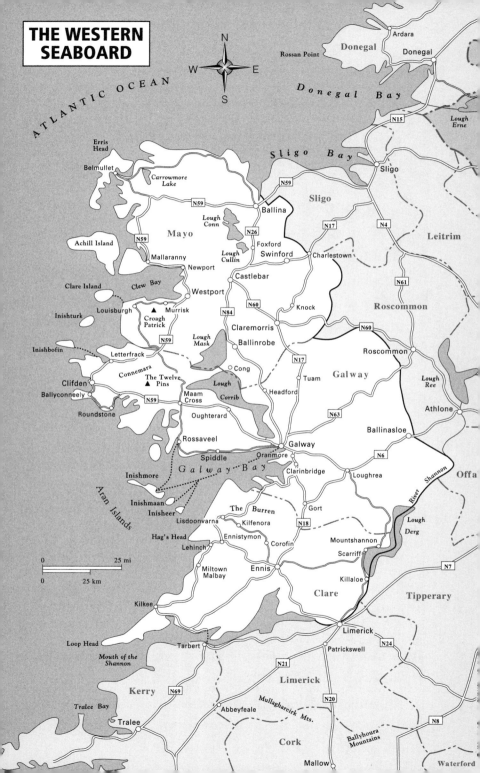

© Steenie Harvey

The Western Seaboard

Aland of stone-walled fields and melancholy mountains, Ireland's wild west offers all the wilderness you could ever wish for. If you're nostalgic for the "traditional Ireland" of ancient ways and curious festivals, this beautiful region will almost certainly fit the bill.

As spring turns to summer, pale water lilies brocade the loughs and the countryside explodes in a pink bonfire blaze of wild rhododendrons. Follow the whiff of ozone westward and the colorfest is completed by white coral strands and shadowy humped islands that drift like whales in the blue-green swell of the Atlantic. Galway, Mayo, and Clare are all maritime counties.

For many people, the very essence of Irishness seems rooted in the far west. County Galway is a very popular location for both foreign buyers and wealthy Dubliners seeking holiday homes—and Mayo and Clare are catching up fast.

Do you prefer the buzz of city streets to scenic beauty and tradition? Well, the wild western wilderness could still provide you with an ideal new home. Numerous people, both Irish and foreign, cite music-mad Galway city as being their very favorite urban location.

County Galway

THE LAY OF THE LAND

Few counties rival Galway for scenic splendor, particularly on cloudless days when the mirror-clear light lends everywhere the qualities of feyness and illusion. Forty shades of green? Galway's canvas is painted in myriad changing hues: the mountains of the Twelve Bens etched in delicate blues and violets, the uplands a bronzed carpet splashed with golden gorse and the white flecks of sheep.

Foreign buyers tend to yearn for old-fashioned cottages and farmsteads in the legendary lands of Connemara, the name given to the county's scenic northern region. For local buyers, proximity to Galway city is a top priority and most prefer modern homes, usually a newly minted bungalow. While it's true that these type of residences hold little appeal for traditionalists, there's no denying that they're far warmer and cozier than the thatched dwellings of times past.

Although house values within the county are considered expensive, there is a two-tier market. An hour's drive from the coastline, the small sleepy towns of agricultural eastern Galway aren't on the tourist trail and houses are thus a lot more affordable. Even if Connemara is beyond your price range, you can still have a piece of Galway at prices that won't break the bank. Look to the "Fields of Athenry" (yes, Athenry exists) and countryside areas around towns such as Ballinasloe, Headford, Loughrea, and Tuam.

WHERE TO LIVE

Galway City

The west's self-styled "cultural capital" is a medieval seaport city of twisty, atmospheric laneways and scores of traditional music pubs. Galway's origins date back to the 13th century, when a settlement grew up around a castle built by Richard de Burgo. As a trading port, the city developed strong links with other European maritime cities and it's widely believed that Columbus came here before his epic voyage to the Americas.

Near the bus and railway stations, the hub of today's city is Eyre Square. Here you'll find all of the big banks and building societies, the grand old Great Southern Hotel, and also a monument to the Galway Hooker—not an infamous lady of the night, but one of the local sailing boats! Interesting pubs and little specialty shops are found on Shop Street, which links Eyre Square to Spanish Arch and the Corrib River, where old wharfside warehouses have been transformed into attractive apartments. Delve into the adjoining laneways and you'll come across tempting little courtyard restaurants and bistros, many specializing in seafood.

University students add all-year vibrancy to the place, but things get really hectic in summer. Galway's arts, music, and theater scene has gained

Galway's arts, music, and theater scene has gained legendary status and legions of tourists arrive to experience festival fever—everything from horse racing to oyster extravaganzas.

legendary status and legions of tourists arrive to experience festival fever—everything from horse racing to oyster extravaganzas. July's 12-day arts festival is always tremendous fun, so don't miss it. Its highlight is a colorful street pageant and previous themes have centered on Noah's Ark and the Fairy Horde.

House prices in Galway City and its suburbs reflect the fact that there has been a population explosion: up from 25,000 inhabitants in the 1960s to more than 66,000 today. (In County Galway as a whole, the population numbers 209,000.) With growth expected to increase further, the city is constantly drawing people into its employment orbit. Once sleepy communities such as Oranmore, Spiddal, and the oyster village of Clarinbridge have become an inextricable part of the western commuter belt.

Official statistics put the average price of a home in the Galway region at €240,831 ($298,630). However, that's the average for the whole county. Estate agents' guideline prices for solid family homes near Galway city center are more likely to be pitched higher. In sought-after residential neighborhoods such as Taylor's Hill, Kingston Road, Bushy Park, and Threadneedle, the price of Victorian and Edwardian town houses can easily soar above $800,000. A Bushy Park house with 1,280 square feet of living space was recently advertised at €695,000 ($862,000).

Within the city, the only kind of properties you are likely to find for under €170,000 ($211,000) are former "corporation" houses. These were built by the council to rent to needy families who couldn't afford their own homes. During the late 1980s/early 1990s, many were sold to sitting tenants who have since resold in the private market. Being on estates, these lookalike homes are not particularly attractive, but now some sell for as much as €210,000 ($260,000).

If you're looking to rent, furnished one- and two-bedroom apartments mostly fall into the €650–950 ($806–$1,178) per month range. Furnished three- and four-bedroom houses are mostly between €890 and €1,000 ($1,104–1,240).

Move away from Galway city's environs and prices vary from $50,000 for an isolated cottage in *extremely* sad repair to $600,000 or more for a lovingly restored Georgian mansion in a desirable setting. If you like the idea of building a dream home here, location also dictates the price of sites. Sites on the market at the time of writing included a 1.62-acre plot with full planning permission for a detached house near Tuam for €75,000 ($93,000). But you can pay more than twice that for a half-acre site with sea views.

Depending on size and location, refurbished cottages and houses mostly fall into the $120,000–450,000 bracket. The typical two-/three-bedroom cottage or bungalow usually fetches at least €85,000 ($105,500) in the eastern half of the county and carries a substantial premium if in a prime scenic area.

To cite some typical examples, €90,000 ($111,600) will buy you a tiny two-bedroom cottage in a quiet rural area in the mountainous Inagh Valley near Kylemore Abbey. However, for a two-bedroom bungalow on the coast road between Barna and Spiddal (seven miles from Galway), asking price is €280,000 ($347,000).

Prices fall the farther you get from Galway city—anything more than 10 miles is considered a lengthy commute by locals. Thirty-five miles from the bustle of the city, a 1,000-square-foot modern bungalow with almost an acre of land is €170,000 ($211,000) through the estate agent Heaslips.

Connemara

County Galway's mountainous fringe, Connemara, lies west of Lough Corrib and has long been a popular location with foreign buyers. More a state of mind than a map reference, its haunting beauty can inspire

The Claddagh Ring

Although Claddagh village is now just another of suburban Galway's housing estates, the fame of this former fishing community lives on in the shape of Claddagh rings. Usually made of gold, these unusual love tokens have a 300-year-old history. Tradition tells of a local boy, Richard Joyce, who was kidnapped by Barbary pirates while traveling to the West Indies. The corsairs sold him to an Algerian master who taught him the secrets of the goldsmithing trade.

When Richard Joyce returned to Galway in the 1690s, he founded his own goldsmith's shop and designed the Claddagh ring. The clasped hands signify friendship, the crown symbolizes loyalty and—depending on which way you wear it—the heart motif stands for love. If the heart points inward, you are telling the world that your own heart is spoken for. If it points outward, you are available and seeking a new suitor!

both joy and melancholy as well as the urge to grab a paintbrush. Many first-time visitors are always surprised that Connemara isn't a county in its own right for this seems to be the Ireland of donkeys, turf stacks, and little whitewashed cottages that imagination promised.

The well-trampled routes are in north Connemara, mostly around Clifden and the villages of Roundstone, Ballyconneely, and Letterfrack. As Connemara's main tourist center, Clifden is an area where you can expect to pay premium prices. It's renowned for its beautiful beaches, its Connemara Pony Show, and a further attraction is the nearby championship golf course at Ballyconneely.

Clifden is exceptionally pretty with houses color-washed in an artist's palette of forget-me-not blue, salmon pink, and pale primrose yellow. The town's plethora of craft shops, sweater outlets, pubs, and restaurants suggests that it isn't exactly virgin territory and estate agents' listings soon confirm that there's no such thing as bargains hereabouts. Newly built modern houses of 1,195 square feet are fetching €285,000 ($353,500). Modest three-bedroom cottage-style homes list for €152,000 ($188,500).

Even one-bedroom cottages "in need of renovation" near the villages of Cleggan and Roundstone can achieve prices of more than $125,000. Roundstone is particularly easy to fall in love with—it's a quaint fishing village with a toy-town harbor where you can watch nets and lobster pots being repaired.

Another Connemara village that demands buyers to have fairly deep pockets is Oughterard. Its location is magical—on the western shore of Lough Corrib, which is peppered with uninhabited wooded islets and home to flocks of wild swans. This is the heart of thatched-cottage country but unfortunately these storybook dwellings command very high prices and tend to get snapped up like hotcakes.

Heaslips of Galway city had a sweet two-bedroom thatched cottage with walled orchard not far from Lough Corrib and Headford village. It was fully refurbished, and the asking price was €270,000 ($335,000). In good condition, a three-bedroom traditional farmhouse with around three acres of land will fetch at least €295,000 ($366,000).

Properties for long-term rental through Matt O'Sullivan's Oughterard office include a four-bedroom fully furnished apartment in the Roscahill area of town for €660 ($818) monthly.

Iar Connacht

The countryside south of Maam Cross remains more of a wilderness. Here Connemara's coastline breaks up into a filigree fretwork of peninsulas with islands chained fast to the mainland by stone causeways. This is Iar Connacht—wild, isolated, and veined with some of Ireland's most penitential roads.

Time was when Iar Connacht was the place to snap up bargains, but those days have gone. "Renovation project" cottages occasionally surface for under $150,000, but expect to pay more like €165,000 ($204,600) for the cozier comforts of a modernized cottage. At the time of writing, a refurbished cottage with just 572 square feet of living space was listing for €180,000 ($223,000). Most houses in this mazy land of waterscapes have at least one view of the sea—this cottage does too.

On an elevated half-acre site on the Renvyle Peninsula, a three-bedroom modern bungalow with some of the best views in Ireland is for sale through Connemara Properties. You can see four islands (Inish Turk, Clare Island, Achill Island, and Inish Bofin) as well as across to County Mayo's coastline and the pilgrimage mountain of Croagh Patrick. The price is €280,000 ($347,000), but again, though, it's not huge—only around 800 square feet.

The Irish word for "west," *Iar*, also means "the end," a place where everything runs out. A Gaeltacht enclave where most inhabitants speak Irish as their first language, *Iar Connacht* can evoke fear and dread in urban teenagers. During the summer holidays, scores of city schoolkids are packed off here to improve their language skills. Boarding with local families, both eager and reluctant students are thoroughly immersed in their native tongue.

Not every youngster appreciates the south Connemara experience. No cable TV or discos, just Gaelic games, *ceilidh* nights, and the jabber of Radio na Gaeltachta. Irish summer schools bar English-speaking for the duration and also frown on what is quaintly termed "keeping company" with the opposite sex. Rebellious offenders are sent home and, as fees are nonrefundable, parental reaction can easily be guessed at.

The Aran Islands

Irish is also the day-to-day language of Inishmore (Arainn), Inishmaan (Inis Meain) and Inisheer (Inis Oirr), the Aran Island trio cast adrift in Galway Bay. Leaving aside Aran sweaters, the islanders' most outstanding achievement is how they have managed to create minuscule fields from barren rock, a centuries-old endeavor involving seaweed, shelly soil, and animal dung. Cleared stones built the hundreds of miles of gateless walls that prevent the islands' precious soil from being blown away by the Atlantic's buffeting gales.

Farmers and fishermen on the Aran Islands have long been waging battle against the elements. Their stark lifestyle inspired numerous Celtic Revival dramas as well as 1932's classic documentary, *Man of Aran*. Its American director, Robert Flaherty, certainly believed in artistic license: He wanted to show the islanders' continuing dependence on the basking shark industry, even though it had expired half a century before. And so the fishermen set out to capture a monster of the deep, braving a storm in a fragile hide-coated canoe, shaped like a new moon and known as a currach. During the tourist season, the documentary is shown three times a day in Kilronan, Inishmore's main village.

You're not coming here as a starry-eyed tourist so don't make the mistake of thinking that everything that appears in those lavishly illustrated coffee-table books is gospel fact. Sorry, but Aran women no longer dress in scarlet flannel petticoats and their menfolk wear jeans rather than homespun trousers. Their homes are lit by electricity, not lamps filled with oil squeezed from the liver of the poor old basking shark. And as for drowned fishermen being identified through sweaters that carry a unique, personalized pattern, the sad truth is that the story is pure balderdash. This particular item of folklore originated with J. M. Synge's play, *Riders to the Sea,* in which a corpse is recognized by four dropped stitches in a woolen sock.

But Aran sweaters are big business and it would be commercial suicide to let on that high-powered knitting machines now create the vast majority. Aran women only started knitting them in the late 1920s, which rather quashes the notion that the distinctive raised patterns are as ancient as Ogham script. Even so, the carefully fostered myth that designs such as Tree of Life, Honeycomb, and Trinity have been handed down through the generations as a kind of heirloom is harmless enough—it certainly helps Ireland's export industry!

Because of the high transportation costs of building materials, houses on the Aran Islands and County Galway's other islands aren't cheap— offers above €253,000 ($313,700) were recently sought for a thatched cottage with just three rooms on Inishmore. Few properties are still available for renovation. When homes do change hands, they are usually marketed through agents in Galway city or Clifden.

At the time of writing, Connemara Properties had a small traditional cottage (426 square feet) on the island of Inish Turk, half a mile off the Galway coast. Reflecting the fact that these kind of properties are highly sought after, it was priced at €127,000 ($157,500), but it does have its own boat mooring and almost an acre of land.

Island living won't suit everybody. Winter's storms mean that you can be cut off from the mainland for days at a time, trusting that an army helicopter will manage to get you to hospital in Galway city if you are ill. Shops are few and the price of day-to-day essentials is eye-watering. And, like your new neighbors, you'll have to stoically suffer the annual influx of anthropologically minded visitors armed with camcorders and highly romantic expectations.

Galway has a lot more to offer than just its coastal fringe and offshore islands and bargain hunters should definitely check out the eastern parts of the county. If the sound of "alternative-style country living" appeals, this cottage may suit. On three acres, it's a stone-built cottage with new galvanized roof near Gort, 25 miles from Galway city. Simply rather than luxuriously renovated, it has one large room with two sleeping lofts, a detached bath house with solid fuel heater, a compost toilet shed, and another guest shed with woodstove. There's also an organic vegetable garden.

The property is bordered by a stream and wooded gully. A short walk brings you into the Slieve Aughty mountains, with panoramic views over counties Clare and Galway. A planning application has been made to extend the cottage and add a septic tank. It was €125,000 ($155,000) through County Clare agents Green Valley Properties.

Deep in the countryside's green heart, Ballinasloe is a trim little town of 6,000 souls drowsing away in the flat limestone pasturelands that mark the county border with Roscommon. Traditional-style slate-roofed cottages in reasonable condition can be had for €100,000–145,000 ($124,000–180,000).

Although you'll not be getting spectacular scenery, what makes Ballinasloe special is that it's the location for the Great October Fair, Ireland's oldest horse fair whose origins date to the 1100s. Fair Week is a snorting, stomping spectacle of horseflesh with around 4,000 beasts passing through the town and dealers engaging in the time-honored language of nods, winks, spits, and handshakes. As horse-trading is thirsty work, it's not uncommon for the town's pubs to actually run out of beer!

From dawn until dusk, the Fair Green becomes a heaving sea of hunters, heavy Irish drafts, shaggy-coated Connemaras, tiny Shetland ponies, and eye-catching black and white piebalds. Known in Ireland as "colored horses," piebalds are prized by the traveling people (gypsies) for whom Fair Week is the highlight of the year. In that long-gone era of cavalry troops and horse-drawn carriages, Ballinasloe's Fair Green was Europe's biggest marketplace for horseflesh. It's said that a French officer bought Marengo, Napoleon's magnificent white charger, here in 1801. And although times have moved on, the October Fair provides visible proof that Ireland still possesses more horses per head of population than anywhere else in Europe.

County Mayo

THE LAY OF THE LAND

Shaped like a great stone tent, County Mayo's most mesmeric landmark is undoubtedly Croagh Patrick, Ireland's "holy mountain." Its reputation as a sacred site dates to at least the time of the pagan Celts. Saint Patrick is believed to have spent 40 nights in vigil on its summit in A.D. 441, but whether he performed any snake-charming feats is another matter entirely. Each Garland Sunday, the last Sunday of July, around 50,000 people go on pilgrimage to a mountaintop oratory, some still making the climb barefoot.

Here too are the renowned fishing waters of Lough Conn and Lough Mask. Wealthy anglers often base themselves at Ashford Castle, a fairytale fantasy of a hotel. A walk through Ashford's woodlands brings you to Cong, a time-stood-still village of crystal rivers, low stone bridges, and a market cross. If it looks strangely familiar, that's probably because much of the filming of *The Quiet Man,* the John Wayne and Maureen O'Hara movie of the early 1950s, was shot here. One of the most historic of Irish villages, Cong also has a ruined abbey, founded in 1134 by Turlough O'Connor, the high king of the time.

A walk through Ashford's woodlands brings you to Cong, a time-stood-still village of crystal rivers, low stone bridges, and a market cross.

If you were putting together a list of Mayo highlights, you would certainly have to include Achill Island too. This is the country's largest island and it encompasses all that's best in Irish scenery: dramatic cliffs and mountains, silvery beaches and wild moorlands.

WHERE TO LIVE

Mayo's island-strewn coastline switchbacks from Killala Bay down to Killary Harbor, where it meets Galway's Connemara region. Connacht's regional airport, at Knock, provides an easy link to Dublin as well as to a number of English cities. You can also take a train to the capital from the Mayo towns of Westport, Claremorris, Ballina, and Castlebar, the county town. The average house price in the county is €181,000 ($225,000).

However, in most inland areas, small bungalows in good condition can still be found for $130,000–150,000. For example, in Ballinrobe village, Castlebar agents Collins has a neat bungalow (514 square feet) with garden for €108,000 ($134,000).

In contrast, Castlebar, the county town, has become very expensive in recent years. Here you can expect to pay around €190,000 ($235,500) for a three-bedroom semidetached house. Detached houses are usually upward of €250,000 ($310,000).

Many foreign buyers elect to buy homes in and around seaside Westport. Laid out in Georgian times, it's an attractive town of wide, tree-lined streets, set-piece squares, and a canal flanked by tall, narrow town houses that give one the vague feeling of being in the Low Countries. Then again, that could be all the Dutch accents—Westport is a summer tourism mecca and a high proportion of visitors come from Holland.

Tourist towns tend to be fairly expensive and Westport's house prices reflect its status as an employment honeypot, too. There is no one major

Knock, Knock, Knocking on Heaven's Door

Ireland's spiritual power plant, Knock is one of the world's foremost Marian shrines and a place of continuous prayer. The village draws vast crowds during the May to October pilgrimage season and some pilgrims spend their entire summer vacations here, taking part in torch-lit rosary processions and all-night vigils. Sundays are particularly hectic, often with around 10,000 of the faithful patiently waiting to take Communion in the huge Basilica of Our Lady, Queen of Ireland. Holy days are even busier as almost every Catholic parish organizes a coach trip for parishioners.

Knock's fame stems from the evening of August 21, 1879, when 20 villagers claimed to have seen an apparition of three figures near the gable wall of their church. Bathed in a golden glow, the central figure was recognized as the Virgin Mary. Her unearthly companions were adjudged to be Saint Joseph and Saint John the Evangelist, holding the Book of Revelation and accompanied by a lamb. Hovering two feet above the ground, the apparition apparently lasted for almost two hours.

employer in the Mayo area but rather a mix of small industries that take in everything from pharmaceuticals to eye care products, seaweed processors, and electrode and paintbrush manufacturers. Within Westport, don't expect much change from €240,000 ($297,500) for a 1,300-square-foot restored town house. And while you can find modern bungalows of the same size for €250,000 ($310,000), you'll be a 20-minute drive from town.

Within a few miles of Westport, habitable "Land Commission" cottages of around 900 square feet surface for €110,000–145,000 ($136,500–180,000). As they were mostly built during the 1950s, these are generally more plain and boxy rather than picturesque.

Strung out along the ocean like beads on a rosary, some of the most sought-after coastal villages within easy reach of Westport include Lecanvey, Murrisk, Newport, and Louisburgh. In these communities, buyers are paying substantial sums for a particularly good lookout on Clew Bay and its islands. At Murrisk, O'Donnell's had a 912-square-foot modern bungalow on a half-acre site for €270,000 ($335,000).

Murrisk is the nearest village to Croagh Patrick and the Garland Sunday pilgrim trail. It's intriguing to discover that the village derives its name from the Muir Iasc, a one-eyed sea serpent that was apparently worshipped by the local inhabitants during druidic times. Makes you

© Steenie Harvey

Killary Harbor marks the county border between Galway and Mayo.

wonder if there was some truth in the legend of Saint Patrick banishing the snakes after all!

A poignant, real-life story is attached to Louisburgh village, a little farther up the coast. It's that of the Doolough tragedy, commemorated every year by a sponsored walk for famine victims of developing nations. At the height of Ireland's own Great Famine, when the potatoes rotted in the fields, a number of starving families banded together and trudged across the Doolough Pass from Killary Harbor to Louisburgh. There they sought admission to the old workhouse but entrance was refused. Almost 600 people died on the hopeless journey back across the Doolough Mountains, dark and lonely peaks that fully epitomize the brooding savagery of "the scenic west."

Achill, Ireland's largest island, is linked to the mainland by a road-bridge. Although wintertime weather can be quite squally, here you can still find some nice homes at a reasonable price—most island properties are sold through agents on the mainland. Newport agent Frank Chambers has traditional-type Achill cottages to restore from €70,000 ($87,000). A cottage you could move into is 110,000 ($136,500), but it is small—only 551 square feet. With spectacular views of Keel Island

and the Atlantic Ocean, a modern bungalow with 1,800 square feet of living space is €260,000 ($322,500).

In north Mayo, the area around Ballina, Killala Bay and the remote Belmullet Peninsula is your best bet for tracking down seaside snips: Small coastal bungalows occasionally pop up for under $200,000. On the Belmullet Peninsula, Castlebar agents Collins was offering a pretty 860-square-foot whitewashed bungalow (two bedrooms) with sea views for €125,000 ($155,000).

Although not as fashionable as Westport, Ballina is a pleasantly old-fashioned town on the Moy, one of Ireland's noted fishing rivers. Just a few minutes' drive away, pretty cottages can be found for around the €120,000 ($149,000) mark. You can buy cheaper—semidetached former corporation homes still go for €110,000 ($136,500) in Ballina town—but most foreign buyers don't find these type of estate houses very appealing.

Or consider the county's agricultural heartland, laid out in a patchwork quilt of emerald-green fields and brown velvet boglands, all sewn together with gray drystone walls. Around little farming communities such as Swinford, Foxford, Ballinrobe, and Claremorris, you can still find do-it-uppers starting at €20,000 ($25,000) and small cottage-type properties in fairly habitable condition from €60,000 ($74,500). Note, though, that the $25,000 figure relates to cottages requiring "extensive repairs"—and to be honest the ones you'll see for that price are nothing other than a heap of old stones. Cottages requiring "repair" rather than "extensive repair" go for upward of €50,000 ($62,000).

On the main Galway to Sligo road, Claremorris and its satellite villages are the best place to look for bargain properties: Local agent Martin Finn usually has a wide selection. A habitable two-bedroom country cottage, three miles from Knock shrine, is €63,000 ($78,000). A 1930s-built bungalow with five rooms on a .7-acre site is €90,000 ($111,500). A three-bedroom country house with 2.75 acres near Claremorris is €102,000 ($126,500).

Why are prices in the Claremorris area substantially cheaper? Well, the first thing that strikes you when strolling around the town is the complete absence of craft stores, gift shops, and other tourist outlets—evidence that coach tours never see the place. House values haven't been artificially inflated by either foreign buyers or city dwellers in the market for holiday homes, undoubtedly because the landscape doesn't offer the Ireland of loughs and mountains that exists in most people's dreams. There are no major employers in this area, another factor that always sends house prices upward.

County Clare

THE LAY OF THE LAND

From the mighty Cliffs of Moher to the starkly beautiful uplands of the moonscaped Burren and the lush green pastures around Lough Derg, Clare packs a lot into a compact area. Although prices have risen—the county average is €200,195 ($248,000) prime coastal properties aren't quite as expensive as in neighboring Galway. Most Irish people would agree that Clare is a kind of spiritual home for traditional music and enthusiasts will already know about the legendary music pubs of Doolin, Miltown Malbay, Ennistymon, and Kilfenora.

Yet there's more to this county than first meets the eye. Strolling the streets of Ennis, Clare's county town and commercial center, take a peek at the window displays of bookshops and newsagents. If you're expecting to see the standard fare of books on local history, the Cliffs of Moher, and the wildflowers of the stony Burren region, you'll probably wonder why self-help guides to using computers and the Internet are given such a high profile instead. The reason? Well, sleepy old Ennis won the prize to become Ireland's first Information Age town.

Ennis has a population of around 18,000. One of the projects for the millennium was that 80 percent of households would have computers and be connected to the Internet. For a substantial saving on the normal retail price, every family was entitled to collect a computer, a bundle of software packages, and obtain Internet access. The only criteria was that one member of the household could show that he or she could perform five simple computer tasks—83 percent of Ennis households applied.

WHERE TO LIVE

If you like the idea of living in Ireland's most technologically adept community, apartments in Ennis range from €90,000 ($111,500) for a studio to €172,500 ($214,000) for a two-bedroom apartment on Bank Square, the town center. Small bungalows and semidetached houses start at €145,000 ($180,000), but €180,000 ($223,000) is a more realistic price for nicer residential neighborhoods. Better value lies out of town. In Crusheen village, eight miles from Ennis, a ready-to-move-into cottage with two bedrooms and a half acre of land is €137,500 ($170,500).

Local agent Philip O'Reilly also has a good choice of rental properties.

One-bedroom furnished apartments are from €450 ($558) monthly; three-bedroom furnished town houses from €625 ($775).

Clare's countryside is home to a host of abbeys, castles, and ancient monuments, and also a host of inexpensive cottages (Green Valley Properties is a great source of bargain-priced country hideaways). Yes, some are nothing other than a tumbledown "pile of stones," others are totally unmodernized and require bathrooms fitted, but you can find sound cottages for under €120,000 ($149,000).

Here's a listing for a typical fixer-upper in a hamlet called Lack East: Simple, stone-built, slate-roofed cottage in rural location in the heart of Clare. Situated at the end of a single-track, tarred road, this cottage is in good, sound condition. Just four rooms, with no bathroom or septic tank at present. Otherwise habitable with electricity and water supplied. Sale includes good-quality stone-built outbuilding with new galvanised roof and approximately one-half acre. Large hilly views over open countryside. €75,000 ($93,000).

The Cliffs of Moher

At one of Ireland's most famous scenic landmarks, you can take an exhilarating five-mile walk along these vertigo-inducing cliffs from the observation point of O'Brien's Tower to Hag's Head. The cliffs tower above crashing Atlantic breakers to a height of almost 200 meters (656 feet) and offer views to take your breath away. Out in Galway Bay, beyond the rocky sea stacks and natural arches, are the three misty humps of the Aran Islands. To the south you can glimpse the faraway hills of Kerry; look northwest and you'll see the brooding mountain fastnesses of Connemara. Fringed by a flowery sward of sea pinks, campions, and bird's-foot-trefoil, the path to O'Brien's Tower is made of hefty slabs of Liscannor flagstone.

It's easy to escape the crowds as most camera-toting coach-tour visitors simply spend a quick 20 minutes walking from the visitors center to O'Brien's Tower and back again. Head instead to the distant Moher Tower and—apart from the odd backpacker—you can relish the views in complete solitude. The path also forms part of the much longer Burren Way, marked by little arrows on stone markers--as they can sometimes be hard to identify be careful not to stray too close to the edge.

Birds nest all along these cliffs: kittiwakes, guillemots, razorbills, fulmars, and various other species of gulls. You may also spot clownlike puffins and the occasional red-legged chough. Look out too for wildflowers such as the white scented flowers of lady's tresses, dainty pink fairy foxgloves, and cushion-like mossy saxifrage with its abundant clumps of star-shaped flowers blooming among the sea-sprayed rocks between May and August.

The coastline will prove a big draw but the north of the county is more expensive than the south. In north Clare, right on the shores of Galway Bay, Ballyvaughan is a picturesque harbor village with some excellent pubs and restaurants—don't miss the seafood at Monk's on the quayside. From here you can explore the traffic-free "Green Roads" of the Burren, old drovers' tracks that lead up into a mysterious world of caves, dolmens, ring forts, and the sad remains of famine villages.

Springtime is especially magical for it's then that the Burren's limestone pavements are transformed into a flowery carpet of rare wildflowers: Species include purple spotted orchids, mountain avens, and vivid blue gentians. Although properties are more expensive than in less well-known parts of the county, you can still find reasonable value. For example, €74,000 ($91,800) buys a three-room cottage with an acre of land. Very small and a bit primitive, but it would scrub up into a sweet vacation home.

Look around Kilfenora of the high Celtic crosses and you can find old-fashioned Burren cottages—in habitable condition—for €137,000–165,000 ($170,000–204,500). However, modern bungalow residences change hands for far more. In the heart of the Burren, a new three-bedroom stone bungalow styled like a traditional cottage is €375,000 ($465,000).

Doolin is another desirable coastal village between the Burren and Cliffs of Moher. As well as traditional music every night, villagers have unrivaled views of the Aran Islands. Again, it's a brilliant location for botanists and ramblers who enjoy seeking out the remains of historical churches, castles, and prehistoric ruins.

At the lower reaches of North Clare are the seaside resorts of Liscannor and Lahinch. Liscannor is the more traditional of the two: You can still see black-hulled currach boats in the harbor and the curative powers of Saint Brigid's Well continue to attract local people on February 1. Lahinch is more of a golfer's hangout—here the championship links course along the dunes dates to 1893. It was originally intended for the sole use of officers of the infamous Black Watch regiment.

Lovely location but prices will probably seem staggering, especially for properties with sea views. Built in traditional style, a three-bedroom Liscannor cottage is €317,000 ($393,000). Three miles from Liscannor (a mile from the Cliffs of Moher), another three-bedroom cottage with exposed timber beams and views of Lahinch Bay is €375,000 ($465,000).

Most folks in this area go into Ennistymon for their main shopping.

Its streets are lined with old-fashioned shop fronts and market traditions date to the Napoleonic wars. Come on a Tuesday for the weekly street market, come on Friday for the cattle market, come anytime to take a scenic walk along the riverbank to the Cascades, where you can occasionally see leaping salmon when the waters are in full spate. Within the town, terraced town houses (you probably know them as row houses) needing some modernization are €108,000–125,000 ($134,000–155,000).

For one of Clare's most attractive inland locations, make tracks for Killaloe and the shores of Lough Derg. Sheltered by the Slieve Bearnagh and Arra hills, Killaloe perches on a neck of land where the River Shannon flows out of the lough on its journey toward Limerick; you can walk into County Tipperary over the 13-arched bridge spanning the river.

The locality is littered with historical remains: medieval churches, round towers, and those bibles in stone, high Celtic crosses, one of which carries inscriptions both in old Irish ogham lettering and Norse runic script. Locals claim this was once Ireland's capital—the most famous of the high kings, Brian Boru, is said to have had a palace known as Kincora where the present-day town now stands. Best known as a sailing and water-sports center, Killaloe does a good summer tourist trade with visitors who enjoy messing about in boats. Three-bedroom holiday houses with berthage rights were listing for €235,000 ($291,500) through Hamptons.

For a two-bedroom cottage in good order and a distant lake view, expect to pay in the region of €165,000 ($204,500). It's even more if you want to look on to the lough and glimpse Holy Island. Laden with legends, Holy Island's other name is Inishcealtra. Marked by a high round tower, it has a collection of ancient chapels, an anchorite's cell, and gravestones dating back to the 7th century. Thought to have been founded by Saint Colm, the island was an important monastic site until it fell to Viking raiders. Until the 1830s, the island's holy well was a popular place of pilgrimage, but the church discouraged visits after revelries got out of hand. Some local girls were carried off by men intent on what you might describe as "inappropriate relationships."

If Killaloe seems too expensive, look to the nearby communities of Scarriff, Tuamgraney, Mountshannon, and Whitegate, where village houses start at around $130,000. For example, a two-bedroom semi-detached house on Whitegate's main street is €110,000 ($136,500). At Scariff, a three-bedroom home in good decorative order is €130,000 ($161,000).

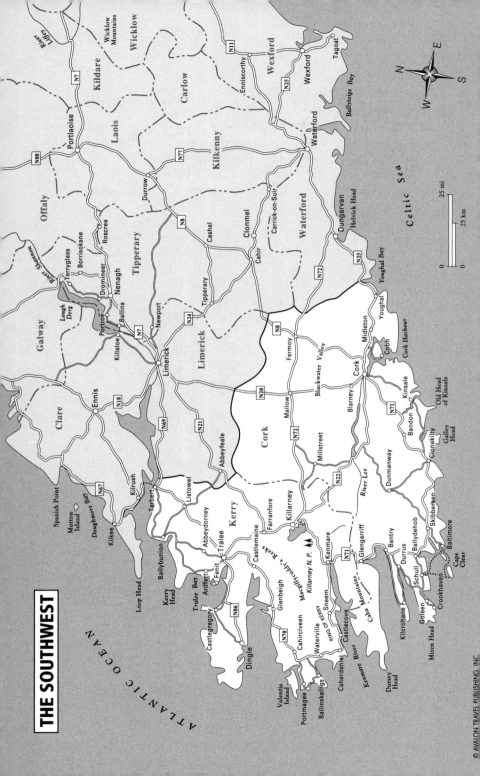

The Southwest

The paintbox villages of the southwest are a favorite hunting ground for foreign home-buyers. You may also decide that the counties of Cork or Kerry, rich in folklore, music, and wildly seductive landscapes, are perfect for raising a young family, starting a new business venture, or simply enjoying your retirement.

The Gulf Stream climate ensures that winters are mild and cottage gardens rarely see snowfalls. Primroses start blooming in the hedgerows in February and shops stock the new season's vegetables sooner than anywhere else. An added bonus is the wide range of sporting activities, which include everything from golf to yachting, hill walking, fishing, and foxhunting. Outside of Dublin, the southwest coastal region is the country's main tourism mecca so there are plenty of opportunities for anyone considering a business venture.

Scenerywise, it's impossible to favor one county over the other. When it comes down to it, a lot depends on just how near you want to be to the big city. If that's important to you, you'll probably plump for Cork.

Ireland's second city, Cork city offers an array of cultural delights from film festivals to jazz festivals to top-class theater. In 2005 it was actually rewarded with the title of European Capital of Culture.

County Kerry

LAY OF THE LAND

Despite the annual horde of summer visitors, Kerry delivers sheer poetry. Nothing detracts from the bewitching beauty of its landscapes, where mountains are reflected in looking-glass loughs, and flotillas of islands drift out of a muslin mesh of sea mist.

You'll never forget the first time you actually see this enchanted kingdom for yourself: the silver-thread waterfalls spilling down from the Slieve Mish, Derrynasaggart, and Macgillyguddy's Reeks mountain ranges, the mirror-bright lakes of Killarney, the rocky Atlantic peninsulas with their basking seals and occasional frolicking dolphin.

In general, the view factor dictates the price of all Kerry properties. For residences with a lookout onto the seashore, you can expect to pay almost double what you would for a similar property inland. As a yardstick, the average price of a Kerry property is now €192,180 ($238,300).

WHERE TO LIVE

With a population of around 20,000, Tralee is Kerry's main town and home to the whimsical Rose of Tralee festival. "Roses" of Irish descent from all over the globe come to take part in what is more of a celebration of Irishness than a straightforward beauty contest. However, few of its residents would describe it as Kerry's most scenic location.

For many visitors, the county is more synonymous with the famous Ring of Kerry, the 112-mile circuit around the Iveragh Peninsula. This drive holds the bulk of the county's scenic goodies. With the national park on its doorstep, Killarney is where most of them stay. The town itself (population 13,000) is almost entirely given over to the tourism trade.

But although Killarney undoubtedly makes an excellent holiday base, there's not the same sense of intimacy that you'll find in many of the other towns and villages strung around the Iveragh Peninsula. As you travel clockwise, the litany of lovely coastal towns and villages includes Kenmare, Sneem, Caherdaniel, Waterville, Ballinskelligs, Portmagee, Valentia Island, and Cahirciveen.

Ring of Kerry

My own favorite Ring of Kerry location is the Derrynane-Caherdaniel-Castlecove area. You don't have to choose between mountain and coastal vistas—here you've got the full glory of both and the hauntingly desolate monastic island of Skellig Michael is only a boat ride away. For ramblers, this is one of the way stations on the 135-mile-long Kerry Way and the surrounding area is an archaeologist's playground of forts, *soutterains,* and standing stones. Those fascinated by the natural world will come across unusual flora such as the Kerry lily, kidney saxifrage, bee orchid, and blue-eyed grass. It's not uncommon to meet the local wildlife either—foxes, stoats, hares, seals, and otters abound in this area.

As with all such heavenly places, house prices tend to be quite high. But if you've got time and enthusiasm, dilapidated cottages in the mountain foothills of the Iveragh Peninsula often sell for under $100,000. Not all may fit your idea of a dream home, though. Real estate agents tend to describe any sad-eyed hovel as a "fixer-upper." Be warned that even a heap of stones can fetch €80,000 ($99,200) if in a desirable location.

Most three-bedroom modern bungalows sell for €200,000 ($248,000)

Killarney's Lakes

Nestling within the 27,000 acres of Killarney's national park, girdled by mountains, are the three magical lakes that conjure one of Ireland's most quintessential images. The largest is Lough Léin, the Lake of Learning, which gained its name through the scholars who were rowed over to Inisfallen Island, a renowned center of education in medieval times. Boatmen still take visitors to this tumbledown monastic settlement, originally founded by Saint Finian the Leper in the 7th century. As well as being the place where the *Annals of Inisfallen* were written, it's said that Brian Boru, high king of Ireland, studied here during his youth.

Muckross Lake is the middle lake. Stopping points include the ruins of a 15th-century abbey that was laid to waste by Cromwell's soldiers in 1652, the Victorian magnificence of Muckross House and gardens, and the Torc waterfall that cascades off the mountains. Following the track around the north shore of the lake brings you to the Old Weir Bridge and the Meeting of the Waters, where a small river tumbles from the Upper Lake. The entire area is excellent walking and cycling country—you can hire a bike from many outlets in Killarney town. If you're traveling by car, a grandstand panorama over the Upper Lake toward the Purple Mountain can be had from Ladies View, where Queen Victoria and her ladies-in-waiting came to picnic.

upward—but for that price, you're unlikely to get a sea view. Refurbished farmhouses and cottages seem better value. For a very reasonable €160,000 ($198,500), Daly's had a two-story restored farmhouse with three bedrooms on a half-acre plot. On a quiet country lane, and with mountain views, it's just over a mile from the village of Sneem with its shops, school, church, pubs, and restaurants.

If an ocean lookout isn't a priority, €185,000 ($229,500) buys an old-style refurbished cottage with cut-stone front. It has three bedrooms and nestles in a bowl in the mountains near Waterville. In excellent condition, this cottage is only a few miles from the colorful town of Kenmare. Local agent Daly's has a good choice of long-term furnished rentals in and around Kenmare. Two- and three-bedroom properties are mostly €520–700 ($645–868) monthly.

In the Killarney area, between Castleisland and Ballydesmond, €160,000 ($198,500) was sought for a two-bedroom cottage with newly installed kitchen, two acres of land, and countryside views. Five minutes from Killarney town center, a three-bedroom modern bungalow on a half-acre plot was €195,000 ($241,800).

With those kinds of prices, you may wonder how local people on low incomes can afford south Kerry properties. Well, town suburbs provide some answers and it's still possible to buy semidetached modern row houses in Cahirciveen, Kenmare, Tralee, and Killarney for under €120,000 ($148,800). These aren't the kinds of properties that most foreign or holiday-home buyers want, so the market is purely local and not subject to the same ever-upward pressures. That said, some urban properties can be attractive. Well-maintained and overlooking a green area, a 1990s-built two-bedroom house on a mature Kenmare housing estate was available through Daly's for €132,000 ($163,600).

For an affordable slice of County Kerry at a bargain price, the best hunting grounds are in the north of the county, around Listowel and Tralee. Much of this part of North Kerry is constructed of hilly green fields rather than dramatic mountain scenery. If this is your first view of the county, you'll wonder what all the fuss has been about. There isn't much to distinguish it from the rural parts of County Limerick, linked to North Kerry by the county border and with much similarity in house prices.

The landscape alone explains why you can buy two-bedroom cottages in good structural condition that only internal modernization for €85,000 ($105,400). If you're seeking a cottage you can move straight into, there are some rich pickings in the €115,000–150,000 ($142,600–

186,000) range. Cottages requiring a major upgrade start at around €50,000 ($62,000), three-bedroom country bungalows from €155,000 ($192,200). You're likely to come across such properties in the rural hinterland of villages such as Abbeyfeale, Ardfert, and Abbeydorney.

In the town of Tralee, William Giles was offering a well-maintained semidetached bungalow (two bedrooms) for €95,000 ($117,800). This seemed a very good buy, particularly as it's wheelchair-friendly throughout.

North Kerry

The North Kerry coastline between Tarbert and Fenit is nowhere near as breathtaking as the Iveragh Peninsula, but many Irish families holiday in this area and there are a number of golf courses here. The most popular golf resort is Ballybunion, where a centuries-old family vendetta resulted in an estimated 3,000 eager participants' battling it out on the beach in 1834! Interesting buys around this little seaside town included a two-bedroom refurbished cottage for €145,000 ($179,800) and a modern semidetached bungalow with two bedrooms for €125,000 ($155,000).

North Kerry isn't entirely bereft of gorgeous seascapes and mountain fastnesses—you'll find plenty to enthrall you on the wild Dingle Peninsula. Thirty miles long and with a backbone of mountains, it reaches

Stormy skies over Dingle, County Kerry

into the ocean to the west of Tralee and is one of western Europe's richest sites for monastic beehive huts and other archaeological curiosities. The Dingle Peninsula sees far fewer package tourists than the Iveragh Peninsula, largely because its ribbon-thin roads just weren't designed for coach-tour traffic.

With around 1,200 inhabitants, 52 pubs, and some excellent seafood restaurants (try Doyle's), the main settlement is harbor town Dingle, which has a thriving fishing fleet and does a lucrative trade in taking visitors out to spot Fungie, the famous resident dolphin. The villages scattered west of Dingle town are Irish-speaking, so this is a bilingual town and you'll certainly hear the chatter of Irish in An Café Liteartha (the Literary Café), which sells books as well as coffee.

Small town houses within Dingle town start from €220,000 ($272,800). Note "from." A 1,372-square-foot refurbished town house on Goat Street with views of Dingle Harbor from all its street-facing rooms is €395,000 ($489,800).

Elsewhere on the Dingle Peninsula, you can buy traditional two-story rural houses and refurbished farmhouses from €200,000 ($248,000). For €250,000 ($310,000), O'Connors had a gorgeous sunshine-yellow farmhouse with five bedrooms that's within a mile of Ventry Beach— you can see Ventry Harbor from the rear of the property.

Modern bungalows are quite expensive, perhaps because just about everything here comes with a lookout onto both mountains and ocean. Want the kind of silver-screen views seen in the movie *Ryan's Daughter?* It was filmed at Inch Beach, a spectacular spot where four-bedroom bungalows change hands for more than $450,000. Two miles from Dingle town, beside Beenbawn beach, a three-bedroom bungalow with views toward Dingle Harbor is €292,000 ($362,000).

County Cork

LAY OF THE LAND

Sandwiched between Waterford and Kerry, cosmopolitan Cork is Ireland's largest county. Like neighboring south Kerry, the scenery is simply dramatic—imagine a hinterland of mountains, loughs, and wooded river valleys, all fringed by a craggy coastline of cliffs, coves, and pristine beaches. That's Cork.

House values within the county vary enormously, though as a yardstick the average is €218,038 ($270,000). The dearest locations are villages within easy striking distance of Cork City, high-profile harbor towns such as Kinsale, and pretty color-washed villages such as Eyries on the Beara Peninsula, where all the village houses are painted in rainbow colors: mint green, sky blue, primrose yellow, pale lavender. You would be surprised at how many buyers fall in love with a coat of paint—in Eyeries, the quintessential beauty-spot village, even fixer-upper cottages list for €100,000 ($124,000).

WHERE TO LIVE

The biggest problem with County Cork is its sheer size—it can be hard deciding on the best place to begin a house-hunting quest. In general, real estate agents in Cork City are more likely to deal with properties in the eastern half of the county, between the border with County Waterford and Kinsale, which has its own local agents. If you're more inclined toward west Cork, try Clonakilty, Skibbereen, or Bantry for the widest choice of properties and agents.

Ireland's second city, Cork City offers an array of cultural delights from film festivals to jazz festivals to top-class theater.

Location, location, location. As always, it will dictate the price. Habitable period cottages (800 square feet) with exposed wooden beams and slate floors start at €120,000 ($148,800) in the inland Bandon/Dunmanway area. In a small coastal village called Timoleague in west Cork, Beet Cottage is similar, but has views over an inner bay. This was priced at €220,000 ($272,800). But go looking in the popular Skibbereen area and you can expect to pay around €275,000 ($341,000) for such a cottage.

Cork City

Although you perhaps haven't come to pound the city streets, it's hard to resist spending a day or two in Cork City, wandering the engaging laneways around the River Lee. With a population of around 180,000, this is the republic's second-largest city and has its own university as well as a thriving arts and culture scene. Early birds find the best bargains at the flea market on Coal Quay, or go to the covered English Market, which at one time was barred to Irish traders. Produce varies from locally made cheeses to *drisheen,* a sausage made from sheep's blood.

The average price of a property within the city stands at €243,766 ($302,000). Nowadays, it's almost impossible to find a three-bedroom

The Big Fella

Many scenes in Neil Jordan's movie *Michael Collins* were shot in the west Cork area. Played in the film by Liam Neeson, Michael Collins was born in 1890 near Clonakilty. Often referred to as "the Big Fella,"' he was a major figure in Ireland's War of Independence (1919–1921). Using "flying columns" and assassination squads, he organized a ruthless campaign of guerrilla warfare against the British that eventually resulted in bringing the old enemy to the negotiating table.

Sent to London by Eamon de Val-era to negotiate a truce, Collins put his signature to the treaty that partitioned the island of Ireland. In doing so he signed his own death warrant. Southern Ireland split into pro- and antitreaty factions and former comrades-in-arms were soon spilling their own blood in a bitter civil war. On August 22, 1922, the antitreaty forces caught up with Collins at Beal-na-Bleath, near the west Cork village of Macroom. His car was ambushed, and rather than fleeing, Collins engaged in a shoot-out that resulted in his death.

semidetached home in a desirable area for less than €300,000 ($372,000). In the city center, one-bedroom apartments (570 square feet) in a new development on North Main Street are €205,000 ($254,000).

The Coast

As you journey east to west along the coast road, the first of the county's old harbor towns is Youghal (YAWL). Its town walls date from the 13th century and Sir Walter Raleigh was the mayor here in 1588.

Next comes Cobh (COVE), whose huge natural harbor was the embarkation point for around 2.5 million of the 19th century's emigrants. The Heritage Center chronicles some of their sad stories and also remembers the days when the transatlantic liners, the *Titanic* among them, put into port here. Under British rule Cobh's name was Queenstown and its 19th-century terraces have something of the look of an English seaside town. Three-bedroom terrace (row) houses here fetch €169,000 ($209,500) upward. At the top end of the range, a former Church of Ireland rectory was listing for €950,000 ($1.17 million).

Under British rule Cobh's name was Queenstown and its 19th-century terraces have something of the look of an English seaside town.

On to fashionable Kinsale, which has its own seafaring history—pubs carry names such as the Spaniard and the Spinnaker and if you walk along its cliff-tops to Old Head, you can gaze out to where the *Lusitania* went down in 1915 with the loss of 1,500 lives. A center for yachting, sea angling, and golf, the town's alleyways are steep and cobbled, houses are painted in a rainbow of pastel colors, and 11 of its 35 restaurants are of the gourmet variety.

With only 2,500 year-round residents, Kinsale really comes to life as a summer port resort and almost half of its properties are sold for investments. Modernized two- and three-bedroom town cottages mostly go €195,000–300,000 ($241,800–372,000).

Advertised as being ideal for a professional, a retired couple, or an investor looking for sure-fire rental properties, a modern home built in traditional cottage style in the "World's End" quarter of Kinsale was €240,000 ($297,600). It has three bedrooms and is a 10-minute walk along the waterfront to the town center. At Rose Abbey, a three-bedroom/three-bathroom stone-fronted cottage with a Mediterranean-style terrace looking toward 12th-century Saint Multose Church and Kinsale town center was €280,000 ($347,000).

If you want to live in the Kinsale area for a while, it may make more sense to rent a property. One-bedroom furnished apartments and two-bedroom cottages start at €750 ($930) per month. Duplex apartments with harbor views are more expensive: around €1,150 ($1,425) monthly for a three-bedroom property. Sheehy Brothers always has a good selection of rentals.

Six miles from Kinsale, one mile from Garretstown beach, Ballinspittle village has a school, church, and lots of services and amenities. SWS was selling a three-bedroom town house here for €190,000 ($235,600). For the same price, Keane Mahoney Smith had the Old Posthouse, a two-bedroom town cottage painted sky blue and with wooden paneled ceilings. It has both a roof garden and an enclosed courtyard.

Farther to the west is color-washed Clonakilty, a pretty heritage town with a magnificent array of traditional hand-painted shopfronts. Accessible by an archway from McCurtain Hill, a three-bedroom mews house painted strawberry-pink seemed very reasonably priced at €152,000 ($188,500). Most modernized town houses fetch at least 180,000 ($223,000). A few miles away, at Rosscarbery Beach, two-bedroom apartments with sea views in a new beachside development were €165,000 ($204,600).

Incidentally, Clonakilty's citizens are very proud of their local delicacy—Clonakilty Black Pudding. If you feel queasy about tucking into pig's blood sausage, a good place for a pub seafood lunch is An Sugan. Much of Neil Jordan's film *Michael Collins* was filmed hereabouts and it was in Clonakilty that the Free State general went to school.

Protestants founded bustling Skibbereen but its name became a by-word for Catholic suffering and the severe hardships endured by the peasantry during the famine years. Even though today it's a prosperous farmers' town, memories never fade and visitors are encouraged to follow the Skibbereen Trail around sites associated with the An Gorta Mor, the Great Hunger.

Simple two-bedroom row houses in Skibbereen start at €120,000 ($149,000), but expect to pay around €225,000 ($279,000) for a three-bedroom modern bungalow. Long-term furnished rentals in town and the surrounding villages begin at €550 ($682) monthly for two-bedroom cottages, from €700 ($868) monthly for three-bedroom bungalows. Local agent Liam Hodnett has a good selection.

Skibbereen's nearby coastal villages are a big draw for foreign buyers. Although most village populations in west Cork number fewer than 500 year-round residents, they're always swollen with summer visitors and so have a good choice of traditional music pubs and restaurants.

South of Skibbereen, Baltimore is a lively port and sailing center with a ruined castle that goes by the magical name of Dún na Sead, the Fort of the Jewels. Its former inhabitants, the O'Driscoll clan, enjoyed a million-dollar view over Roaringwater Bay and Carberry's Hundred Islands. Ferryboats make the journey over to Sherkin Island and Cape Clear Island, a noted site for bird-watching as it lies on one of the migratory passage routes. One of the strangest events in Baltimore's history occurred in 1631, when 200 of the inhabitants were snatched by Barbary pirates and shipped off to Algiers as slaves. I haven't got a clue what homes sold for in those days, but today you can easily pay €295,000 ($365,800) for a detached bungalow of around 2,000 square feet.

Other sought-after villages on Roaringwater Bay include Ballydehob and Schull. Lovely villages, without doubt, but if you want a good-quality hideaway with harbor views, expect to pay for it. A three-bedroom pink-washed two-story residence near Schull certainly has the picturesque panoramas—and also a €375,000 ($465,000) price tag to match. Some of west Cork's best beaches are to be found along this stretch of the Mizen Peninsula—the queen of them all is Barleycove, on the road between the villages of Crookhaven and Goleen, where you often see artists trying to capture the beauty of the place on canvas. Farmhouses to modernize in this area go for around €220,000 ($272,800).

With Dunmanus Bay on one side and Bantry Bay on the other, remote Sheep's Head Peninsula takes a 12-mile plunge southwestward from Durrus village. It's another splendid spot to get out the easel and paintbrushes. (And it also provides a good example of how prices have risen.) Four years ago, you could have bought a fully restored two-story farmhouse here for $130,000. Nowadays it costs around $150,000 for a farmhouse on half an acre needing substantial renovation. Unmodernized two-bedroom cottages with a quarter acre of land cost roughly the same price. Modern bungalows of around 1,000 square feet cost around €275,000 ($341,000).

Near Cork's border with County Kerry, the Bantry Bay village of Glengarriff is noted for its lush gardens and picturesque harbor. It's very popular with vacationers as there are lots of activities, including fishing, sailing, shooting, pony trekking, mountain climbing, golf, and forest walks. Only five minutes' drive from the village are thousands of acres of forest with freshwater lakes.

Key Properties had a one-bedroom cottage in Glengarriff village for €135,000 ($167,500). It's recently modernized, in excellent repair, but is probably only suitable as a vacation home. Total living space only amounts to around 340 square feet. In the vicinity of Glengarriff, and also on the Beara Peninsula, the same agents also had some habitable small stone farmhouses of around 1,000 square feet for €190,000 ($235,600).

If you decide to check out properties away from the coast, avoid County Cork's best-known village: Blarney. Too twee for words, it's a real tourist trap and traffic is simply horrendous. Coach tour after coach tour delivers hordes of would-be stone kissers, all convinced the Blarney Stone has the power to turn them into silver-tongued charmers. Personally, I wouldn't spend $5 to bend over backward from a great and giddy height to slaver over some lump of rock! On the other hand, if you've got a money-spinning idea, it may be just the place—it's a village where tourists are very easily parted from their cash and Blarney Woolen Mills alone manages to sell 900,000 sweaters to convoys of the credulous every year.

Elsewhere, Midleton is a 17th-century market town and home to the Jameson whiskey distillery. Town houses here can be found for €140,000–150,000 ($173,600–186,000). Or look to the Blackwater Valley, dotted with castles and ancient sites. Main towns and villages along the valley include Fermoy, Mallow, and Millstreet, which hosts one of Ireland's largest horse shows. On the Bandon River, the countryside surrounding Dunmanway and Bandon delivers plenty of habitable properties in the $100,000 to $150,000 range and is especially good for hunting down bargain cottages for refurbishment.

THE SOUTHEAST

The Southeast

Gorgeous green meadows, ancient abbey ruins, pretty villages, and horses galloping along sandy beaches. Despite the savage Viking and Norman past, this is Ireland at its most gentle. Even the weather here usually decides to be kind!

The mix in Ireland's southeast is essentially maritime and countryside fringed by mountains. Even if you choose to live in an inland county, the sea is likely to be a two hours' drive at most. Here you really can have the best of both worlds.

Kilkenny's verdant landscape is pastoral perfection. An added bonus is Kilkenny town, the country's best-preserved example of a medieval city. Filling the region's southeast corner, Wexford of the big sandy beaches also has a strong agricultural base and has been inhabited since prehistoric times. Again with excellent beaches, Waterford is the Crystal County, renowned throughout the world as the home of the exquisitely crafted crystal that shares its name. Or, if peace and tranquillity top your shopping list, take a trip to Tipp and check out the sleepy market towns and even sleepier villages of County Tipperary.

County Kilkenny

THE LAY OF THE LAND

This lovely county is dotted with picturebook villages, shady woodland copses, ramblers' tracks, and winding rivers banked by lacy white clouds of cow parsley. Lost in the fields are some hauntingly beautiful monastic settlements and you'll also stumble across a wealth of high crosses, round towers, and castles dating from Norman times.

South Kilkenny's countryside brims with enticements, particularly if you concentrate on the small towns and villages besides the banks of the Barrow, Nore, Munster, and Suir rivers, all excellent fly-fishing rivers. If your new neighbors aren't involved in farming, chances are they'll be doing something arty with clay, crystal, wool, gemstones, wood, or leather—this part of the country has a high concentration of craft-workers.

There's always room for new blood and new ideas and just because you've never done anything remotely crafty in your life doesn't mean it's too late to start. The Crafts Council of Ireland runs courses in jewelry-making and pottery from its training center in the Castle Yard in Kilkenny town. Whether you're an existing craft-worker looking for a new market or are interested in taking a course, it's worth looking at its website at www.ccoi.ie.

WHERE TO LIVE

Kilkenny Town

Sometimes called the Marble City, Kilkenny town is the place to head for first. Although wandering around its castle, abbeys, and maze of crooked laneways can make you feel as if you're trapped in a time warp, the modern world is there when you need it. Kilkenny has good train and bus services to Dublin, or if you're driving, it's 70 miles from the capital by road.

With around 20,000 inhabitants, this is a large town by Irish standards and thus laden with all the essentials: excellent shops, health services, restaurants, the Watergate theater, and three annual arts festivals. And, if you suddenly develop an arid throat, you'll find 68 pubs an Saint Francis's Abbey, now the headquarters of Smithwicks Brewery.

The Witch of Kilkenny

Born in Kilkenny in 1280, Alice Kyteler was the daughter of a wealthy Norman banker who established a money-lending venture in the town. The business eventually passed into Alice's hands through inheritance, but the ecclesiastical authorities of the day were staunchly opposed to women's being in trade and she made many enemies. As in many other witchcraft cases, money may have been the reason behind her eventual downfall. Seemingly a woman of healthy appetites, Alice worked her way through four husbands, all of whom mysteriously expired for no apparent reason. Some townsfolk believed that she had poisoned the lot of them, others whispered that it was the work of the devil.

At her trial in 1324, the bishop of Ossory accused her of heresy and of trafficking with his satanic majesty. Witnesses swore that they had seen Alice and her maidservant slaughtering cockerels and sweeping dust from the town's streets to the house of William Outlawe, Alice's son. In the murky world of medieval magickry, this was a form of transference whereby dust represented gold and Kilkenny's wealth would all fall to William. In other words, witchcraft.

The court found the defendants guilty. Alice and her servant, Petronella, were sentenced to be burnt at the stake, William to be hanged. However, Alice managed to engineer an escape and fled to England while William bought his pardon by funding the reroofing of the choir stalls in Saint Canice's Cathedral. Only the poor servant girl paid the ultimate penalty. Petronella was burned at the Tholsel, outside Kilkenny's City Hall, along with many of her mistress's possessions. The house on Saint Kieran's Street where Alice and Petronella lived now goes by the name of Kyteler's Inn.

Rather than demolish their ancient buildings, Kilkennians simply give them a new lease on life. The tourist office is in the Shee Alms House on Rose Inn Street; it was built as a pauper's hospital in 1582 and was still being used as such until 1830. Dating from 1284, the home of the infamous Witch of Kilkenny on Saint Kieran's Street is now a popular pub-restaurant. On Parliament Street, the Archaeological Society and the genealogical county records have found a home in the Rothe House, built by a merchant for his young bride in 1594. One of the more recent architectural ventures was the construction of the castle's new coach-houses and stables. Set in a flower-filled courtyard, these buildings are now used by local craftspeople and the Kilkenny Design Center.

Although Kilkenny's old black marble pavements were lifted in 1929, much else remains to distract you from your house-hunting plans: riverside walks below the castle, Saint Canice's Cathedral, the Black Abbey, and the Tholsel where medieval villains were publicly burnt at the stake. No one knows how long people have been walking through the dark passageway of the Butterslip but records show that in 1616 market traders were using it. Older residents can still recite a traditional rhyme about the Butterslip:

If you ever go to Kilkenny,
Look for the hole in the wall.
Where you get 24 eggs for a penny
And butter for nothing at all.

Unfortunately houses within Kilkenny town don't sell for "nothing at all" kinds of prices. It's an affluent community with people employed in the service industries, brewing, and food production. Prices vary considerably and, as always, much depends on location and the type of home sought. To give you a yardstick, the average price for a home within the county is €210,187 ($260,600).

One of Kilkenny town's most sought-after residential addresses is Sion Road, which tracks the River Nore's broad, bosky vale. Here an elegant four-bedroom residence with 1,765 square feet of living space and spacious garden was on the market for €450,000 ($558,000). If you're seeking a business opportunity, real estate agents SF McCreery also had a 10-bedroom residence on Sion Road for €650,000 ($806,000). The current owners have obtained planning permission to turn it into a crèche (day nursery) with capacity for 28 children.

At the other end of the price scale, midterrace row houses in the city's outer suburbs start at around €105,000 ($130,000); modern semidetached and detached family houses with 3–4 bedrooms in attractive residential neighborhoods mostly fall into the €212,000–300,000 range ($263,000–$372,000). In the city center, off the High Street, a one-bedroom apartment is €150,000 ($186,000).

Oakwood House is a Georgian home with four bedrooms, five reception rooms, walled courtyard, and 18 acres. In a sylvan setting overlooking the Nore Valley, it was priced at €1 million ($1.24 million). Expensive, but any Georgian house is likely to prove a good investment in the long run. Built in simple classic style, these types of residences will never go out of fashion—after all, nobody is making them any more!

Homes on the city's rural outskirts can be fairly expensive—for example, a 3,000-square-foot house in a village two miles from the city was €550,000 ($682,000). However, the deeper you move into the countryside, the more prices fall. Thirteen miles from the city, at Ballyhale, a three-bedroom village house in good repair was €130,000 ($161,000) At Maddoxtown, a modern two-bedroom bungalow with garage and well-maintained garden was €145,000 ($180,000).

Along with ancient Thomastown, Kilkenny's main craft clusters are the villages of Goresbridge, Stoneyford, Bennetsbridge, and Graiguenamanagh. Most Kilkenny real estate agents have properties in these villages. In medieval Graiguenamanagh, modest town houses start at €105,000 ($130,000), but you can easily pay €195,000 ($242,000) for a two-bedroom riverside apartment. Looking like a traditional cottage, but only built a couple of years ago, a modern four-bedroom home was €265,000 ($328,600).

Thomastown takes its name from Thomas Fitzanthony, a Welsh-Norman knight who founded this place of time-toppled medieval walls and castles in 1197. Less than two miles down the road, Jerpoint Abbey silhouettes the skyline. Today its towers and cloisters are in ruins but this was once one of the finest Cistercian abbeys in Ireland. As an example of typical prices in the surrounding area, €365,000 ($452,600) was being sought for a three-bedroom ivy-covered cottage (1,432 square feet) close to Jerpoint Abbey. This is a grand location with all the history you ever wanted within walking distance.

The medieval monks couldn't get enough of County Kilkenny's real estate. Five miles west of Stoneyford, they took over Kells Priory, a former Norman castle with seven gray towers and massively thick curtain walls that perches above the King's River, a tributary of the Nore. Now abandoned to time and the elements, Kells is made even more atmospheric by the fact that the government seems to have forgotten its existence—there are no ticket office, no guided tours, no designated visiting hours. Just you, the sheep, and maybe a ghost or two.

Nor did the holy men neglect to colonize the banks of the River Barrow. With the 13th-century Cistercian splendor of Duiske Abbey on the doorstep, Graiguenamanagh's name actually means "the grange of the monks." At nearby Kilconnely, a quadrangle of seven stone buildings for restoration was on the market for €180,000 ($223,000). Totaling a massive 7,747 square feet, these courtyard buildings once formed part of an estate. They include a former gamekeeper's lodge, a coach house, and a lofted barn.

If you're seeking a farmhouse, obviously a lot depends on location, state of repair, and the amount of land being sold with the property. Your €80,000 ($99,000) will buy a two-story renovation-project farmhouse, but you'll probably pay at least €150,000 ($186,000) for one you can move into immediately. And at that price it's likely to be fairly compact and have no land included.

Inistioge (Inishteeg) is an adorable village backdropped by dark, goblin woods on the banks of the River Nore. An 18th-century 10-arched bridge spans the river and around the grassy square, lined with a canopy of lime trees, most pubs and shops have kept their original facades. The village has featured in a number of recent movies—one was the romantic weepy *Circle of Friends,* adapted from a novel of the same name by Irish writer Maeve Binchy.

This is a popular area—the Mount Juliet Estate with its world-famous golf course is only 10 minutes' drive away—and properties sell for premium prices. Inistioge properties on the market included a restored two-bedroom cottage with an acre of land. The price was €175,000 ($217,000). A modern three-bedroom bungalow was €300,000 ($372,000).

County Wexford

LAY OF THE LAND

Although converted to Christianity by Saint Ibar in the 5th century, Wexford's name comes from the Norse word *waesfjord,* meaning "sandy harbor" or "harbor of mud flats." The Viking invaders who settled here were followed in 1169 by the Normans, for whom Wexford was their first Irish port of call. Then, as now, the county's main settlement was Wexford town. Unfortunately relatively few traces of the distant past remain—for that you can thank Cromwell, who attacked the town in 1649, putting many of its citizens and all of its Franciscan friars to the sword.

Golden sandy beaches are County Wexford's star attraction and many have been awarded the European blue flag for excellence.

Golden sandy beaches are County Wexford's star attraction and many have been awarded the European blue flag for excellence. Near Gorey, in the north of the county, you'll find beautiful strands beside the villages of Ballymoney and Courtown; the endless golden chain then continues through Morriscastle, Kilmuckbridge, Blackwater, and Curracloe, which featured in the Tom Hanks movie, *Saving Private Ryan.*

As nowhere within the county is more than a two-hour drive from Dublin, Wexford is favored by second-home buyers. Prices are fairly buoyant and, depending on whether it has sea views or not, the typical three-bedroom family home falls somewhere into the €185,000–225,000 category ($229,000–279,000). For example, €185,000 ($229,000) buys a two-story detached house in Blackwater, a coastal village with pubs, shops, church, and school only a mile from the golden sands of Ballyconnigar Beach.

WHERE TO LIVE

Wexford Town

Around 16,000 people live in the Wexford town area with smaller numbers in Gorey, Enniscorthy, New Ross, and Rosslare Harbour, the main ferry port to South Wales in Britain. Over a quarter of the population is aged between 25 and 44 and employment is found in a diversity of enterprises—everything from food production to data processing and light engineering to the manufacture of pharmaceutical products and car components. In addition, Wexford has benefited from the government's decentralization program. A number of state departments have relocated here—they include the Environmental Protection Agency and Teagasc, the state's agricultural research center.

Although Wexford town is no longer a commercial port—the Slaney estuary is too silted up with centuries of river mud—it still has the feel of a seafarers' hangout. One of its most famous sons was John Barry, who emigrated to America and founded the United States navy. Its ribbon-thin streets can get very roisterous during summer's Viking Festival, though for classier entertainment you should come for October's Opera Festival.

County average for a home is €189,910 ($235,500). If you're taken with Wexford town, two-bedroom row houses can still be had for under $160,000, and new semidetached bungalows start at €145,000 ($180,000). Large showpiece apartments in top locations around the harbor and quays can cost a lot more—often more than €200,000 ($248,000) for a two-bedroom unit with sea views.

If you are looking to rent, one-bedroom furnished apartments mostly fall into the €460–560 per month range ($570–695). Two-bedroom apartments run €560–700 ($695–868). In nearby seaside villages, two-bedroom furnished bungalows average around €650 ($806) monthly.

Vicinity of Wexford

An easy drive from Wexford town, the Courtown area has both great beaches and three 18-hole golf courses. Sought after? You bet. Here you

A Night at the Opera

Even non-operagoers have probably heard of Bizet's *Carmen* and Strauss's *Die Fledermaus*. But have you ever had the chance to enjoy *Fosca, I Cavalieri di Ekebu,* or *Sarlatan,* the tragicomic tale of a quack doctor who falls in love with a beautiful hypochondriac? Yet at the Wexford festival, an 18-day October extravaganza of opera and much else besides, you could have seen all of the above-mentioned operas in recent years.

Along with its Nordic setting, the hammers, fire, and alcoholic Lutheran pastor of *I Cavalieri di Ekebu* had given this particular opera something of a cult status in Sweden. But the Wexford performance of *Sarlatan* was the first on stage since its last outing 60 years before, at Brno in Czechoslovakia. The career of its Czech composer, Pavel Haas, was cut brutally short when he went to his death in the gas chambers of Auschwitz in 1944.

Since Wexford's Opera Festival began in 1951, the focus has been on bringing to light obscure operas that for one reason or another have been unjustly neglected or forgotten. It attracts an international crowd of opera lovers and you can also sample street theater, poetry readings, choral recitals, lectures, stand-up comedy, and music that varies from foot-tapping Irish traditional to the haunting strains of gypsy violins. Wexford town itself takes on a carnival atmosphere with storekeepers competing for the kudos of having the best festive window display, and artists and audiences alike thronging the cafès and bars along Main Street and the Quays. No other small-town Irish festival offers such a perfect excuse for revelers to get out their evening dresses and dinner jackets!

Tickets for the three showpiece operas aren't cheap: Last year's prices were pitched at €75 ($93) for weekday performances and €95 ($118) at weekends. Daytime and late-night events are more affordable, costing €10–15 ($12.50–18.50). For booking and information about this year's October Festival, contact Wexford Festival Opera Box Office, Theater Royal, High Street, Wexford Town, County Wexford; tel. 053/22144.

can pay as much as €400,000 ($496,000) for a well-maintained home on half an acre with around 1,850 square feet of living space.

Along with miles of forest walks and sand dunes, there are excellent marina facilities here and residents are right beside one of Europe's most renowned nature reserves: the North Sloblands. During the winter, the Slobs provide a feeding ground for around 10,000 migratory Greenland white-fronted geese, more than half the world's entire population. South of Wexford town lies Rosslare Strand and Carne; round the corner to the south coast proper and you'll come across Kilmore Quay, Fethard, Hook Head, and Duncannon.

In a village called Ballyhogue, around 30 minutes' drive from Wexford town, a two-bedroom modern bungalow with a quarter acre of garden was on the market for €105,000 ($130,000). However, living space amounts to only 650 square feet. If you prefer to buy a plot of land within telescope sight of the coast and build a home, .75- to 1-acre sites with planning permission mostly go €120,000–150,000 ($149,000–186,000).

If your heart is set on a thatched property, the area around the fishing village of Kilmore Quay is your best bet. Lining the main street, many local houses are pictures of whitewashed, thatched perfection.

Like every visitor who turns up for July's seafood festival, you too will probably want to own one. All well and good if you have deep pockets but are you prepared to part with €375,000 ($465,000)? That's the price Kehoe's was quoting for a two-story traditional thatched cottage in the village center. With three bedrooms, it had been fully refurbished, but still had its beamed ceilings and slate floors.

I also like the Duncannon area, though again, properties are quite expensive: Three-bedroom bungalow properties are mostly selling for more than €200,000 ($248,000). South of Duncannon, some lovely walks crisscross the largely deserted Hook Peninsula, pointing into the ocean like a witch's bony finger. The lighthouse on the headland dates to the 12th century and the peninsula itself is dotted with crumbling castles, forts, and abbeys.

This area has another and very curious historical claim to fame. Ever heard the phrase "by hook or by crook" and wondered how it originated? Cromwell coined it during his campaign to capture Waterford city, which lies a few miles west across the county border. What he was referring to was two possible landing points: Hook in Wexford and Crooke in County Waterford. The city would fall to his army by Hook or by Crooke.

In Wexford's hinterland, there's a good choice of attractive cottages and small houses in a "move-into-tomorrow" condition for around €150,000 ($186,000). From many inland locations, if you look due south you can see the ocean and the distant smudge of the Saltee Islands, whose surrounding treacherous waters gave rise to the nickname "the graveyard of a thousand ships."

At the top of the cottage price scale, €400,000 ($496,000) could buy a chocolate-box pretty cottage at Edenvale, three miles from Wexford town. Stone-built, 250 years old, and with 1,281 square feet of living space, it has beautiful gardens and is set in woodland. A freshwater fishing river is only 50 yards away.

Carry on northward along the road through the heart of strawberry-growing countryside and you'll come to Enniscorthy, a little town on the banks of the River Slaney. Twenty minutes' drive from the beaches and backdropped by the Blackstairs Mountains, this busy little town has plenty of waterfront inns, brightly painted shop fronts, a 13th-century castle, and an annual summer strawberry festival. "It's the biggest small town in the world," claims one enthusiastic local realtor, "a town that's rocketing from nowhere."

Within the town, starting price for one-bedroom apartments of 400 square feet is around €110,000 ($136,400). In the surrounding countryside, €95,000 ($118,000) could buy an unrenovated cottage (1,300 square feet) backing onto the River Slaney.

One of the nicest villages is Ferns with yet another collection of castle and abbey ruins. This was once the base of the kings of Leinster; their number included the notorious Dermot MacMurrough, who invited the Normans over to Ireland and thus brought about centuries of English rule. Four-bedroom modern bungalows here are mostly fetching over €200,000 ($248,000).

County Waterford

LAY OF THE LAND

With County Cork to the west and County Wexford to the east, Waterford's coastline has sandy coves, cliff-top walks, and some particularly attractive harbor towns and fishing villages. Coastal property prices tend to be fairly high as everywhere is within easy commuting distance of both Waterford city and Cork city.

It's so mild here that palm trees grow in gardens—and if you fancy trying your hand at wine-making, it's also possible to grow certain varieties of grapes. Not that you have to break your back digging and delving—I always like seeing gardens that resemble wildflower meadows, and there are lots of those around here too.

WHERE TO LIVE

Waterford City

With around 44,000 people, Waterford city is the county's main population center and also the southeast's biggest commercial port, always busy with freighters and container ships. Although much of Waterford's outskirts are a featureless sprawl of industrial development, it's proud of its reputation as a working city. Thanks to its strategic location on the River Suir estuary, this is a true trading settlement and has been for more than a millennium.

While you might not want to live within the city confines, do pay a visit for at its heart lies a fascinating kernel of historical heritage. Surrounded by the remnants of medieval walls, streets and laneways track back through the centuries to the time of the Victorians, the Georgians, and even the Anglo-Normans who wrested the settlement of Vadrafjord from the Vikings in 1170.

The city's most famous Norman landmark is Reginald's Tower, a stone replacement for the original wooden watchtower, built by Reginald the Dane in 1003, where guard could be kept over the longships in the harbor. The tower has witnessed an incredible amount of history: The all-conquering Norman lord Strongbow and the Irish princess Aoife held their wedding feast here above the rubble and ashes of

The Crystal Connection

As an object of desire, Waterford crystal is just about unsurpassable. It rings sweet as a bell and gleams with an almost magical silvery brilliance—the great mystery is how something so beautiful can be created from such mundane mineral products as red lead, silica sand, and potash. Producing this luxury crystalware demands great skill and it takes 8–10 years for the glassblowers, cutters, and engravers to fully learn their art.

Waterford's connection with crystal-making dates back more than 200 years, to 1783 to be precise, when George and William Penrose founded the Waterford Glass House on the city quayside. The new crystal business quickly flourished and went on to win a number of gold medals at the Great Exhibi-

tion in London. Unfortunately for the Penrose family and their workers, the firm went out of business in 1851, mainly through the British government's imposition of a crippling import tax on the raw minerals needed to produce this heavy crystalware.

With Irish independence came the urge to breathe new life into old crafts and Waterford Crystal was reborn in 1947, relaunching its wares on the world market four years later. So successful was the revival that the company had to move to larger premises on the Cork Road. Today the factory employs around 1,600 people and visitors can take a workshop tour and do serious damage to their credit cards in the Crystal Gallery. Even a tiny crystal napkin-holder will cost you at least $30.

Kiinsale, County Cork

the fallen Viking city; it has served as a royal guesthouse, a military arsenal, a mint, and a gaol (jail). And although the motto on the city's coat of arms is *Urbs intacta manet Waterfordia* (Waterford remains unconquered), the besieged townsfolk did eventually surrender to Cromwellian forces in 1650.

The average price in Waterford County as a whole is €202,494 ($251,000). Within Waterford city, row houses with three bedrooms are mostly fetching €110,000–145,000 ($136,000–180,000). A three-bedroom home in semidetached suburbia would cost you around €200,000 ($248,000). If you were looking to rent, the O'Shea O'Toole agency was quoting €600 ($744) per month for a two-bedroom apartment on Adelphi Quay.

Vicinity of Waterford City

If you want to be near Waterford city, but not pay the proverbial earth, the most affordable area is inland, tracking westward along the Suir River Valley. Look around villages such as Portlaw and you can find refurbished terraced village houses with four bedrooms for around €150,000 ($186,000). Three miles from the city, a quaint two-bedroom terraced cottage at Dunkitt was €170,000 ($210,800).

In the southeast of the county, eight miles from Waterford city, Dunmore East is a lovely fishing village and holiday retreat with plenty of thatched cottages and a busy harbor that entices many oceangoing yachts from Europe. The village seems to have the lot: a 12th-century castle, a 19th-century lighthouse, some good inns and restaurants, cliff-top and woodland walks, and great beaches. Ladies' Cove is right in the village while a short stroll south brings you to Counsellor's Strand, a beach that flies the much-coveted EU Blue Flag, awarded for cleanliness and safety.

Although no thatched properties were for sale at the time of writing, three-bedroom semidetached homes were on offer for €220,000–300,000 ($273,000–372,000). It's a highly sought-after area, and prospective residents are willing to pay over the odds to bask in the mild Gulf Stream weather.

Traveling west, the next place you'll come to is Tramore but unless you have kids in tow, you'll probably pass straight through. A traditional blue-collar seaside resort, its safe golden beach is perfect for the bucket-and-spade brigade to build elaborate castles and bury snoozing dads in the sand. The huge Trabolgan "holiday village" is here and when it rains the crowds descend on Splashworld, an indoor leisure center with swimming pools, water slides, and chutes. Two-bedroom bungalows around the town can be had for €135,000 ($167,400).

Leave Tramore behind, drive across Great Newtown Head, and you're back in the world of deserted coves and sleepy-hollow fishing villages.

In the southeast of the county, eight miles from Waterford city, Dunmore East is a lovely fishing village and holiday retreat with plenty of thatched cottages and a busy harbor that entices many oceangoing yachts from Europe.

Anywhere around Annestown, Bonmahon, Stradbally, Clonea, or Ballinacourty makes an idyllic retreat but the location factor means you can pay as much as €350,000 ($434,000) for a four-bedroom bungalow with sea views. Yet move a short distance inland and you can still find old-style cottages in decent repair for €95,000–135,000 ($118,000–

167,500). Along with a good selection of cottages, the Eurobond agency in Cappoquin was also offering a restored three-bedroom farmhouse for €155,000 ($192,000).

Next stop along the coast is Dungarvan, the administrative center for County Waterford. It's a good base for making property forays into east Cork, the West Waterford hinterland, and around the Nire Valley and Comeragh Mountains straddling the county's northern border with Tipperary.

Habitable homes in the Nire Valley area can also be found for reasonable prices. One €150,000 ($186,000) gem I liked the look of was a four-bedroom bungalow in Lemybrien village—sitting on a quarter acre, it has gorgeous mountain views and is on a walking trail to the Mahon Falls. Near the County Tipperary border, the Nire Valley qualifies as a "secret place," perfect for anybody wanting to live off the beaten track.

I took a walking holiday in this unspoiled area in the fall of 2003, staying in Ballymacarbry village and hiking the lavender ridgetops of the Comeraghs, gentle mountains that rise to only 800 meters (2,625 feet) maximum. Steeped in legend, dark jewel-like loughs lie deep in corries in the mountains' rocky flanks and local lore whispers of fairy cattle emerging from the waters on moonlit nights. Although part of County Waterford, the Nire Valley's nearest town is Clonmel in Tipperary. Check out agents there for local properties—you'll still find old stone farmhouses to renovate for around €80,000 ($99,000).

County Tipperary

THE LAY OF THE LAND

"It's a long way to Tipperary" goes the old World War I marching song. Certainly it's far enough away to have escaped becoming part of the Limerick, Cork, or Waterford city commuter belts. Although this is Ireland's largest inland county, its charms are understated by most tourist guides and so it still has the air of a well-guarded secret.

However, house prices are by no means inexpensive. The county is becoming increasingly popular with affluent Dublin buyers looking to buy weekend homes and take up the traditional rural pursuits of hunting and fishing. Although it's still one of Ireland's cheapest counties, the average price of a home is now €178,501 ($221,300).

The Age of Wonders

Great ones for lists and catalogs, the long-bearded sages of the Middle Ages weren't content with just seven wonders of the world. Two miles east of Roscrea town is a place that used to be known as the 31st Wonder of the World: a sacred Celtic isle called Monaincha or Insula Viventium, the Island of the Living. Reputed to hold the secret of everlasting life, its only hint of past glories is a little ruined church and sadly, the site has long been dispossessed of its island status by drainage schemes.

In previous centuries only the wealthy could afford the services of a doctor and the Irish peasantry was more concerned with having a pain-free life than in traveling to remote islands in a quest for immortality. The high crosses of Ahenny and one of the crosses at Kilkieran are crowned with removable capstones, sometimes known as miter stones or bishop's hats. Tipperary lore suggests that headache sufferers sought to relieve their pain by placing these capstones upon their own pates. It seems a curious notion. There you are with a throbbing migraine and you want to balance a *boulder* on your head? Should the aspirins run out, you may be better off seeking relief from the waters of Saint Kieran's Well, beside Kilkieran churchyard. It too reputedly cures headaches.

WHERE TO LIVE

Tipperary

Walled on its southern horizon by the smudgy blue bastions of the Galtee and Comeragh mountain ranges, in the west by the Silvermine Mountains and Lough Derg, Tipperary is essentially farming country. Its central Golden Vale produces prime herds of beef and dairy cattle and local agents often find it hard to keep up with the demand for good quality pasture. As this is also excellent hunting country, any period-type property with a couple of paddocks and outbuildings for stabling generally finds plenty of eager buyers.

I know it sounds ludicrous, but by Dublin values, a Georgian residence priced below $2.5 million is seen as a steal. They are undoubtedly romantic: You can easily imagine a harpsichord tinkling away in the drawing room, a frock-coated master of the house writing his journal in the study, and ladies in frothy muslin dresses playing croquet on the lawn. At the foot of the Knockmealdown Mountains, a six-bedroom/five-bathroom Georgian home with gate lodge, stable yard, and extensive paddocks recently sold for €1.8 million ($2.23 million).

Away from the grand country house market, smaller properties throughout Tipperary are rather more affordable. Many habitable rural cottages and small bungalows fall into the $90,000 to $150,000 range. However, those sort of price levels indicate that a property will be very much off the beaten track. You'll pay rather more to gaze over Lough Derg or be within easy striking distance of the county's prettiest towns: Clonmel, Roscrea, Cahir, Cashel, and Carrick-on-Suir. Just because of its name, you may feel it's worth having a look at Tipperary town but to be honest, it's rather drab and disappointing. The only real reason to come here would be for the twice-weekly cattle mart or if a horse-race meeting is scheduled.

Vicinity of Tipperary

Cashel is a heritage town that's home to one of Ireland's most splendid historical sights. Once the seat of the kings of Munster, the Rock of Cashel rises above the Tipperary countryside like the mirage of some Celtic Acropolis, crowned with an array of ecclesiastical stonework dating to medieval times: a round tower, intricately carved high crosses, a ruined cathedral, and a castle tower house. It was from this lofty eyrie that Saint Patrick reputedly plucked a shamrock to illustrate the doctrine of the Holy Trinity.

Below the rock, most attractively old-fashioned town houses and small urban bungalows sell for €110,000–140,000 ($136,400–173,600). At this price, though, don't expect much space—only around 560–680 square feet. But if you're a minimalist looking for a low-maintenance home, a 517-square-foot terraced bungalow for €95,000 ($117,800) might just be the home for you.

For €175,000 ($217,000), newly built homes in Cashel town provide a more reasonable 1,000 square feet. In the suburban housing estates, the starting figure is €130,000 ($161,200) for homes of similar size. Within a five-mile radius of the town, plenty of modern three-bedroom country bungalows can be found for €100,000–140,000 ($124,000–173,600). Note though, that a three-bedroom bungalow may not always be as big as you may think. Bedrooms can be tiny—one that was on the market for $124,000 comprised a mere 797 square feet in total.

Cashel is the one Tipperary town to which tourists flock in any great numbers, so it may prove a good location for anyone seeking a guesthouse opportunity. Butler's was seeking offers of around €450,000 ($558,000) for a Bord Failte–approved bungalow-style guesthouse with eight ensuite bedrooms. A four-bedroom home with views of the Rock of Cashel from its garden was €245,000 ($303,800).

On the county's southeastern border, surrounded by cider apple orchards, Carrick-on-Suir (population 5,500) sees far fewer visitors than Cashel. A riverside market town, its history goes back to the Middle Ages when it was an important center for the wool trade. Within the town, three-bedroom row houses are fetching €82,000–120,000 ($101,700–148,800).

A traditional Irish cottage with all modern comforts? At the time of writing, Gleesons was selling one of 10 traditional thatched cottages. These were built in the 1970s in a small development in Holycross village, on the banks of the River Suir. This one had three bedrooms and a traditional half door—designed to let the light in and keep the chickens out. With around 750 square feet of living space, it was priced at €160,000 ($198,400).

In a development of newly built modern homes in Holycross village, a three-bedroom property with 1,292 square feet of living space was €134,000 ($166,000). Not much mystique about "the Hermitage" development, but the village itself has plenty: Its magnificent Cistercian abbey dates back eight centuries.

South Tipperary's main town for work, shopping, restaurants, and real estate agents is Clonmel: With around 20,000 inhabitants this is as close as the county gets to big-city lights. Ten miles west of Carrick-on-Suir, it's another riverbank town of atmospheric backstreets and quayside mills surrounded by good hill-walking territory.

There's still a quaintly old-fashioned air to Clonmel and it gives a good inkling of what a Georgian coaching town must have been like. Down from the turrets of the West Gate, Hearns Hotel was once the home and headquarters of Charles Bianconi, who came over from Lombardy in Italy to found Ireland's first coach service in 1815. "The Bian" was a horse-drawn two-wheeler that carried both the mail and up to six passengers who sat back-to-back facing the roadside.

Within the town, three-bedroom midterrace houses—row houses—start at €90,000 ($111,600). Nearby villages include Clogheen, on the road leading to the Knockmealdown Mountains. On its main street, a double-fronted family home (three bedrooms) with a large rear garden was €150,000 ($186,000). Like many other villages in Ireland, Clogheen now also has new developments of starter homes—this is commuter country for people who work in Clonmel. Brand-new houses with 1,540 square feet of living space are selling for €205,000 ($254,200).

If you're seeking something more traditional, Pollard's had a four-bedroom cottage in Kilsheelan village, midway between Clonmel and Carrick-on-Suir. Priced at €190,000 ($235,600), it was in pristine condition and had an acre of land, stables, hay shed, kennels, and orchard. Other renovated cottages can be found for much cheaper in this part of Tipperary, but a realistic starting level is still €100,000 ($124,000); €70,000–80,000 ($86,800–99,200) will get you something in fairly good structural condition but needing modernization.

At Glengall near Thurles, the same agents had a two-bedroom renovated cottage with an acre of landscaped garden for €110,000 ($136,400), and €156,000 ($193,400) would buy a three-bedroom cottage with a three-quarter acre garden at Killenaule. Both were in perfect condition. Another pretty three-bedroom cottage was being offered for €105,000 ($130,200) in Kilsheelan village, but this had just been snapped up. But it shows bargains are still there if you're prepared to seek them out.

North Tipperary's chief town is Nenagh. Although the town is not particularly picturesque, its real estate agents generally have a good supply of inexpensive cottages in the rural hinterland where narrow forested roads climb from Newport into the Silvermines Mountains. As their name suggests, this was once a center for silver mining though the term "mountains" is something of an exaggeration. The highest point (Keeper Hill) towers to a rather underwhelming 676 meters (2,218 feet). The range links with an intriguing-sounding plateau called the Devil's Bit and most local kids can reel off the story about how this gap in the hills came by its strange name. Long ago, the devil himself flew over Tipperary and just for the hell of it decided to bite a chunk out of the mountains. Finding that it wasn't the most palatable of snack foods, he spat it out and that's how the Rock of Cashel was formed. Or so the legend goes.

In this part of north Tipperary, cottages needing internal modernization but in good structural condition start at around €75,000 ($93,000). Some really tempting homes are available if you're willing to go up toward €125,000 ($155,000). At the time of writing, that was the price sought for a pretty, whitewashed "village street" cottage with threebedrooms and a flowery garden at Borrisokane.

Near Roscrea, one characterful home on the market was Timoney Lodge, the original stone gatehouse to Timoney House. On a half-acre site, it was totally refurbished and had 1,830 square feet of living space.

Priced at €360,000 ($446,400) through Fogarty's of Roscrea, it's a chance for someone to snap up a piece of Ireland's Georgian heritage for under $1 million.

West of Nenagh and the Silvermines Mountains is the Tipperary shore of Lough Derg, part of the famous River Shannon navigation scheme. Always busy in summertime with boating visitors, the shore is strung with little marinas and attractive lakeside villages such as Terryglass, Dromineer, Garrykennedy, Portroe, and Ballina, the latter linked to Killaloe in County Clare by an arched stone bridge. The two counties and their lakeshore villages are in friendly competition to win the tourism battle so there's no shortage of good restaurants, curio shops, traditional music pubs, and summer festivals.

House prices are similar to the Clare side of the shore: upward of €250,000 ($310,000) for luxury bungalows with four bedrooms near the lough. Refurbished Old World cottages mostly fetch €165,000–185,000 (approximately $204,000–229,000). Hamptons in Killaloe (County Clare) also handles properties on the Tipperary side of Lough Derg.

THE NORTHWEST
AND LAKELANDS

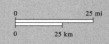

0 _____ 25 mi
0 _____ 25 km

N
W E
S

Tory Island

Malin Head

Fanad
Head

Malin

ATLANTIC OCEAN

Dunfanaghy
Inishbofin

BLOODY
FORELAND

Gola

Errigal
Mtn.

Ramelton

Buncrana

Lough
Foyle

A2

Cruit I.

Burtonport

Inch I.

Londonderry

Aran
Island

Letterkenny

Donegal

Lifford

A5

NORTHERN
IRELAND
(UK)

N56

Glen
Columbkille

Ardara

N15

A505

Omagh

Lough
Neagh

Rossan Point

Donegal

Lough
Derg

Lower Lough
Erne

A32

A5

Rossnowlagh

Donegal Bay

Ballyshannon

N15

Lough
Melvin

Grange
Cliffoney

Drumcliff

Enniskillen

Sligo Bay

Sligo

N16

Upper
Lough
Erne

Monaghan

Enniscrone

N59

Swanlinbar

N54

Monaghan

Lough
Conn

Ballina

Sligo

N4

Lough
Arrow

Lough
Allen

N87

Cavan

N26

Tubbercurry

Lough
Key

Lough
Oughter

Cavan

Lough
Cullin

Boyle

Carrick-
on-Shannon

Leitrim

Castlebar

Lough
Gara

N61

Mayo

Roscommon

Kilglass
Lough

Longford

N55

Claremorris

N60

Lough
Sheelin

Meath

Lough
Mask

N17

Roscommon

Longford

Lough
Derravaragh

Tuam

N4

Lough
Ree

N55

Lough
Owel

River Boyne

N4

Lough
Corrib

N63

Westmeath

N61

Athlone

Lough
Ennell

N6

Galway

Kildare

Galway

N6

Loughrea

Offaly

Kildare

Galway Bay

N18

Laois

N9

Clare

Lough
Derg

N62

N7

© AVALON TRAVEL PUBLISHING, INC.

The Northwest and Lakelands

ar from the well-worn tourist trails, the underrated counties of Ireland's northwest and Lakelands are an ideal choice for getting away from the usual stresses of modern life. Perhaps more so than anywhere else, it's here that bargain hunters will find some of the country's most affordable properties.

Small cottages in fairly good structural condition start at around €50,000 ($62,000), but not all will necessarily come with the trappings that most of us expect nowadays. Even in soundly structured cottages, with electricity and water already connected, you may find there's no bathroom or septic tank for getting rid of the waste. I remember inspecting such a cottage in County Sligo when I was looking for my own Irish home to buy. I asked the agent why he was showing it to me—how was I expected to manage without a lavatory?

"Do what folks have always done," he said. "Use the field." Incredible though it seems, there are still some older people living in old-fashioned hermit's cottages who see nothing odd about not having a bathroom. One has to presume that they bathe in a tin tub in front of the fire.

County Sligo

LAY OF THE LAND

A land of literature and legend, Sligo is synonymous with the poet William Butler Yeats; he spent many childhood summers here. Tagged "Yeats Country," its most distinctive landmark is Benbulben, a flat-topped table mountain famed in Irish mythology as the site where the hero Diarmuid met a sticky end on the tusks of a magic boar.

Here too is Knock-narea, traditionally held to be a hollow hill and one of the strongholds of the Sidhe (the fairies).

Many places throughout the county resonate with eerie magic: the Lake Isle of Innisfree, shimmering Lough Arrow and Lough Gill, the bluebell glades of Slish Wood, and the dolmens and stone circles of Carrowmore—a mysterious necropolis whose secrets date to Bronze Age times. Here too is Knocknarea, traditionally held to be a hollow hill and one of the strongholds of the Sidhe (the fairies). Crowned by a cairn, Knocknarea is also reputed to be the final resting place of Maeve, a tempestuous goddess-queen who waged battle against Ulster's warriors for possession of the Brown Bull of Cooley.

WHERE TO LIVE

Sligo Town

With 19,000 citizens, Sligo town is the county's only sizable settlement. On the quality-of-life scale it has all the right ingredients: a good general hospital and services, train links to Dublin, and a vibrant array of cultural activities. It also has a wonderfully unvamped center that retains much of the character of times past. Visit a time-warp pub such as Hargadon's on O'Connell Street and it feels as if you've been transported back a few centuries, especially during winter when a pot-bellied stove blazes in the main bar.

On the banks of the Garavogue River, Sligo's shopping streets are always busy, drawing in people from Leitrim, Roscommon, and south

The Fairy Folk

Sligo's folk heritage chronicles countless strange stories about apparitions of the land. In his *Fairy and Folk Tales of the Irish Peasantry,* W. B. Yeats concluded that when the pagan gods of the Celts were no longer worshipped, they diminished in the popular imagination until eventually they turned into "the good people,'" or fairies. During the 19th century, it was also reputed that fairies were fallen angels, or alternatively, the heathen dead. Barred from heaven, they weren't wicked enough to deserve a place in hell and so had to live out a shadowy existence in secret places: caves, hollow hills, burial mounds, and the ancient earthen forts known as *raths.*

Superstition warned that it was important to treat these ancestral spirits with respect. Fairies held the power to bring wealth to a farm or to give fishermen a good catch. When neglected or badly treated, they could turn spiteful. Thanks to *pishogues* (fairy spells), hens stopped laying eggs, milk turned sour, and livestock fell sick. And anyone who cut down a fairy thorn tree or built a new dwelling across a fairy path could expect to suffer an unpleasant accident. But naturally every spell had its counterspell and the four-leafed shamrock, a motif of good luck, was thought to guard against otherworldly bewitchments.

The best-known character in folklore is the leprechaun, or fairy shoemaker. Legend claims that if you catch one he'll lead you to a crock of gold. However, if you take your eyes off him for just one second, he'll disappear. A more menacing figure is the banshee *(bean sidhe),* for it's said that the sound of her eldritch wail outside a house signifies a death in the family. In some tales the banshee appears as a beautiful young woman wearing fine clothes; in others she is described as a wizened old crone draped in a shroud. Sighting the *bean nídhe,* the fairy washerwoman, is also a premonition of disaster. In heroic myths, warriors doomed to fall in battle often see her beside water. She is wailing and washing out bloodstained clothing—theirs.

Donegal whose own little towns aren't quite so well-stocked. Cinemas, restaurants, and the Hawk's Well theater give the town a year-round bustle; regular summertime events include the Arts Festival and the Yeats' Summer School, attended by scholars from all over the world.

Within Sligo town's environs, terraced row houses can be had for €100,000–125,000 ($124,000–155,000). It's a good place to find rental properties—the town's estate agents enjoy a lively market, thanks to sizable numbers of hospital staff and students from the Regional Technical College seeking accommodation. Depending on size and location, good-quality country properties can be had for €700–800 ($868–992)

© Steenie Harvey

Lough Arrow, south Sligo

a month. Apartments within town generally let for €500–700 ($620–868) monthly.

Cottages and small country houses in fairly good condition can still occasionally be picked up for as little as €60,000 ($74,500) in more remote corners of the county. And you'll also find habitable farmhouses needing modernization for €125,000 ($155,000). For this price, though, you'll have to search in the south of the county, well away from the ocean. As everywhere else, the price of homes usually depends on proximity to town or coastline. In rural backwaters, there are still quite a few traditional-style cottages in various states of repair selling for less than $100,000. However, move the exact same cottage to the coast and there's every likelihood its price will have doubled.

Vicinity of Sligo

Attractive north Sligo villages for living the country lifestyle include Carney, Cliffoney and Grange. At Drumcliffe, W. B. Yeats is buried in the Protestant churchyard—his great-grandfather was once rector here. Under the shadow of Benbulben, the gravestone bears an epitaph Yeats penned himself:

Cast a cold eye on life, on death. Horseman, pass by!

The south of the county has more of an unexplored feel. A good place in south Sligo to find fairly inexpensive bucolic bolt-holes is in the countryside around Tubbercurry, Curry, and Gurteen villages. Priced at €150,000 ($186,000) Schiller's had a renovated two-story farmhouse near Curry with a half acre of land. With Lough Gara as a backdrop, a newly built four-bedroom bungalow on .75 acre was €190,000 ($235,600).

For €60,000 ($74,500), McCarrick's had a one-bedroom cottage with bathroom, electricity, and water supply at Ballyglass, five miles from the small town of Tubbercurry. As it's on an acre plot, this seems a very good buy—there's ample room for extension.

The two main seaside villages in the north of the county are Rosses Point (site of an 18-hole links course that holds regular tournament events) and Strandhill, which is popular with surfers. At low tide you can walk across from Cummeen Strand to Coney Island and look out to sea from the Wishing Chair in which Saint Patrick reputedly sat. This, I hasten to add, is not the Coney Island in New York! Properties in these two villages are very expensive: Three-bedroom family homes start at €230,000 ($285,000) and go up from there. A five-bedroom residence with sweeping views of Sligo Bay was recently advertised at €850,000 ($1.05 million).

Farther south, Enniscrone is trimmed by a five-mile stretch of golden sands and is another stop for golfers on the western links trail. Believers in the powers of thalassotherapy come to immerse themselves in the village's curious seaweed baths, here since Edwardian times. Two-bedroom holiday homes in fairly uninspiring complexes are on the market for €125,000 ($155,000), but look to the immediate countryside and you can find small but mint-condition bungalows for the same price.

County Donegal

LAY OF THE LAND

The distance from Dublin to Donegal's heartland is barely 150 miles but it really can feel like traveling to the opposite ends of the earth. Best known for its tweeds, Donegal's name means "Fort of the Foreigner" (Dún na nGall), a reference to the 9th-century Viking invaders who established forts here. Geographically part of Ulster Province, this is the republic's northernmost county, a place of blue, windswept mountains, heathery moorlands, and small communities where the welcome is warm and generous. The

Saint Patrick's Purgatory

Do you like the idea of a three-day break on an island marooned in the middle of a remote lake for just €40 ($49.50)? Accommodation, food--and the boat ride too? Of course you do, so let's set sail with the ferryman to Station Island and a retreat wryly described by past visitors as "Ireland's holy health farm." Six miles north of Pettigo, the island with its cluster of grim buildings known as Saint Patrick's Purgatory is the location for the toughest pilgrimage in Christendom: Lough Derg.

Donegal's Lough Derg isn't to be confused with the lake of the same name in Clare. This isn't a place where you find cozy pubs, pleasure crafts, and watersports--what you get instead is a chance to quite literally renounce the world, the flesh, and the devil. The three-day course in pain and suffering is almost shockingly medieval and would undoubtedly test the ascetic resolve of a Trappist monk. When you arrive on the island, the first thing that happens is that you are deprived of your footwear--socks and shoes aren't given back until you leave the island. Your bare and bloody

Irish language remains in daily use along its western fringe, particularly around Gweedore (Gaoth Dobhair) and it's still fairly common to hear hand-weavers' looms clattering away in many a little cottage.

Ramblers soon discover that Donegal is a walkers' paradise with more than 400 miles of jigsaw-puzzle coastline. Toy-town fishing ports give way to long pristine beaches punctuated by cliffs, caves, and rocky promontories that absolutely teem with birdlife. Scenic splendors include the Bloody Foreland, Horn Head, and the giddy heights of Slieve League, whose sea cliffs (1,972 feet) are the highest in Europe. At the center of the county is quartz-tipped Mount Errigal and Glenveagh National Park—25,000 acres of blanket bogs and forested mountains with roaming herds of red deer.

Ramblers soon discover that Donegal is a walkers' paradise with more than 400 miles of jigsaw-puzzle coastline.

One factor that has helped keep the cap on the property market is Donegal's remoteness. Trains don't come this far north and most local bus services can only be described as infrequent. But while the county's sense of separateness has an undoubted charm, prospective new residents ought to weigh all the pros and cons of buying a property here, particularly if planning to live in Ireland year-round. Yes, summers can be glorious but the gray gloom of wintertime is another proposition entirely. You're in for a dose of Ulster weather—mist feet spend the next three days stumbling over the jagged remains of beehive cells where monks of the early Celtic church lived out their days in lonely isolation.

Chanting long patterns of prayer, pilgrims also take part in a vigil, which effectively means being deprived of sleep for 36 hours. Nor can they take any comfort in the pleasures of the table-- there's only one meal a day served at Saint Patrick's Purgatory and it consists of dry toast and black tea. First chronicled back in the 1100s, the Lough Derg pilgrimage used to be even tougher than it is today-- pilgrims once spent the vigil inside a cave instead of the basilica.

No booking is necessary for these pilgrimages, which take place between June 1 and August 15. (The last one of the year starts on August 13.) For less hardy pilgrims, one-day retreats costing €25 ($31) also take place at certain times of year and do need to be booked. For more information contact The Prior, Saint Patrick's Purgatory, Lough Derg, Pettigo, County Donegal; tel. 071/986-1518; info@loughderg.org.

rolls in, rain drizzles down, and you may come to feel that your little home feels rather like a prison. Donegal isn't the ideal location for anyone suffering from SAD (seasonal affective disorder).

WHERE TO LIVE

Donegal

Donegal is very popular with Dutch and German buyers who seem to like the idea of living in a place where sheep outnumber people. The best places to begin a house-hunt are in the county's main towns: Letterkenny, Buncrana, Moville Ballyshannon, Donegal town, and the seaside resort of Bundoran. All have a good choice of real estate agents with properties spread over the county.

Donegal covers a huge area (this is the second-largest county after Cork) and it can take hours to get from the commercial fishing port of Killybegs to the county's northernmost tip, Malin Head. Its footloose flocks of sheep, its Irish-language signposts, and its extremely narrow roads laced with scary hairpin bends make for extremely slow driving times, so don't go thinking that you'll be able to inspect any more than a handful of homes in a day or two.

The map also shows that Donegal shares a border with Northern Ireland. How close you are to what is euphemistically termed as "the other tradition" is evidenced by the 12th of July celebrations in Rossnowlagh, a seaside village just north of Ballyshannon town. Rossnowlagh is home to the republic's only Orange Order Parade, when Protestant men wearing bowler hats and orange sashes march through the village to pay tribute to King Billy—William of Orange, who defeated the Catholic King James II at the Battle of the Boyne in 1690. The village boasts wonderful beaches—just 250 yards from the strand, three-bedroom beach cottages (1,130 square feet) in a new development were priced at €198,000 ($245,500).

But don't start thinking all Donegal homes are so expensive. You can still find enticing bargains. I was amazed to see an asking price of just €65,000 ($80,600) for a three-bedroom cottage (1,368 square feet) with new roof and all services in place. Being sold through Sligo agents Schillers, this traditional stone-built cottage—70 years old but in good condition—was on Tory Island, served by a modern ferry from the mainland. Views of the sea and the Donegal Mountains... an island with rich folklore and music... I'd say this represented the best bargain in Ireland at the time.

Of course, not everybody wants to live on an island, which probably explains its good value. Just about all of Donegal's western coast is holiday-home territory, so be aware that you'll be in competition for prize properties with city buyers from Dublin, Belfast, and many other places too. The good news is that most second-home buyers seek modern properties in sight of the sea. They tend to ignore the habitable little cottages in the folds of the hills that you can still unearth for less than $120,000.

Vicinity of Donegal

Just four miles from Donegal town, a refurbished farmhouse on an acre of land was €160,000 ($198,500). It dates to the early 1900s and has two bedrooms, lounge, kitchen, bathroom, utility room, and toilet. Five miles from Donegal town, on the shores of Donegal Bay, three-bedroom village houses in Mountcharles village were selling for €75,000–80,000 ($93,000–99,000).

Also in south Donegal, Ballyshannon is a lively town of steep characterful streets that hosts a big folk festival during the August Bank Holiday. Three-bedroom row houses here can be found for €85,000 ($105,500). Nearby Bundoran is one of Ireland's most popular summer resorts. Prices reflect this: One-bedroom apartments (400 square feet) were fetching €135,000 ($167,500).

Yet for only a little more money—€140,000 ($173,600)—Killybegs agents Kees had a two-bedroom thatched cottage in first-class condition near Dunkineely village. In previous years, it has been rented out to vacationers.

Once you hit the house-hunting trail, one western Donegal village where you might want to look for properties coming up is Glencolumbcille, an Irish-speaking community of whitewashed cottages on the sheltered side of the Slieve League peninsula.

Credited with converting Scotland to Christianity, Saint Columbcille (also known as Saint Columba) lived here during the 6th century and the hilly neighborhood is studded with holy sites and prehistoric curiosities. On the saint's Pattern (Patron) Day, June 9th, villagers take part in an evening pilgrimage around the sacred places. Summers can be quite lively with tourists coming to check out the village's traditional music pubs and wandering around the open-air folk museum for a glimpse into the rural past. Refurbished cottages around here and Glenties village can be had for €124,000 ($154,000); a four-bedroom house with adjoining grocery store business was €300,000 ($372,000).

Following the coastal road northwestward, you'll come to the Bloody Foreland—it takes its name from the setting sun that paints the peninsula a fiery crimson. This is a wonderful drive, full of twists and turns and glimpses of the islands of Inishbofin, Inishdooey, Arranmore, and Tory. A little farther on, at Sheephaven Bay, Dunfanaghy village is one of the most captivating stops on the magical seven-mile-long Atlantic Drive that links Rosguill Peninsula to the giddy heights of Horn Head. To help attract visitors to this remote corner, local people have transformed Dunfanaghy's former workhouse into a heritage center that chronicles the hardships of the famine years of 1845–1847.

Those who enjoy outdoor pleasures will find an 18-hole links course here along with wonderful walks around Killahoey Beach, Ards Forest Park, and out to crumbling Doe Castle, built in the 16th century by Scottish mercenaries. It's a much sought-after location and compact three-bedroom holiday cottages sell for around €150,000 ($186,000).

Across the bay, Downings is another engaging little hamlet where fishing boats land catches of salmon, lobster, and crab. Small bungalows requiring modernization start at €129,000 ($160,000), dormer bungalows with three and four bedrooms are mostly priced €230,000–250,000 ($285,000–310,000). "Dormer" is a word you'll come across fairly often in relation to cottages and houses. If you're puzzled by the term, what it generally refers to is an original single-story dwelling that now has a loft conversion, whereby extra rooms have been built into the roof space. A four-bedroom dormer home can often have 2,000 square feet of living space.

The next spit of land is the Fanad Peninsula, separated from the Inishowen Peninsula by Lough Swilly. The lough has many myths associated with it: One is that its name comes from Suileach, a 400-eyed water monster that was slain by the local hero, Saint Columbcille. To cross from one peninsula to the other first entails a southerly journey back through Ramelton (sometimes spelt Rathmelton) to Letterkenny. More a village than a town, Ramelton dates to the 17th century and was the setting for *The Hanging Gale,* a major 1995 TV drama that commemorated the onset of the Great Famine. Town houses here can still be had for €100,000 ($124,000). In the countryside around Greencastle, you can find good-condition one-bedroom cottages for €76,000 ($94,200).

The Inishowen Peninsula (Inis Eoghain—Owen's Island) takes its name from Owen, son of Niall of the Nine Hostages, who is credited in some folktales with capturing Saint Patrick and taking him from Wales to Ireland. Once part of the great northern kingdom of the Ui Neill clan, it's one of the wildest and most beautiful spots in the whole country, with evocative prehistoric sites such as the circular stone fort at Grianan Aileach. For properties in this area, look to agents in Moville and Carndonagh.

At Ireland's most northerly point, Malin Head, a traditional white-washed cottage was on sale through McCauley's for €95,000 ($118,000). However, it was small—it had only 600 square feet of living space. Small farmhouses in good condition occasionally surface for around €130,000 ($161,000), while two-bedroom bungalows of 1,200 square feet are fetching €145,000 ($180,000). Although you don't always get a sea view, most areas are scenic. On the outskirts of the town of Moville, a fully restored farmhouse overlooking Lough Foyle was €195,000 ($242,000).

Another of my favorite villages is Ardara, a stone's throw from the wild Atlantic shores of southwest Donegal. If you've a yen for huge deserted beaches and mysterious sea caves right on the doorstep, then this is one of the most perfect locations in the whole of the northwest. Ardara itself is protected from the sea breezes by steep, heather-clad hills, its cluster of pink, white, and teal-blue dwellings nestling in their valley like some secret forgotten settlement. Long renowned as a center for tweeds and knitwear, it's a place where spinning wheels aren't regarded as museum-piece objects.

Each June the village hosts an old-fashioned weaver's fair with displays of spinning, carding, and loom-weaving. The hub of village social life is Nancy's, a historic inn whose labyrinthine passageways lead to tiny rooms where traditional musicians gather around open fires. Compact three-bedroom bungalows with gardens on the Killybegs road are priced €135,000–140,000 ($167,000–174,000).

The Lakelands: Counties Roscommon, Leitrim, and Cavan

LAY OF THE LAND

Sparsely populated and with very little in the way of tourist "sights," the low-key Lakelands are worth considering if you yearn for an Ireland where you can get even further away from it all. Apart from anglers and boating enthusiasts, these counties see few foreign visitors, probably because the scenery is serene rather than spectacular. Along with dozens of little loughs, the border county of Cavan has an undulating landscape of drumlin hills, shaped for the entire world like upturned eggboxes. Leitrim is another border county of forested glens and rushy wetlands where smart white cruisers lazily drift along the Shannon River and its tributaries into Lough Ree and the more pastoral landscape of Roscommon. Lough Ree is a place where it may pay to carry a camera—old folktales whisper of the Lough Ree Monster, a humpbacked creature that seems to be a cousin of the equally shy and elusive monster in Scotland's Loch Ness.

This really is small-town Ireland, steeped in old-fashioned ways and provincial pastimes. Most "towns" number around 2,000 residents, so you soon get to know local names and faces. Go into a remote country pub and conversations will be revolving slowly around the weather, local politics, and the price that sheep are fetching at Tulsk and Drumshanbo markets. You often see locals playing the 25-card game, an unfathomable combination of whist and brag, in which winners compete for "fierce prizes" that sometimes take the form of livestock. Don't get involved unless you want to go home with a heifer!

Individuals who buy properties here tend to have renounced the consumer-driven world and exchanged the rat race for drowsy tranquillity and a very simple lifestyle. Unless you are perfectly happy with a dearth of good restaurants, theaters, and fashion stores, it may be too laid-back for most American tastes. However, this is a part of the country where many properties have remained at fairly affordable levels. In 1988, I bought a little mint-condition cottage (two bedrooms, kitchen, sitting room, and bathroom) on an acre of land overlooking Lough Key in County Roscommon for just $13,000. Although you will have to pay more than that for a similar cottage in this area nowadays, it's still fairly good value compared to other parts of Ireland.

Parts of the Lakelands region are still likely areas to track down rural cottages for €30,000 ($37,000). But don't get excited—nowadays you're likely to find one only in the middle of nowhere—and it will undoubtedly require a lifetime's work to refurbish it to anything resembling modern requirements. At the time of writing, you could have bought a ramshackle cottage for this price at Ballinameen in the unscenic half of County Roscommon. But (and it's a big but) you only get what you pay for. And that price is unlikely to buy even a scrap of basic home comfort.

What exactly do you get for $37,000? Alas, not a lot—probably a corrugated iron roof covering a poky sitting room, a kitchen with an old-fashioned cooking range, and one bedroom. Perhaps best described as "something to suit a desperate man," cottages such as these were built in the days when farm laborers weren't concerned with bathroom facilities and were happy to use an outhouse toilet or the fields.

However, most Lakelands areas can be good bargain-hunting territory if you're looking for a house you can call home. For example, the Arigna Hills in north County Roscommon—here €79,000 ($98,000) could buys a traditional-style cottage of 650 square feet on a 1.8-acre site. In good structural condition—though needing some modernization—the cottage had views of the Arigna Valley and was near the Miner's Way walking trail down into Keadue village.

Every August Keadue hosts a harp festival in honor of Turlough O'Carolan, a blind 18th-century harpist who was the last of the great Irish bards. His grave lies a mile from Keadue, at Kilronan, where pilgrims still visit Saint Lazair's holy well. The sacred spring reputedly holds the cure for backache and you can walk through shadowy woods beside Lough Meelagh, where an ancient court cairn evokes the mysteries of the Celtic past.

WHERE TO LIVE

Roscommon
Roscommon town is the county town of Roscommon, but to be honest it doesn't have the best scenery to boast of in these parts. That said, it

Lady Betty

Roscommon town's Old Gaol housed plenty of accursed characters in its heyday, the most infamous being Elizabeth Sugrue. Widely known as Lady Betty, she practiced an unusual profession for her time: that of a hangwoman. One deliciously creepy rumor says that if you stand outside the gaol walls when the moon is full, it's possible to hear the futile cries of former inmates who had an appointment with the Lady Betty.

Betty gained the position in 1780 and you could say it was through being in the right place at the right time. Convicted of the murder of her own son at Roscommon Sessions, she had been sentenced to death along with 25 other assort-

ed ruffians. The prisoners thought they had won a reprieve when the hangman didn't turn up at the appointed hour, but they hadn't bargained on Betty. Hoping to save her own neck, she volunteered to dispatch her fellow sinners.

The ploy worked. On condition that she continued to ply the hangman's duties without reward, black-hearted Betty got her own death sentence withdrawn. A zealous soul, she devised a more effective gallows system and took over the task of public floggings. If tales are to be believed, she also indulged in torture, drank whiskey from a skull, and became a dab hand at drawing charcoal portraits of her victims.

is on the railway line between Dublin's Heuston Station and Galway. And its real estate agencies have properties all over the county.

Laced with bluebell woods and studded with islands, the Lough Key area of County Roscommon is increasingly popular with Dubliners seeking holiday hideaways, so prices here aren't the cheapest in the Lakelands. However, it is fairly accessible—even if you're without transport it's easy enough to reach this part of the world. Trains run south to Dublin's Connolly Station and north to Sligo from the nearby town of Boyle. Here you'll find a reasonable selection of stores for day-to-day shopping and its own summer arts festival.

At the time of writing, Boyle agents Egans was marketing a four-room rural bungalow/cottage near the County Roscommon village of Croghan, about 12 miles from my own home. Priced at €80,000 ($99,000), the house looked very similar to the one I bought. It was lived in until recent years, so it didn't need major repairs—just modernization and decoration. Cottages to modernize in this area start at €65,000 ($80,500).

The star buy through Castlerea agents Cleary's was a two-bedroom restored and modernized thatched cottage near Ballinagare. On one acre, the cottage had a stream flowing beside it. Thatched homes are quite rare finds in County Roscommon, so don't be surprised if it has sold by the time you read this. The vendors were seeking in excess of €100,000 ($124,000). The same agents had good-condition three-bedroom bungalows in the village of Frenchpark for €70,000 and €80,000 ($87,000 and $99,000).

Close to the River Shannon, with an abundance of fishing lakes and country walks nearby, a traditional three-bedroom country cottage with outbuildings on a one-acre site was €125,000 ($155,000). Beside the road, in an attractive sylvan setting, the cottage was within a few minutes drive of Carrick-on-Shannon.

Leitrim

Carrick-on-Shannon is the Lakelands region's main pocket of affluence. The county town of Leitrim's marina is one of the biggest on the Shannon and provides a base for cruiser-hire companies. The area has become even more popular with the recent opening of the Ballyconnell Canal, which links the Shannon with the River Erne in County Fermanagh. Unlike a decade ago, holidaymakers can now continue their boating odyssey upriver through Leitrim's countryside into Northern Ireland. Naturally enough, many break their journey to stock up on supplies and discover Carrick's waterfront pubs, so the town is always full of good-natured bustle.

French and German visitors adore boating holidays and quite a few return to buy homes in the area. Riverside properties always find eager buyers from both home and abroad so vendors take full advantage: The premium can be as high as 25 percent for a Shannonside residence. Another factor that has pushed up house values around Carrick has been the opening of a wood-pulp plant that employs around 500 people downriver at Drumsna.

New one-bedroom apartments of around 580 square feet in Carrick can now fetch as much as €150,000 ($186,000). If you're seeking to rent, expect to pay around €500 ($620) per month. Despite prices ranging €205,000–390,000 ($254,000–484,000), a new development of three- and four-bedroom houses in a "marina village" setting on the banks of the Shannon were all snapped as soon as they were released.

But hunt around and you can find better value. Just over the border in County Roscommon—but still within a few minutes' drive of Carrick-on-Shannon town—Farrell's had a 1930s-built home of 1,000 square feet for €135,000 ($167,500). The same price would buy an immaculate 700-

© Steenie Harvey

Hoylwell at Tobernalt, county Sligo

square-foot home built in 1914 on an acre plot in the village of Croghan. However, country cottages in good condition around Carrick's satellite villages tend to fetch more than in remoter corners of the Lakelands—for example, a two-bedroom Old World cottage of 600 square feet for €115,000 ($143,000). Overlooking Annaghearly Lough, six miles from town, it was neat and pretty with whitewashed walls and turquoise trim.

A little north of here, at Mohill, you could buy a sound little cottage to modernize for €85,000 ($105,500). It's within walking distance of the town. There are some grand walks in this area, and I've seen pine martens, foxes, and badgers in the woods bordering the road to Lough Rynn. Four miles from Mohill, the Lough Rynn estate's most notorious owner was William Clements, the third earl of Leitrim, who treated his 19th-century tenant farmers as little better than slaves and allegedly exercised the *droit de seigneur* on local brides-to-be.

The Lough Rynn estate is getting a makeover with a Nick Faldo–designed golf course, marina, leisure center, spa, restaurants, conference facilities, children's amenities, and Victorian gardens restored to their former glory. The earl's house is being converted into a top-quality hotel, and there's also a development of 69 new three-bedroom houses. Prices started at €225,000 ($279,000).

Less expensive properties available through Mohill agents Lloyds included a two-bedroom cottage on the Lough Rynn road for €75,000 ($93,000). A traditional-style country house (three bedrooms and in good condition), a short drive from the village of Kiltyclogher, was €165,000 ($204,600). A two-bedroom bungalow with 1.5 acres of gardens in the Shannonside village of Rooskey was €135,000 ($167,500).

County Cavan

County Cavan can be a good hunting ground too. On the outskirts of Belturbet, a market town on the River Erne, neat two-bedroom town houses start at €115,000 ($142,600). Near the border village of Swanlinbar, agents O'Reilly's also had a pretty two-bedroom cottage for €100,000 ($124,000).

And in the town of Virginia, €150,000 ($186,000) would buy you a two-bedroom duplex apartment in a converted stone mill. The apartment faces onto a courtyard and has a rear garden fronting onto the Blackwater River with scenic views of Virginia's town bridge. The town has many attractive stone town houses, a number of which have been converted into apartments. A 900-square-foot apartment with three bedrooms on the Ballyjamesduff road was also €150,000 ($186,000).

© Steenie Harvey

Daily Life

© Steenie Harvey

Making the Move

When moving to an English-speaking country such as Ireland, it's easy to assume the words "culture shock" don't apply. OK, Irish people use a few weird words and speak with peculiar accents but day-to-day living will be pretty much the same as back home, won't it? After all, you're simply exchanging a frenetic big-city existence for that idyllic life you've been dreaming about for years. You can picture it already—an old-fashioned farmstead on a dozen emerald acres, walking your dogs along the beach, maybe even getting a little part-time job in the local bookstore.

Hmm. Some clouds are looming over the horizon if that's your plan. Do you realize that your pets will be quarantined? Or that you cannot buy more than five acres of land without seeking special permission? And there'll be no job in the bookstore or anywhere else for that matter—not unless you have special skills, buy your own business, or have claims to Irish or any other EU citizenship.

Culture Shock

If you've been used to a city lifestyle, the reality of rural Ireland may provide you rather more than you bargained for. The countryside isn't a picture book, it's a working environment. Cows smell, pigs smell, and you'll undoubtedly smell a bit niffy too if your next-door neighbor is a farmer who regularly sprays slurry (a fertile mix of animal dung and urine) on his fields. The joys of rural life don't only include cockerels crowing away at the unearthly hour of 5 A.M., but the summertime sounds of agricultural machinery grinding away at 2 A.M., 3 A.M., and 4 A.M. too. Because of the fickle weather, farmers often work through the entire night to get the hay in. You'll just have to put up with a few nights of disturbed sleep.

Countryside properties don't come with quite the same services as in towns or cities. Unless you buy a village house, it's most unlikely that there will be any streetlamps on the laneway and everywhere may seem rather spooky on moonless nights. Of course, the great benefit of living in a place with no light pollution means you'll be able to step outside and look at the stars--when was the last time you did that? Another surprise to city dwellers is the complete absence of sidewalks: A country stroll usually entails leaping into the hedgerow every time a car whizzes past.

No streetlamps, no sidewalks, and no sewage-treatment plants either. Rural Ireland hasn't got a proper sewage system and even if you've bought a trophy property costing more than $1 million, you'll still be in the same position as a buyer with a $50,000 cottage--you'll need a septic tank in which to store all that stuff most people don't talk about in polite society. Connected to the house by a waste pipe, septic tanks are buried in the ground: You'll know if yours needs emptying when the contents start to seep into the garden or back along the outflow pipe. Though it

Although the subject of employment is dealt with in the employment chapter, it's worth pointing out here that all non-EU nationals need work permits to take up paid employment within Ireland. This isn't something you can obtain yourself—applications must be made by *employers* before a prospective employee even arrives in Ireland. However, if you have a historic entitlement to Irish or any other EU citizenship, then the door to employment is wide open.

sounds a bit of a nightmare, it isn't something to constantly fret over. In general, a septic tank needs emptying only once every 10 years.

Thought chimney sweeps belonged only in the pages of Dickens? Think again. If you have open fires, chimneys need to be swept free of soot twice a year. For around €60 ($75) you can buy rods and brushes and do the task yourself. Alternatively, contact a chimney-cleaning service or an old-fashioned local sweep, who will charge around €120 ($149) for the average-sized cottage or bungalow.

Dressing for the Occasion

Ireland is a jeans-and-sweaters type of country: Casual gear does for almost all occasions. Even in cities such as Dublin and Cork, there are few fashion victims and most people dress very informally. Of course, different standards apply to management and professional people so you should certainly wear something a bit more formal if you intend conducting any business here. People generally make an effort to dress up for weddings, special social functions, theater trips, and dinner at a classy restaurant. Otherwise the rule is "come as you are."

Leaving aside Dublin's chattering classes, Ireland doesn't really have a dinner-party culture (in rural areas dinner is the meal you eat at midday) and most social contact with neighbors is down at the pub. Village pubs operate as community centers and you'll often find they're the venue for quiz nights, charades, and card games as well as live music. You don't have to drink alcohol if you don't want to—it's quite common to see people with soft drinks, tea, or coffee. In the west of Ireland especially, many pub-goers give up alcohol completely for the 40 days of Lent. Well, almost completely--the church allows a special dispensation to break the Lenten fast on March 17, Saint Patrick's Day.

Red Tape

VISAS AND IMMIGRATION

Citizens of the United States will not need a visa to enter Ireland. However, unless you're claiming dual Irish nationality, all non-EU citizens planning to stay in Ireland for longer than three months need to register with the authorities. You must obtain what is known as "Permission to Remain" from the minister of justice. This can be done by calling on your local An Garda Siochána (police) office in the district where you're living. Dublin is a bit different—here all formalities are handled by the Immigration and Registration Bureau, Garda Headquarters, Harcourt Street, Dublin 2.

"Permission to Remain" is affixed by way of a stamp in your passport. You will also be issued a residency document. There is no fee for registering. You need to supply the following documentation with your application for Permission to Remain:
• A valid passport
• Evidence (bank statements) that you have sufficient funds with which to support yourself and any dependents
• Any information requested in connection with the purpose of your being in the state

STUDENTS
In addition to the above documentation, individuals entering Ireland to study or to sit an examination must present to the immigration officer at the port of arrival a letter of registration from the relevant educational institution. It should verify the duration/nature of the course or examination and proof that all the fees have been paid. Prospective students must also provide evidence of full medical insurance to cover their stay in Ireland.

Traditional farmhouse

© Steenie Harvey

STAYING

You will normally be given permission to remain for the duration of your stated purpose in the state up to a maximum of 12 months for any single period. This permission is renewable. People who have been issued work authorization/student permits will be granted residency for the duration of the work or study term.

The onus is on you to ensure that your Permission to Remain is not allowed to lapse. Once you have been legally resident in Ireland for five years, you may then apply to obtain a stamp giving permission to remain in the state for a further five years. During this period, there is no requirement to keep registering on an annual basis.

People who have been legally resident in Ireland for 10 years can then apply for a stamp giving them "residence without condition." However, this entitles a person only to residency without going through all the red tape. All the other "alien" requirements such as work permits and business permission remain.

Citizenship

Irish citizenship is a valuable thing to have as it brings with it a whole range of economic and social benefits, including the right to live and work in any part of the European Union. And maybe one day your grandson may even play for the Irish soccer team—most of our heroes who wear the green jersey are in the team through the "Irish granny" rule. More prosaically, as an Irish citizen you'll have the right to vote (and be a candidate for elective office) in elections for both the European Parliament and at national level.

Irish citizenship is a valuable thing to have as it brings with it a whole range of economic and social benefits, including the right to live and work in any part of the European Union.

There are four ways to claim Irish citizenship:
• Citizenship through birth in Ireland
• Citizenship through descent
• Declaration of postnuptial citizenship
• Naturalization

CITIZENSHIP THROUGH BIRTH

First, the easiest way to become a citizen of Ireland is to be born here, with at least one parent being an Irish citizen or entitled to Irish citizenship.

Genealogy

What were your great-grandparents' names and where did they come from? Quite possibly the Emerald Isle for it's estimated that 40 million Americans are of Irish descent. If you too have Irish forebears somewhere in your background, why not take the opportunity to find out something about their lives and communities? Just imagine the thrill of glimpsing something of the world they knew--their town or village, the fields the family tilled, maybe even the local school or holy well that would have been visited on the patron saint's day. You may even find distant cousins you never knew existed.

Where do you begin if your Irish background is all a bit hazy? Well, you'll certainly need more information than just a family surname so the more information you can garner about maiden names and the names of siblings, the better. There are more than 70,000 listed townlands throughout Ireland and it's vital to be able to pinpoint the county where your ancestor(s) was born. If you're not sure, the best place to begin your research is in the United States. The National Archives (700 Pennsylvania Avenue, Washing-ton, DC 20408; tel. 202/501-5400) possess-

However, having a child born here no longer confers automatic rights of residency to the foreign-born parents. In recent years, Ireland was flooded by economic refugees—and many women took advantage of the country's liberal laws by giving birth as quickly as possible. As a result of a Supreme Court decision, the immigration division no longer accepts applications for residency from individuals based purely on their parentage of an Irish-born child.

CITIZENSHIP THROUGH DESCENT

If either parent was born in Ireland, you're automatically deemed Irish by right of birth (the *jus sanguinis* principle). There is no need to register a claim or even to take up residency to acquire citizenship. To obtain an Irish passport, all you have to do is to submit the necessary documentation to the nearest Irish embassy or consulate. Along with passport photos, you'll be asked to produce your own birth certificate, your parents' birth certificates, and their marriage certificate.

Again, you don't have to be resident in Ireland to claim citizenship through a grandparent. However, the procedure is a little different and needs to be undertaken by what is known as "foreign birth registration." Applications are processed through the local Irish embassy or consulate, or (once you are resident in Ireland), through the Department of Foreign Affairs.

es an extensive collection of immigration records and passenger lists. Those from 1883 onward generally include the last place of residence in Ireland. Another source is the Washington National Records Office (4205 Sutland Road, Washington, DC 20409; tel. 301/457-7010). which holds naturalization records. These may contain the date and place of birth, occupation, and previous place of residence for each immigrant.

Armed with that sort of information, you will be able to search through Ireland's census returns, parish records, national school records, and many other resources, which will give clues about other family members. You can even search transportation records to discover if any unfortunate relative was shipped away on a convict hull to Australia. Each Irish county has its own computerized genealogic database, though some are more comprehensive than others. Those interested in undertaking research work but who aren't too sure where to start should first contact the Genealogical Office at Kildare Street, Dublin 2; tel.: 01/661-8811, which runs a general consultancy service.

A great deal of paperwork will need to be produced, both the original certificates and two copies of each document. You'll need your own birth certificate, the birth certificate of the parent you are claiming Irish ancestry through, and also that of your Irish-born grandparent. If his or her birth certificate is unobtainable, a baptismal certificate may be acceptable, though this is likely to slow down the process somewhat. You'll also need to produce marriage certificates for yourself (if applicable), parents, and grandparents. Death certificates are also required if a grandparent or the relevant parent is deceased.

Along with two passport-sized photos, you must also submit a photocopy of a current passport (if you have one), and photocopies of three more forms of identity such as a driver's license, social security number ID card, pay slips, or bank statements. You may have heard that Irish citizenship can be claimed through a great-grandparent. This was so until 1984. Unfortunately, the legislation was altered and it's no longer possible for great-grandchildren to benefit from the *jus sanguinis* principle.

CITIZENSHIP THROUGH MARRIAGE

Marriage is another route to Irish citizenship. It used to be that if you had been married to an Irish citizen for three years, you could also claim citizenship. However, the law has been changed. Now any non-national

© Steenie Harvey

across Toormore Bay to Mount Gabriel, from Spanish Point, West Cork

who married an Irish citizen on or after November 30, 2002, can apply for citizenship only through the naturalization process.

CITIZENSHIP THROUGH NATURALIZATION

Ireland's Department of Justice handles applications for naturalization and citizenship is granted at the minister's "absolute discretion." It's a slow process and generally takes between 18 and 24 months before any decision is reached. To be considered for Irish citizenship, the following criteria have to be satisfied: The applicant is resident in the state and is 18 years of age or older. During the preceding nine years, the applicant must have lived legally in the state for five of those years. The last of those five qualifying years must have been one of continuous residence, though an absence for vacations or business won't generally be regarded as a break in residence.

Applicants must satisfy the minister of their good character and also of their intention to live in Ireland after naturalization. The following documentation has to be submitted with an application, both the originals and a photocopy of each:

- A passport
- Garda Síochána certificate of registration (green residency permit book)
- Birth certificate with a certified translation if not in English
- If applicable, a marriage certificate—again with certified translation if necessary
- Statement from the revenue commissioners that all due taxes have been paid
- Depending on circumstances, details of personal tax, company tax, PRSI contributions, and VAT payments
- Documentary proofs of financial status such as bank or building society statements
- If applicable, pay slips or statement of earnings from an employer

Should the minister grant your application, you'll be required to stand in open court before a district court judge and make a declaration of fidelity to the nation and loyalty to the state.

For more information contact the Department of Justice, Immigration and Citizenship Division.

Holding Dual Nationality

Unlike in some European countries, taking up Irish citizenship doesn't require renouncing another citizenship. Ireland's Department of Foreign Affairs has no objection to anyone's holding dual citizenship, but it does advise individuals to clarify the position with home governments first.

Looking at it from the reverse angle, the U.S. government will not deem you to have committed an expatriating act simply by becoming a dual national. To lose your legal status as a U.S. national, you would need to have committed treason or have formally renounced your citizenship.

One specification is that you are required to use your U.S. passport when leaving or entering the United States. However, even if you decide to use your Irish passport when traveling elsewhere, you can still call on the assistance of U.S. embassies and consulates. Another point to note is that the U.S. government still expects its overseas citizens to file tax returns, even if no tax is payable. Even so, one congressional report estimated that around 61 percent of Americans living abroad are flouting this rule. In an attempt to keep track of its wayward citizens, every U.S. national applying for a passport is supposed to file an IRS information report listing foreign residences and other details that the taxman may find interesting.

RIGHTS AND OBLIGATIONS OF CITIZENSHIP

The main obligation for Irish citizens resident in the state is the requirement to undertake jury service if called upon to do so. As a citizen you'll have full voting rights which, for others, depends on status.

At present, only Irish citizens can vote in presidential elections or a referendum. The only resident foreigners entitled to vote in elections to the Dáil (the Irish Parliament) are U.K. citizens—that's because Irish citizens living in the United Kingdom also have the right to vote there. Voting in elections to the European Parliament is open to any resident holding citizenship of an EU member state.

However, you don't need to hold Irish or any other kind of EU nationality to vote in local elections—you simply need to be resident here and have your name on the electoral roll. Those who are entitled to vote only in local elections have the letter "L" after their names on the register.

A new register of electors is compiled each year. To get on the register, either contact your local council offices or fill in a form at the post office. The process of compiling the register starts in September/October and comes into effect the following February. To make sure you're on the electoral roll, you can check the draft register that is published on November 1. It's available for inspection in post offices, libraries, *Garda* stations, and local authority offices.

Moving with Children

It is undoubtedly a very good idea to include your children in any plans you have for relocating to Ireland. Take them with you on your fact-finding or house-hunting trips. When you do relocate, take the time to listen to what they have to say about their new school and friends. Keep track of their progress in their new school. If your children are very young it might help ease their tensions if you accompany them to school for the first few days.

Bringing your children to Ireland isn't likely to produce any major problems. Crimes against children are rare. Depending on the age group, kids in Ireland face the same sort of problems at school as they would in the United States. Although there is little danger of a child turning up at school with a gun, you do get instances of bullying and of high school kids being targeted by drug dealers. (General education issues are discussed in the *Language and Education* chapter.)

If you have very young children and intend to work here, then childcare will be important. Unfortunately, at the moment, crèche facilities in Ireland can only be described as abysmal and expensive. In Dublin, if you can find one with spaces, a crèche is likely to be charging €100–150 ($124–186) a week.

Other than basketball, your kids will have to get used to a new set of sports. Gaelic games are popular, as is soccer, but there is little in the way of tuition in sports such as tennis. You would need to arrange that privately. Teenage culture will not be much different either. Most of the U.S. rap stars are popular here as well. One potential problem you will have to keep an eye on, though, is "teenage drinking." Ireland does not have the same tough laws as some U.S. states. Although a voluntary "prove your age" card system has been widely adopted by publicans, teenage drinking remains a problem.

It is undoubtedly a very good idea to include your children in any plans you have for relocating to Ireland.

Moving with Pets

Ireland has strict rules and regulations on the importation of pets. If you intend to bring a dog or pet from any countries other than the UK, the Channel Islands, and the Isle of Man, you must have an import license. In order to obtain one, the animal must:

• be put in approved quarantine in Ireland for at least six months
• be put in approved quarantine for one month, then in approved private arrangements for a further five months. Depending on the facility you can provide for the animal, the "private arrangements" could be a quarantine facility in your own back garden.

However, the "private option" is feasible only if the animal has been vaccinated against rabies and has a current certificate. For an animal to be "quarantined" at your own residence, you'll need to obtain prior approval from the Veterinary Inspectorate of the Department of Agriculture and Food before bringing the pet to Ireland. The pet (and the premises) will be subject to further inspection by private veterinary surgeons during the five-month period. You should apply for approval of private quarantine premises at least three months before bringing the animal to Ireland.

At present there is only one public quarantine facility: Lissenhall Quarantine Kennels and Catteries, Lissenhall, Swords, County Dublin.

What to Take

Briefly, in the words of one American friend who moved here some years ago: "as little as possible."

Apart from clothing and some personal items, everything else you will need can be sourced in Ireland. The trauma and cost involved in shipping all of your household belongings across the Atlantic is probably not justified. However, if you do want to move everything, there are some things to bear in mind. To start, remember that the average-sized Irish home is smaller than you are used to. So you will need to decide if you want to bring any or all of your furniture. If you are bringing electrical goods, you will need to buy transformers in the United States to take account of the different current in Ireland.

Use your airline allowance to the maximum, although you will probably find it will not be enough for all your clothing. Use FedEx or UPS for other essential items, as they can normally make deliveries to Ireland within 3–4 days. If you are planning on bringing all your furniture, crockery, and so on, then you will need to plan well in advance. Shipping goods across the Atlantic can take 5–6 weeks.

There are hundreds of relocation/shipping agencies throughout the United States that will ship to Ireland. Although it will be time-consuming, the best place to begin your search for a mover is in the shipping/freight-forwarding section of your local telephone directory. Choose at least three companies that can provide all the services you need. You will need to decide just exactly what you want done. Will you want them to pack for you, provide packing materials, pick up your consignment, handle customs clearance, arrange for delivery, and maybe even unpack? Arrange a time for each of them to visit your home, consider the options, and prepare an estimate.

You will need to use discretion on what to ship overseas. Unlike a domestic move, when you are likely to take everything, you need to consider the economics involved. For example, apart from the fact that the electrical system in Ireland is different, do you really want to take an aging freezer or washing machine with you? How much do they weigh and what will it cost? Will you be able to get them modified or serviced in Ireland?

My American friend certainly regrets shipping over her king-sized bed. She's searched in Waterford, in Cork city—she's even made a special shopping trip to Dublin. But she still cannot find king-sized sheets to fit. Although "king-sized" beds are sold in Ireland, they are anything but king-sized in American terms.

If you have not yet decided on the location of your permanent new home, you may have to consider putting some of your goods into storage on arrival. Check with your chosen freight forwarder to see if it can organize this for you.

Customs and Excise

If you're relocating from outside the European Union (e.g., from the United States), you're allowed to import, duty-free, any belongings that you have owned for at least six months. You can continue to import your personal possessions for up to one year after relocating. The only real proviso is that should you decide to sell any of your imported belongings within the first year of residence, duty becomes liable to be paid. There are some items that you'll not be allowed to import—handguns, for example.

Language and Education

Céad Míle Fáilte. Ceol agus Craic. Sláinte is Saol. If you believe that the Irish language is merely English spoken with a soft brogue, surprises are in store. For starters, we don't have a prime minister, we have a Taoiseach. Our biggest political party is called Fianna Fáil, the Soldiers of Destiny. Ever received an Irish Christmas card? Look at the special seasonal stamps—they aren't marked "Christmas," they're marked Nollaig.

"An labhraíonn tú Gaeilge?" If you haven't already guessed, the phrase means "'Do you speak Irish?'" Not everybody realizes that the republic's first official language is Irish, or to give it its proper title, Gaeilge. Often also referred to as Gaelic, it bears little resemblance to English—like Scots Gaelic, Breton, and Welsh, it belongs to the Celtic language group.

Until the 17th century, nearly all the population spoke Irish, but

Weird Words

No parking lots for drivers, no sidewalks for pedestrians. Restrooms? Forget it. Nor are we familiar with gas stations, drugstores, or diapers. As a blow-in (foreigner), you'll need to get used to some strange new terminology.

Want to fill your car with gas? No, no, no. You want petrol or diesel. And you put your messages (groceries) in the car boot, not the trunk. The fender is the bumper and the hood is the bonnet.

Shopping too has a language all of its own. You buy medicines at the chemist and stores are always called shops. Minerals are soft drinks such as cola and lemonade, rashers are bacon, and courgettes are what you call zucchini. Babies will need to get used to wearing nappies, not diapers. A new pair of pants? If you mean trousers or slacks, say so. Pants are something you'll find in the men's underwear department.

Why do you want to go to the bathroom if you don't intend to have a bath? The door marked W.C. (water closet) is a toilet, lavatory, loo (or if you've fallen into rough company, the jacks). It is not, repeat *not*, a restroom.

Any tool that us culchies (country bumpkins) forget the name of is a yoke as in, "Pass me that

English rule undermined most aspects of Ireland's traditional culture, including teaching of the native language. The situation was further exacerbated by the Great Famine and the long decades of mass emigration that drained the country of countless native speakers. Although Irish has been a language in slow decline since that time, there has been an enthusiastic revival in recent years. Every effort is being made to keep it alive and all schoolchildren study Irish as part of the curriculum. Proficiency in the language is a requirement for careers in professions such as teaching, banking, and the civil service.

Learning the Language

Despite its official status, newcomers aren't pressured to learn Irish. While Gaeilge is regarded as a cornerstone of the cultural heritage, most people use English as their preferred tongue. Latest census figures showed that although around 1.4 million people describe themselves as having an understanding of Irish, nearly two-thirds of them either never speak the language at all or use it less than once a week. Even so, you'll soon be using odd Irish words as part of everyday conversation.

yoke." Any person whose name you can't remember is yer man or yer woman. "You know who I mean, yer man beside the lough (lake)."

Naughty kids are bold and anybody who seems unwell probably looks well shook. If you're tired, you're banjaxed. However, if your radio or TV is banjaxed it's broken or damaged. (Though cruder people will tell you it's bollixed.)

And if somebody asks if you're enjoying the crack *(craic)*, don't be alarmed. It's not a reference to illegal substance abuse, but rather a harmless word for sharing a joke or having a fun time.

Scheme is another word that sends American eyebrows into orbit. In Ireland you'll see it everywhere: health insurance schemes, drug-subsidization schemes, community-employment schemes, seaside-resort schemes. Scheme never signifies anything dubious; it's simply an alternative word for a plan or project.

You'll also see numerous spelling differences. Words such as colour, sceptic, centre, traveller, theatre, labour, and honourable aren't an indication of bad spelling—Ireland simply uses the "British English" dictionary as opposed to the "American English" one.

Many of your new friends will have names such as Niamh (pronounced Neev) or Blaithin (pronounced Bloheen). You may want to visit the Fleadh (the feast), Ireland's biggest traditional music festival, or even learn how to play the *bodhrán,* the Irish drum.

You'll soon notice that place-names and street signs are invariably given in both Irish and English. Galway is also Gaillimhe; Cork doubles as Corcaigh; Sligo as Sligeach. Baile Átha Cliath isn't so easy to guess—any bus bound for what translates as "the town at the ford of the hurdles" is actually taking passengers to Dublin.

Follow a direction sign pointing to An Lár and it leads you to a town center. You may also see signs for *an Scoil* (a school), *an Leabharlann* (a library), or *an Ospidéal* (a hospital). A stroll down Sráid Padraig (Patrick Street) could take you past the *Oifig an Phoist* (post office), and if you get lost you can always ask a *Garda* for directions. Colloquially called "the guards," the Garda Síochána is the official title of Ireland's police force.

There are a few places in the remoter parts of Ireland where even Dubliners feel like strangers in a strange land. Counties Donegal, Kerry, Cork, Waterford, Mayo, and Galway all possess little enclaves known as Gaeltacht areas. The inhabitants of the Gaeltacht number only around

8,000 but more than 60 percent of the residents all speak Irish within the home and on the street. During summertime, many city kids are sent here to board with local families—they get a thorough immersion course in Gaeilge as preparation for forthcoming exams.

Gaeltacht roads aren't for the fainthearted. When exploring the country's Irish-speaking pockets, it's well worth having a smattering of the language as here direction signs are not bilingual. Yes, your map book says "Carraroe" but the signposts confusingly point to An Cheathrú Rua. Although everybody in the Gaeltacht does speak English, few concessions are made to the linguistically challenged visitor. If you're seeking the restroom in some little pub, it's handy to know the difference between the doors that read Mná (Ladies) and Fir or Fear (Men). It could save your blushes!

Ireland's best-known bilingual town is Dingle, a color-washed harbor town on County Kerry's wild and witchy Dingle Peninsula. East of Dingle town, the language is English—head west and you'll soon be deep into Irish-speaking territory. Stay in town and the place to head for is An Café Litearta, Ireland's first literary coffee shop where you can puzzle over the Irish menu and also browse for books on Tír na nOg (the Land of Everlasting Youth). Rumor has it that this fairytale land lies somewhere off the Dingle Peninsula, out in the Atlantic beyond the misty hummocks of the Blasket Islands. However, if you go to the Irish-speaking Aran Islands off the County Galway coast, you'll probably hear that it lies somewhere in that part of the western ocean!

Fairy folklore throws up an interesting example of how many Irish words became anglicized through the centuries. Take the *bean sidhe*, whose name translates as "spirit" or "fairy woman." She is, of course, much better known to the English-speaking world as the fearsome banshee. How do you pronounce a tongue-twister such as *bean sidhe?* Exactly the same as you would "banshee."

LANGUAGE SCHOOLS

Should you wish to learn Irish, plenty of summer schools and evening classes offer adults the opportunity to come to grips with this intriguing ancient language. Radio programs and an Irish language television station, Telefis na Gaelige (TnaG), also broadcast into the country's sitting rooms. The majority of TnaG's scheduling is in Irish, but it occasionally carries programs from our Celtic neighbors too.

Foras na Gaeilge is a new body that was set up to promote the Irish language throughout the whole of the island of Ireland in the wake of 1999's Good Friday Agreement. Its main activities include funding Irish language organizations and activities, the distribution and promotion of Irish language and Irish-interest books, and supporting Irish-language education. Its website at www.forasnagaeilge.ie has extensive links. Principal course providers for adults wishing to learn Irish include Gael Linn and Oideas Gael.

Oideas Gael has summer schools in County Donegal's Gaeltacht, where you can also take part in workshops varying from Irish dancing to tapestry weaving, hill walking, archaeology, marine painting, and bodhrán playing.

There is a wide choice of short-term and long-term courses for learners of every level and age group. Most courses in Gaeltacht areas are held during the summer, but an increasing number are now being offered throughout the year—particularly during bank holiday weekends, Easter, and New Year.

Probably the most enjoyable introduction to the Irish language is to attend a course that combines class work in the morning with activities in the afternoon. Oideas Gael has summer schools in County Donegal's Gaeltacht, where you can also take part in workshops varying from Irish dancing to tapestry weaving, hill walking, archaeology, marine painting, and *bodhrán* playing. The morning language classes are designed to give beginners the basics—stating your likes and dislikes, chatting about the weather, and so on. Alternatively you could give the activities a miss and opt for a more intensive language course.

Prices for a weeklong language course (45 hours of study) are €190 ($236); language and culture, €200 ($248); and three-day weekend courses, €95 ($118). Accommodation and board (bed, breakfast, and dinner) with local families costs an extra €210 ($260) per week; €105 ($130) for a three-day weekend. If you prefer self-catering, you can also opt to share a modern house with other course participants at a cost of €125 ($155) per week.

In the Galway area, contact Áras Mháirtín uí Chadain, the Irish Language Center of University College Galway. Its summer courses are more intensive and often draw foreign students wishing to gain university credits. For U.S. students, it would merit six semester credits. Fees for the monthlong beginner's and intermediate courses are €930 ($1,153), plus accommodation costs. Staying with local families, full board costs €800/€1,155 ($992/$1,432) depending on whether you require a single room.

Irish Place-Names

Many place-names are anglicized renderings of original names in the Irish language. Taken down by mapmakers and 19th-century ordnance survey teams, their meanings often describe the landscape, ancient monuments, or important local happenings. Common prefixes are the words *dún* (fort); *cill* (church), which is often written as Kill or Kil; *cnoc* (hill), which usually became Knock; and Bally, which takes its roots from *baile* (town). Clon derives from *cluain,* meaning "meadow." Signposts pointing to Drum this and Drom that are all linked to the Irish word *druim*—a ridge.

The original name of Killarney, the well-known tourist town, was Cill Áirne—the church of the sloes. Donegal derives its name from Viking times when it became known as Dún na nGall, the fort of the foreigner. The fascination in tracing names back to some misty past can be endless—a place such as Gortahork (Gorta Coirce) initially sounds an incomprehensible mouthful but *gort* signifies "field" and *coirce* means "oats." Thus it's fairly reasonable to assume that Gortahork was once renowned for its oatfields. Knockcroghery, a village in County Roscommon, has a

Each course covers intensive instruction in the spoken Irish language, special classes in traditional Irish dancing and singing, and lectures on history, folklore, literature, and society. Excursions and visits are arranged to several Irish-speaking locations: the fishing villages of Carna and Rossaveal, inland Clonbur, which was the birthplace of Thomas Lynch, one of the signatories to the U.S. Declaration of Independence, and the arts-and-crafty village of Spiddal.

COMMON IRISH EXPRESSIONS

You may hear these expressions spoken slightly differently as there are three distinct varieties of pronunciation: Ulster Irish, Connacht Irish, and Munster Irish.

Dia duit (JEE-a ditch)—Good day, hello. (Its literal meaning is "God be with you.")
Conas tá tú? (KUN-as taw too)—How are you?
Fáilte (FAWL-cha)—Welcome!
Tá go maith, go raibh maith agat (TAW gu MAH, GURA MAH ug UT)—I'm fine, thank you.
Cad é an t-ainm atá ort? (KAJ-ay in TAN-yim a-TAW urt)—What's your name?

darker derivation—that of a place of execution. *Cnoc* obviously means "hill" but *crochaire* is the Irish word for "hangman." Anyone with a smattering of Irish knows that Knockcroghery translates as Hangman's Hill.

The word *tobar* within a place-name usually signifies a healing well dating to pre-Christian times. The mapmakers often wrote it down as "tubber" or "tober" and in County Mayo you'll come across Ballintober (Baile-an-tobar), the town of the well. Tubbercurry in County Sligo takes its name from Tobar-an-choire, the well of the cauldron. Interestingly enough, magic cauldrons commonly appear in Celtic mythology and it's also in County Sligo that you find Knocknashee (Cnoc na Sidhe), the hill of the fairies. One of the most malevolent creatures of the Celtic Otherworld was the *púca,* a shape-changing goblin that haunted lonely places and often appeared to travelers in the form of a black horse. On the boundary of counties Limerick and Cork, the bridge at Ahaphuca takes its name from *ath* and *púca,* the goblin's ford. *Poll* signifies "hole," "cavern," or a deep pool of water and in the wild glens of County Wicklow, the River Liffey spills over a ledge into Pollaphuca—the goblin's hole.

(Jim, Sadie, etc.) *atá orm* (a-TAW OR-im)—My name is (Jim, Sadie, etc.)
Slán leat (SLAWN ly-AT)—Goodbye (if you are staying).
Slán agat (SLAWN u-GUT)—Goodbye (if you are leaving).

Education

Within the Republic of Ireland, education is compulsory from 6 to 15 years of age. If you're legally resident here, your children can be educated for free. There is no charge to attend public primary schools (4–12 years) and second-level schools (12–17 years). But although the tuition is free, schoolchildren have to pay for books and extracurricular activities.

Most Irish parents put their children through the state educational system, which comes under the auspices of the Department of Education and Science. This government body administers all aspects of education policy, including curricula, syllabi, and national examinations. However, state schools are generally privately owned and managed by religious orders or boards of governors. Ninety-five percent of schools belong to this sector and they receive their funding allowances from the state.

The school year runs from September until the end of June, with

Dublin's Trinity College dates back to 1592

holidays at Christmas and Easter. In general, you should be able to send your child to the school of your choice. However, state-funded primary schools tend to give priority to children living in the immediate area. Problems can arise if their classes are already full and they have a waiting list. Multidenominational schools, nondenominational schools, and Gaelscoileanna (Irish-speaking schools) all decide their own admissions policies.

Children are not obliged to start school until they reach the age of six, but 65 percent of four-year-olds and almost all five-year-olds are enrolled in infant classes in primary schools. The primary-education sector has just over 3,200 primary schools serving about 500,000 children.

Second-level education takes in secondary, vocational, community, and comprehensive schools. There are about 370,000 students in this sector attending a total of 768 publicly aided schools.

Postprimary education consists of a three-year junior cycle followed by a two- or three-year senior cycle. The Junior Certificate examination is taken after three years. In the senior cycle there is an optional Transition Year program followed by a choice of three two-year Leaving Certificate programs. Students normally sit their Leaving Certificate examination at 17 or 18 years of age.

Further Education for Adults

Whether you're looking for something to do during the day or at night, Ireland has a wide choice of adult education programs. Usually held once a week for a two-hour period, they vary from the academic to the practical. If you're interested in taking up anything from yoga to martial arts, auto repairs to beginner's French, check out the National Education Database at www.night courses.com.

Prices are usually very reasonable. To give a couple of examples, a 10-week course in the lost skill of needlepoint in Dublin is €70 ($87). In Cork, you can take 10 weeks of ballroom dancing lessons for €85 ($105).

When they move into their senior cycle, students must take a minimum of five subjects, including the three core subjects of English, Irish, and mathematics. They can then choose their other subjects from a broad range, including arts, languages, science, and other applied subjects (e.g., mechanical drawing, woodwork, etc.). According to the Department of Education and Science, 81 percent of students complete their second-level education.

Incidentally, if you're concerned about how your children will cope with the Irish language, there is an effective get-out clause. Students entering the education system after 11 years of age are not obliged to take Irish-language examinations.

Before I move on to higher education, here's a quick mention of Ireland's private-sector schools. The majority of nonstate primary schools, international, and specialist schools are day schools, but a small number do offer boarding. You can obtain full listings from the Department of Education and Science. Fees obviously vary, but these are what Saint Andrews College (Blackrock, County Dublin) charges for tuition: preparatory school €5,040 ($6,250) per annum; secondary school €4,015 ($4,979) per annum; international baccalaureate €4,670 ($5,791) per annum. The American College in Dublin charges tuition fees of €7,427 for the full academic year.

THIRD-LEVEL EDUCATION

More than half of Ireland's young people go from second- to third-level education, and 50 percent of these take degree-level programs. Access to third-level courses depends on results obtained in the Leaving Certificate examination. The third-level education sector consists of universities, technological colleges, and colleges of education. All of these are substantially funded by the state and are autonomous and self-governing. In recent years several independent private colleges have opened, offering mainly business-related courses.

There are more than 100,000 students in this sector, and there are seven universities in Ireland. These are the University of Dublin (Trinity College)—Ireland's oldest university, founded in 1592. The others are University College Dublin (UCD), University College Cork (UCC), the National University of Ireland (NUI) in Galway and also Maynooth, the University of Limerick, and Dublin City University.

The Royal College of Surgeons and The National College of Art and Design are also recognized colleges of the NUI. In addition, 14 countrywide institutes of technology offer education and training both full- and part-time in the areas of business studies, engineering and technology, and science and paramedicine. The Dublin Institute of Technology is the country's largest third-level institution with 22,000 students. It has constituent colleges specializing in technology, catering, marketing and design, commerce, and music.

Universities offer degrees at bachelor's, master's, and doctorate levels and undergraduate and postgraduate diplomas. In addition, research is undertaken in many areas and the universities are also involved in continuing and distance-education programs.

Teaching at the undergraduate level is normally by way of a program of lectures supplemented by tutorials and, where appropriate, practical demonstrations and laboratory work. Master's degrees are usually taken by course work, research work, or a combination of both. Doctoral degrees are awarded on the basis of research.

Unless you and your children can claim Irish or EU citizenship, you will have to pay for tuition fees as well as student upkeep. To obtain "Undergraduate Free Fees," an applicant must be both an EU national and have been ordinarily resident in Ireland (or another EU member state) for at least three of the five years preceding entry to a third-level course.

Annual undergraduate tuition fees will vary depending on the course and the institution, but these are the 2004/2005 figures provided by the Department of Education and Science.
- Medicine and related: €22,123–34,250 ($27,432–42,470)
- Law: €9,555–12,305 ($11,848–15,258)
- Music: €9,500–13,801 ($11,780–17,113)
- Engineering, science, and technology: €8,000–16,123 ($9,920–19,993)

- Business and related: €7,500–16,460 ($9,300–20,410)
- Arts and humanities: €7,500–12,305 ($9,300–15,258)

Fees for master's programs range €8,000–15,000 ($9,920–18,600) and upward for some specialized medical programs.

Regarding accommodation, living, and other expenses, the department estimates that during the 8- to 9-month academic year, a student will spend €850–1,200 ($1,054–1,488) per month. The cheapest accommodation is on campus, but a student can still expect to pay monthly rent of €350–450 ($434–558).

STUDYING ABROAD

Students can gain credits for studying at colleges and universities in Ireland, and they can choose to study for a full academic year, a semester, or take a summer program. Despite the name, a good web resource to start your research is www.studyinbritain.com. It covers a wide range of student programs in Ireland too.

For example, the University of Limerick is academically linked with 230 other universities. Taking in Irish studies along the way, the A–Z of courses starts with accounting and ends with zoology and wildlife sciences. Program types vary from short-term summer courses to a full year. Depending on the length of the course and time spent in Ireland, costs are $4,759–22,890. This includes tuition, housing, meals, outbound flight, cultural activities, University Sports Arena membership, field trips to the west of Ireland and Dublin, stopover in London, services of a predeparture student advisory center, and an on-site resident director.

With its lively social and cultural scene, Dublin is the No. 1 choice for native and foreign students alike.

At Galway's College Consortium for International Studies, students can choose from the following disciplines: archaeology, Italian, classical civilization, Latin, economics, legal science, English, mathematics, French, mathematical physics, Irish studies, philosophy, geography, psychology, German, sociological and political studies, history, and Spanish. Offerings in the sciences are available to Americans on a case-by-case basis. A 3.0 GPA is required for participation in this program and students earn 12–15 undergraduate credits for their work at the university. Semester fees are $6,900–7,300 but do not include accommodation or maintenance. The cost in this instance covers tuition, health insurance, and administrative fees.

With its lively social and cultural scene, Dublin is the No. 1 choice for native and foreign students alike. Most of the universities accept applications from foreign students and there is a wide and varied choice of courses on offer.

Trinity College is Ireland's oldest and most prestigious university. More than 100 normal degree courses are available through the college's five faculties. The college also offers a seven-week summer session. The program offers a choice of six minicourses, each worth 1.5 credits. A one-week stay in Northern Ireland is included in the schedule as well as some interesting field trips—an archaeological tour of the most important prehistoric sites in the Boyne Valley, trips to medieval sites in County Wicklow, and a tour of the Antrim coast with its famous Giant's Causeway.

Students have the option of living with a host family or staying on campus in Trinity College. You can apply for a place in the course directly to Trinity College or through an American university study-abroad program. For example, at the time of writing the University of Notre Dame in Indiana was enrolling students for the 2005 summer session. The cost varied from $7,200 to $8,500 depending on choice of accommodation. The price included tuition, accommodation, field trips, and meals (for those students choosing a host family).

Students are required to enroll in at least four of the six following courses: Irish Literature; Irish Drama (19th Century to Present); Post-Famine Irish History; Gaelic Culture; Irish Visual Culture; and Critical Issues in Contemporary Ireland. The Gaelic culture course gives students an opportunity to explore the fascinating world of Celtic mythology and folk traditions.

Elsewhere in the capital, in addition to a full range of degree courses, University College Dublin (UCD) offers a two-week James Joyce summer school each year. Three credits can be earned, and the aim of the school is to consider the numerous contexts of Joyce's work that are of interest to both scholar and the general reader. A variety of social events complements the program of lectures and seminars. Included are tours of Joycean Dublin, visits to concerts, theaters, and historic sights, poetry readings, and of course, informal gatherings in the atmospheric pubs. The fee for the 2005 school course was $903 and $1385 for self-catering campus accomodation. Applications can be made directly to UCD or through the North American Institute for Study Abroad (NAISA).

There are also a growing number of private institutions that offer degree courses to overseas students. One that offers some interesting options is the American College in Dublin. In Merrion Square, the college is a sister school of Lynn University in Boca Raton, Florida. The college offers an extensive program of full-time courses as well as 4- and 6-week summer terms. During each term, students have an option to attend a study tour for academic credit.

Although it's likely to be more of interest to full-time students than to those coming to Ireland for a summer course, one study tour offered most years by the American College is a 10-day art and humanities tour of Italy. Taking in Rome and Florence, students explore Italian art, culture, and society from the Roman civilization up to the present day. Visits include the Colosseum, the Forum, and the Vatican in Rome and the Uffizi Gallery and Duomo in Florence.

The most recent semester fee for the college is $12,500. This includes tuition, room, and board. The Italy tour costs an additional $1,950.

Foreign students are also permitted to work during the course of their education in Ireland. (See the *Employment* chapter for details.)

Health

O ne of the central issues of moving to a new country is the standards and costs of its health-care services. Ireland's are of a high quality for a small country, though it needs pointing out that the range of services is nowhere near as high-tech or extensive as in the United States. While most county towns have a good general hospital, patients needing procedures such as specialized heart surgery invariably have to travel to Dublin. However, general health care within rural communities is fairly well served by family doctors, health centers, and public health nurses.

For administrative purposes, Ireland's National Health Service is divided into a regional system of health boards. They will provide information on local doctors, dentists, and public health centers.

It may come as a surprise to find that Irish GPs (general practitioners or family doctors) are quite prepared to make home visits, even in the middle of the night if need be. Naturally, if you're simply suffering from general aches and pains, he or she will expect you to visit the surgery. This may be in the doctor's own home or at a health center.

Folk Remedies

Like all societies, Ireland has its folk cures and reputed healers with special powers. Although few people would dream of carrying around a haddock's jawbone in their pockets as a charm against toothache, it's still widely believed that the seventh son of a seventh son holds "the cure."

Another long-standing tradition is that the waters of holy wells can relieve anything from sprains to skin diseases. Wells dedicated to Saint Brigid are commonly credited with an ability to cure eye complaints. That people still believe in their curative powers is evidenced by votive offerings left behind on nearby trees and bushes.

Most country youngsters grow up knowing that dock leaves soothe nettle stings and that a cold iron key pressed against the back usually stops a nosebleed. And, despite the fact that every pharmacy stocks chilblain relief cream, countless older folk swear by the home remedy: bathing afflicted toes or fingers in a bowl of fresh urine. Another commonly cited home cure is to treat piles (hemorrhoids) with a poultice of boiled onions.

Remedies vary from mundane doings with butter and cabbage leaves to some very bizarre notions indeed. One old cure for whooping cough started by giving a meal to a ferret—the portion that the ferret left was then presented to the patient. Another strange idea required any would-be healer of burns to first capture a frog or water newt. The main part of what is undoubtedly an ancient magic ritual was to lick the amphibian's back nine times, an act that needed to be repeated on nine successive days. Apparently the licker was thought to acquire some substance with the power to heal burns.

Although science often confirms the value of certain folk remedies,

Most GPs charge around €35 ($43) per consultation. If you belong to a private health insurance plan, part of the cost of GP consultations can be reclaimed under your outpatient coverage. Medical-card holders don't have to pay for GP visits or prescribed medicines.

What are medical cards and would you be eligible for one? In general, if you are under the age of 70, the answer is only if you acquired Irish or other EU citizenship. Current qualifying rates are a weekly income below €142.50 ($177) for individuals under 66; €156 ($193.50) for those between the ages of 66 and 70. For couples in the same age brackets, qualifying weekly income rates are €206.50 ($256) and €231 ($286.50) respectively. Regardless of income and nationality, all legal residents over the age of 70 are eligible for medical cards. If you think you may qualify for a medical card, the scheme is administered through regional health boards.

it's hard to credit how smearing a fox's blood on the groin can dissolve kidney stones. Nor that goose dung boiled in milk is a sovereign remedy against jaundice. In her book of *Ancient Legends, Mystic Charms and Superstitions of Ireland,* Lady Wilde even unearthed a recipe for an Elixir of Potency, perhaps a 19th-century version of Viagra. The ingredients included cochineal, gentian root, saffron, snakeroot, salts of wormwood, and the rind of 10 oranges, the whole lot of which was steeped in brandy.

Ireland's search for a cure for baldness dates to at least the 12th century. In one example of medieval quackery, the follically challenged were urged to fill an "earthen pipkin" with live mice. The opening of the pipkin, a kind of pot, was stoppered up with clay and, along with its squeaking mice, buried near the hearth.

After 12 months had passed, the eager patient could dig up the pipkin and massage the gruesome contents into his scalp. The leech doctor who devised this practice recommended wearing gloves-- so powerful was the mixture that hair was likely to sprout from the fingertips too.

An equally disgusting remedy suggested the use of earthworms. In this scenario a stoppered jar of worms was buried in a manure heap and only a month needed to elapse before the contents could be rubbed into shiny pates. Sounds unbelievable? After writing about these baldness "cures" in the early 1980s, the Irish author Dr. Patrick Logan was astounded to find readers writing in for the actual preparations. One man even found out the retired doctor's address and turned up on his doorstep, presumably hoping to be given pipkins full of rotten mice and worms!

Public and Private Medical Care

You may have heard mention that Irish residents enjoy free hospital care. So they do—up to a point. To qualify for the entire raft of free services largely depends on age, status, income level, and exactly what level of medical attention is required.

To begin with, Americans who are coming to Ireland as holiday-makers or on a short fact-finding mission will need travel insurance to cover any possible medical costs. Free or reciprocal emergency care applies only to EU citizens who can produce what's known as an E111 form.

Irrespective of nationality or age, once you become resident in Ireland the picture changes. Should you need emergency treatment, you are now entitled to free medical attention in all hospitals and it isn't dependent on income levels. If, however, you and your broken finger simply turn up at a hospital casualty department without a doctor's referral, you'll be liable for a charge of €45 ($56) for the initial visit. Obviously, common sense should dictate what constitutes an emergency requiring immediate attention.

As an Irish resident, again irrespective of nationality, age, or income, you'll also be entitled to free inpatient and outpatient services in public hospitals. This includes consultancy services, surgeon's fees, and so on but does not cover the cost of hospital meals and accommodation. The rate charged is €45 ($56) per day, up to a maximum of €450 ($558) in any one year. These rates apply to beds in public wards. People on very low incomes who hold medical cards don't have to pay any accommodation levy.

If, however, you opted for private or semiprivate accommodation in a public hospital, current daily maintenance charges are €401 ($497) and €314 ($389) respectively in regional hospitals; €334 ($414) for private and €269 ($333) for semiprivate in general hospitals. These charges are additional to the daily public hospital accommodation charge.

As free hospital treatment for residents seems such an attractive proposition, you may well wonder why more than 1.5 million people here belong to private health insurance plans. The answer can be summed up in three short words: hospital waiting lists. Treatment and operations for what are described as nonemergencies can sometimes mean very lengthy waits. It isn't unknown for some patients to have spent three years and more waiting for hip replacements.

Joining an independent health insurance plan means you can effectively leapfrog the waiting list and obtain treatment as required. Furthermore, health-care premiums can be offset against the standard rate income tax. Depending on the level of coverage chosen, subscriptions allow for anything from semiprivate accommodation in a local public hospital up to your own room in one of Dublin's private institutions such as the Mater Hospital or the Blackrock Clinic. You can generally assume that premium-priced plans deliver premium-priced hospital accommodation. On the treatment side, all price bands within these plans cover general medical costs, fees for anesthetists, radiologists, surgeons, consultants, and also most outpatient charges.

(Within Ireland, you'll often see health insurance plans referred to as health insurance schemes. Here the word "scheme" doesn't have the same kind of negative connotations as in the United States.)

Ireland's largest independent provider is the Voluntary Health Insurance Board (VHI). However, if you're over the age of 65, you will not be able to join.

A number of different plans are offered. Depending on the coverage selected, annual adult premiums start at €512 ($635) rising to €1,450 ($1,798). Although you don't have to undergo any medical examination, there are some initial limitations. While benefits are immediately available for treatment due to accidents, for other illnesses and conditions there is a waiting period: 26 weeks for those aged under 55 and a full year for those aged over 55. Preexisting medical conditions are subject to a very lengthy restriction period: 5 years for those under 55; 7 years for those aged 55–59; 10 years if you're aged 60 or over.

At present, government legislation ensures that health insurance companies must charge all adults the same for the same level of coverage. Costs are not age-linked and a 30-year-old pays exactly the same as a 60-year-old with the same plan. However, the framework is to be amended. Companies will still have to accept everyone under 65, but they may charge you a late-entry loading fee if you are over 35 when you first join.

BUPA Ireland offers very similar cover. It has a choice of five plans, called Essential, Essential Plus, Health Manager Starter, Health Manager, and Essential Gold. Annual premiums are from €295 ($366); €408 ($506); €432 ($536); €618 ($766); and €1,550 ($1,922) respectively. All BUPA Ireland plans allow access to a private bed in hospital and give full coverage for heart and cancer treatment, outpatient benefits, and maternity coverage.

The main difference with BUPA as opposed to the VHI is that it also allows coverage for alternative therapies such as acupuncture and homeopathy. Additionally, patients needing very specialized attention can receive treatment at an appropriate hospital in Britain. But again, unless you already hold current medical insurance, BUPA won't take you on if your age is over 65.

Dental Care

The costs of routine dental care will have to come out of your own pocket unless you hold a medical card. Fees vary considerably so shop around. My own dentist in Boyle, County Roscommon, charges the equivalent of $31.75 for cleaning and polishing, $50 for a normal extraction, and up to $89 if the tooth requires surgical removal. Depending on the finish, fillings are $57–76. A full set of dentures is $571.

It's possible to take some of the pain out of paying for dental treatment by traveling across the border to Northern Ireland. Fees charged by Belfast dentists are a little lower (around 20 percent), but whether you realize any savings may depend on the prevailing exchange rate. You'll see their adverts in newspapers such as the *Irish Times* and *Irish Independent.*

Alternative Therapies

Twenty years ago, alternative therapy in Ireland meant pulling out a loose tooth by means of a doorknob and a piece of string. Nowadays you're likely to find even small Irish towns have a massage therapist or a holistic health center on the high street.

But go back further and you discover that alternative therapy has a long-standing tradition in Ireland. The current fashion for spa treatments has given a new lease of life to centers such as Kilkullen's Seaweed Baths in Enniscrone, County Sligo. The baths first opened their doors in 1912. If you suffer from rheumatism or arthritis, a seaweed treatment may be worth a try. Your personal bathtub—an Edwardian porcelain monster with solid brass taps—gets filled with seawater fresh from the unpolluted Atlantic. The seaweed is cut fresh each day, but you're not thrashing about in forests of the stuff. Rich in iodine, oils are extracted from the seaweed, which gives the bathwater an amber tint—it almost looks as if you're immersed in olive oil. Prices are very reasonable—around $20 for a combined steam and seaweed bath.

The current fashion for spa treatments has given a new lease of life to centers such as Kilkullen's Seaweed Baths in Enniscrone, County Sligo.

In County Clare, Lisdoonvarna's Spa Wells Center has a history going back to the mid-18th century. At the end of the harvest, farmers came to bathe away their aches and pains in the village's natural mineral springs. (And also to find a wife—Lisdoonvarna holds a long-standing matchmaking festival each September.) The waters of Lisdoonvarna are rich in iron, magnesium, calcium, and especially sulfur. It smells pretty foul—imagine rotten eggs—but people also gulp down glasses of it. Tucked away in woodlands, the Spa Wells has a Victorian pump house, sauna, and massage room as well as mineral baths. More treatments are likely on the way. More than $5 million is being spent on redeveloping Lisdoonvarna into a luxury spa. Most of the money is coming from private investors.

On the shores of Killary Harbor (Leenane, County Galway), the Delphi Mountain Resort and Spa also offers day treatments. The astounding range includes massage, *reiki,* aromatherapy, and hot basalt lava stones for deep muscle treatment. Delphi was featured by *Condé Nast Traveler* in a feature on the "World's 10 Best Overseas Destination Spas." For the full list of treatments and prices see www.delphiescape.com

Critical Illness Insurance

Also known as serious illness cover, critical illness insurance is a stand-alone insurance policy that pays out a tax-free lump sum on diagnosis of a specified illness or medical condition.

A number of insurance/assurance companies in Ireland offer such policies. Canada Life, Hibernian Life, and New Ireland are all major players in the health/life assurance market, but there are many others too. Illnesses that qualify for payment of benefits vary between insurance companies, but most include heart attack/surgery, stroke, cancer, kidney failure, and multiple sclerosis on their critical illness lists. As there are many different types of coverage, you need to study policy conditions carefully to ensure you have the best coverage should you need to make a claim.

Premiums are dependent on age, medical history, whether or not you smoke, and the level of insurance coverage opted for. The amount of coverage normally advised is five times annual earnings. Unfortunately, no Irish insurance company offers this type of coverage to those over 65. Even if you decide to take out critical illness cover before the age of 64, the maximum term that companies will insure you for is 11 years.

Through Hibernian, you can get an online quote. A female smoker aged 64 on her next birthday who takes out an index-linked 11-year critical illness policy worth €100,000 pays monthly premiums of €487.67. A male nonsmoker, aged 60 on his next birthday, pays monthly premiums of €279.48 for €100,000 of index-linked cover.

Pharmacies and Prescriptions

Every small town has at least one pharmacy, better known in Ireland as "the chemist." They generally open during normal shop retailing hours but within larger towns a rota system allows for late night services too. Along with prescription drugs, cosmetic items, and toiletries, they also stock a range of patent medicines—painkillers, cough syrups, and the like—many of which are manufactured by international drug companies.

Plenty of medicines that you'll be familiar with are to be found in Ireland too. In more rural districts, chemists are also the purveyors of animal husbandry products and it's not uncommon to see remedies for cattle fluke sitting above a shelf stocked with shampoos and hair colorants!

If there is a medication you use regularly, bring it along to your local Irish doctor or pharmacist. He or she will probably be able to identify an equivalent European brand. And there's no need to be concerned if you're prescribed a drug/medication with an unfamiliar name. All pharmaceuticals are subject to rigorous EU testing before they are allowed to be sold.

If the medication or its equivalent isn't available in Ireland, your U.S. physician can forward you a prescription, together with a letter stating you require this drug to treat an illness (specified), and that it's for your sole use. The U.S. physician or pharmacist can then mail you the drugs. The doctor's letter and prescription should be retained in case customs officers want further information.

Travelers already on medication should ensure that they bring sufficient quantities of it to last for the duration of the trip. As well as a copy of the prescription, you should also have a letter from your U.S. physician stating that the medication is necessary. This will avoid any potential problems if you are searched by U.S. or Irish customs officials.

Preventative Measures

Whether you're arriving as a visitor or to establish residency, there are no strange and worrying diseases to be aware of. You won't need shots, though if you're of a very cautious nature you may wish to get inoculated against tetanus. Those working on farms and in the building trade are always advised to have inoculations as the Irish countryside delivers hazards in the shape of barbed wire fencing and rusty nails. Keen gardeners won't need reminding that a thorny rosebush can also occasionally yield a nasty surprise and an unwelcome stay in hospital. Tetanus jabs are generally effective for a 10-year period.

You are not going to tread on snakes, encounter any other poisonous reptiles, or meet marauding packs of rabid dogs. Rabies is unknown within Ireland, largely thanks to the country's strict quarantine laws. The bug-life is pretty harmless too: midge bites are just an irritant and the stings of wasps and bees aren't life-threatening unless you're really unlucky and suffer from a rare allergy. In rural areas, the nastiest bite

Irish Herb Lore

• Camphor plant *(Balsamita vulgaris)*. Its dried leaves can be used to keep moths out of wardrobes and linen cupboards.

• Feverfew *(Chrysanthemum parthenium)*. A daisylike cottage garden plant once widely grown to treat fevers, migraine, and headaches.

• Fleabane *(Pulicaria dysenterica)*. As the name indicates, the burnt foliage can serve to drive away fleas. It was also once employed medicinally against dysentery.

• Heartsease *(Viola tricolour)*. An attractive flower with multicolored white, yellow, and purple petals, it's commonly associated with love potions.

• Horehound *(Marrubium vulgare)*. Commonly used by herbalists in syrups for coughs, colds, and lung ailments. Before the introduction of hops, it was one of the bitter herbs used in beer-making. Black horehound was also once used to treat the bite of mad dogs.

• Houseleek *(Sempervivum tectorum)*. Fleshy and rosettelike, its juice is still sometimes used for skin ailments such as sties on the eyelid. Superstition says that if growing on a roof, the houseleek provides protection against fires.

• Mugwort *(Artemisia vulgaris)*. Traditionally associated with magic and warding off evil spirits on Saint John's Eve, its feathery fronds can serve as an insect repellent.

• Rue *(Ruta gravedens)*. One of the most powerful herbs in medieval leechcraft, its best-known use was as a narcotic.

• Self-heal *(Prunella vulgaris)*. Boiled in water, the purple heads were reputedly an effective restringent against internal bleeding.

• Speedwell *(Veronica chamaedrys)*. Low-growing with tiny blue flowers, this creeping plant was once used to treat coughs, asthma, and catarrh.

• Valerian *(Valerina officinalis)*. A tall, red-flowered plant that's pretty enough for the garden, its roots yield a strong sedative.

• Vervain *(Verbena officinalis)*. Apparently an important plant in druidic times and later used as a charm against witchcraft, its qualities include the treatment of nervous disorders, staunching blood, and easing the pangs of childbirth.

you're likely to receive is from a horsefly, colloquially known as a "cleg." Bites result in angry-looking red lumps, which can be quickly soothed with antihistamine cream and shouldn't require a visit to the doctor.

An obvious concern to some people will be Ireland's damp climate, particularly during winter. If you suffer from respiratory ailments or asthma, there's no avoiding the fact that long sojourns in Ireland are unlikely to improve your condition.

On broader health issues, Ireland is a modern country with modern problems. Like everywhere else we have AIDS and HIV sufferers. The most recent figures put the cumulative total of reported HIV infections at 3,408. Despite the government's campaign to practice safe sex, the majority of newly reported cases are sexually transmitted. Yet Irish-born AIDS/HIV patients represent only a small percentage of the total. The number of asylum seekers arriving in Ireland in recent years has risen substantially. Many are from sub-Saharan Africa. As it is estimated that this area of the world is the most severely affected by HIV, it is not unexpected that the majority of diagnosed new cases (82 percent) are among immigrants from sub-Saharan Africa.

Sexually transmitted infections (STIs) are also increasing. This is despite the fact that condoms are widely available and safe-sex programs are taught in schools. More than 11,000 cases of STIs were reported by clinics in the most recently released statistics (2003), an increase of 6.5 percent from the previous year. Perhaps the Irish government needs to invest even more in public-health information if condom use is to become more widespread.

If you suspect you need to be tested for a sexually transmitted disease, most Dublin hospitals and general hospitals elsewhere in the country have STI clinics. Maybe it's to avoid potential embarrassment, but many people choose to go outside of their own immediate area to be tested. The Irish Family Planning Association (IFPA) also provides a private testing service at its medical center in Dublin.

Another issue is BSE, better known as "mad cow disease." There were cases in Ireland, though nothing like the numbers in neighboring Britain. Animal screening measures have been brought in and farm management procedures are subject to rigorous scrutiny by the Department of Agriculture. Nobody wants to take any chances as the country depends heavily on beef export markets. And don't worry about foot-and-mouth disease either—it affects only livestock, not humans. Ireland had a couple of incidents of foot-and-mouth in early 2001, but the disease was quickly stamped out and didn't spread outside County Louth's Cooley Peninsula.

Environmental Factors

One frequently asked question is if it's safe to drink the water. Yes, it's perfectly safe whether from taps or spring wells. In parts of the midlands and western Ireland, you may notice it sometimes has a brownish tinge, a bit like very watered-down whiskey. This doesn't indicate contamination—the color results from the high peat content of the ground it flows through.

Compared to other western industrialized countries, air pollution in Ireland isn't regarded as a major environmental issue. To alleviate winter smog from coal fires, the whole Dublin area brought in a ban on the marketing, sale, and distribution of bituminous fuel back in 1990. Since then, 11 other areas have come under the ban, including Cork city, Wexford, Waterford, Galway, and Limerick.

> *Aside from hotel bedrooms and in the home, the only places where smokers can still legally enjoy a puff are in prisons and mental health institutions.*

March 29, 2004, was a black day for Ireland's smokers. This was the day the government brought in Prohibition. Smoking in public places—including in clubs and bars—is now entirely banned. Aside from hotel bedrooms and in the home, the only places where smokers can still legally enjoy a puff are in prisons and mental health institutions.

While the smoking ban has been welcomed by some people, publicans report a substantial drop in trade. Takings are down by up to 40 percent in pubs near the border with Northern Ireland, where people aren't yet subject to the draconian measures of the Nanny State.

Disabled Access

Many hotels and guesthouses in Ireland are wheelchair-accessible, as are most purpose-built visitor attractions.

In the past few years, there has also been a substantial improvement in transport facilities. All of Bus Eireann's urban fleet as well as 40 percent of its Dublin Bus fleet are low-floor and wheelchair-accessible. By 2005, all stations on Dublin's DART line were to be fully accessible. However, a recent report by the National Disability Authority points out that though there has been progress, existing main-line rail transport still requires substantial investment to make it accessible to all.

Safety

Crime and personal safety issues are important considerations when contemplating relocation. But although Ireland's crime rate is one of the lowest in the European Union, Dublin does have drug problems. Addicts require funds and aren't too fussy about who provides them.

Just as you would in any city, lock your car and keep an eye open for pickpockets, bag-snatchers, and other shady characters.

In rural areas, the crime problem is minimal. Leaf through the provincial papers and you'll see that the "criminals" who've appeared in court are likely to be speeding motorists, the odd feuding neighbor, and pub landlords who've been caught serving drinks at 3 o'clock in the morning. Or indeed their customers—it is actually an offense to be "found on" licensed premises after closing time.

One reported case of homicide in the region covering the counties of Tipperary, Waterford, Wexford, Kilkenny, and Wicklow: it illustrates that murder here is still a shockingly rare event.

The *Gardaí* (police) are a mainly unarmed force. In an emergency dial 999 or 112. These calls are free. Give the address or location where help is needed. Use the same emergency numbers for the ambulance service, fire brigade, lifeboat, and mountain rescue.

Employment

None of us can live on fresh air alone. Unless you have a regular income, think carefully about how you are going to support yourself. In some aspects, Ireland has become a land of opportunity but finding paid employment may depend on the skills you can offer. Although there is no open-door jobs policy for non-EU nationals such as North Americans, a number of possibilities have opened up in the past couple of years. Labor shortages in information technology companies, and also in nursing and construction, have led to restrictions in these sectors being eased.

Another possibility is self-employment. Moving to a new country is a major life change in itself, but maybe now is the time to think about becoming your own boss too. And even if you can afford to bid farewell to the 9–5 grind, not everyone wants to give up work completely. So why not spare a few hours each week for voluntary services?

However, it's not bad news for everyone. Foreign students attending Irish universities and colleges have opportunities for internships—and also the entitlement to earn money in the general workplace without needing a permit.

Ireland's Economy

Many foreign investors still think Ireland's economy is solely agricultural—a place whose only exports are pigs, butter, and potatoes. While it's true that the country is nowhere near as industrialized as the rest of Europe, immense changes have occurred in recent years. Agriculture is no longer the mainstay of the economy, though it does of course remain a key contributor. Within this sector, the emphasis isn't just on livestock farming but also on large-scale production of wheat and barley. The food-processing industry is equally important and major companies such as the Kerry Group have stock market quotes.

Amounting to around 10 percent of all exports, the software sector alone employs around 32,000 people and generates annual revenues of €12 billion.

But did you know that Ireland is the world's second-largest exporter of computer software after the United States? The information technology business is going gangbusters and benefiting both indigenous companies and big multinationals. Amounting to around 10 percent of all exports, the software sector alone employs around 32,000 people and generates annual revenues of €12 billion.

The boom has come about mainly through offering attractive tax-advantageous packages for foreign companies to relocate to Ireland, but successive governments have also operated a tireless policy of promoting the country's advanced technology services. The Industrial Development Agency (IDA) and Enterprise Ireland do much sterling work behind the scenes.

The republic's big advantage in attracting inward investment is through charging multinationals a very low level of corporation tax. Although this rose from 10 percent to 12.5 percent in January 2003, it's still an enticing deal for companies looking for a gateway into the wider European marketplace.

Continuing growth doesn't just depend on the IT sector. Ireland is also a base for many foreign companies involved in telecoms, chemicals, pharmaceuticals, and textiles; exploration companies have found a number of oil and gas deposits off the southern coastline. In the service sector, banking and insurance companies keep churning out huge prof-

Deer farming is becoming a popular agri-business.

its and Dublin itself is the home of an International Financial Services Center, the IFSC. International banking companies in the IFSC operate there on an offshore basis, which means that foreign investors can roll up profits tax-free. However, just in case you're wondering, Irish people cannot take advantage of these offshore accounts in their own country. Residents wanting to hold offshore investments have to look to places such as the Channel Islands or Isle of Man.

THE LABOR FORCE

Although on a definite downward trend, unemployment still blemishes some parts of the country. While only 4.6 percent of the available labor force is currently jobless (160,500 people in total), the percentage figure disguises the fact that unemployment is often extremely high in rural counties and also on inner-city housing estates. Not everyone has the skills to participate in Ireland's technological boom.

Another thing that you may not have realized is that much of Ireland's labor force is unionized and very happy to be so. Any liberal leanings you may have will be severely tested when you find yourself stuck at the airport, unable to leave the country because aircraft maintenance crews have put down their tools. And you're unlikely to be humming *The Red Flag* if your mail has been gathering dust in a sorting office for three weeks and more. These things can and do happen. Although not up to the same level of bloody-mindedness as their French comrades, Irish unions can be fairly "bolshie."

The Job Hunt

Rapid growth in the Irish economy in recent years has resulted in labor shortages in some sectors. Information and computing technologies, building professionals, and health-care workers always seem to be in demand. To ease recruitment of suitably qualified people from non-EU countries, a working visa and Work Authorization Scheme have been put in place. This makes it possible for prospective employees with job offers from employers in Ireland to obtain immigration and employment clearance in advance from Irish embassies and consulates. The new scheme does not replace the old work-permit procedure—it is simply a faster alternative. The working visa is initially valid for two years.

At present, the designated categories are: information and computing technologies professionals and technicians; architects; construction engineers; quantity surveyors; building surveyors; town planners; registered nurses; and dentists.

If you are planning well enough in advance, it may also be well worth registering with some online recruitment agencies. Some are geared up for general employment opportunities; others specialize only in certain sectors. A good place to begin would be with Monster, one of the biggest agencies in Ireland.

With Ireland producing around 40 percent of Europe's packaged software and 60 percent of business applications software, the IT sector has particular need of graduates with technology degrees. Somewhat worryingly, a recent report revealed that there is a 30 percent dropout rate from Ireland's university courses in computer sciences. At present, there is a huge demand for C++ and Java VS developers, systems administrators, and IT consultants. The rewards start at around €24,000 ($29,800) for developers with one or two years' experience, rising to around €45,000–62,000 ($55,800–76,900) for those with four or more years' experience behind them. Senior positions pay more. For example, a chief information officer can expect to earn €120,000–152,000 ($148,900–188,500) annually.

The health services in Ireland also provide some opportunities for non-EU nationals. Registered nurses in particular always seem to be in demand. Nurses have even been recruited from the Philippines in recent years. Vacancies usually exist in all areas, including the specialist areas of medical, surgical, theater, renal, ICU, A & E, orthopedics, pediatrics, midwifery, and oncology. Depending on qualifications and experience, a staff nurse can expect to earn a salary of around $35,000–50,000 per annum.

To a lesser extent there is also a demand for other health-care professionals. One recently advertised vacancy was for a radiographer. The salary scale for this position ranged $43,000–55,000.

Ireland's state health system was being reorganized at the time of writing. However, it should soon be possible to check the latest health-care vacancies on the new Health Service Executive website.

WORKING STUDENTS

International students do not require a permit to work in Ireland. European Union nationals have the exact same entitlement to take up employment as that of an Irish citizen. Non-EU students are permitted to work for up to 20 hours part-time each week. This usually takes the form of bar work.

As a student, you are also entitled to work full-time during the university holidays. Unfortunately, the entitlement to take up employment ceases once your student visa runs out. If on completing your studies you want to continue in employment, you will need a work permit to do so (see below).

Even though you may be working only part-time, you will have to apply for a Personal Public Service (PPS) number. All employees in Ireland need a PPS number for tax and social security purposes. You can make an application through your nearest social welfare office—find where it is by looking in the Golden Pages telephone directory under "Government Departments."

You will need to take the following along with you:
• Passport
• *Garda* registration card
• Proof of address in Ireland
• Letter from your university/college verifying that you are a student

INTERNSHIPS

Another option for students to explore is internships. These are short-term work assignments that offer the opportunity to enhance classroom knowledge with career-related professional work experience. They would normally be related to your academic major and career goals. The benefit of an internship is that it can help clarify if you're heading down the right career path.

Paid or unpaid, internships are now considered to be an integral part of a student's educational experience. In many instances students are awarded credits for successful completion of projects.

If you are a student and like the idea of an internship in Ireland, you should begin by inquiring with the careers office at your own university/college. Many universities have long-standing arrangements with employers and can normally find internships for suitable candidates.

There are a number of organizations in the United States through which students obtain internships abroad. For example, IAESTE can help place technical students in paid internships. To be eligible, though, you must be studying at a university in the United States. Another important condition to be met is whether or not your major qualifies as "technical." If you're not sure, you should contact IAESTE by email.

Foreign students at Irish universities/colleges can also apply for internships. Again, the best place to begin your search would be with your career office. Many of the Irish universities give details of available internships on their websites. Not all the internships will be in Ireland, though—many will be based in the United Kingdom.

To give you some idea of the type of internships available, here are a few examples of internships University College Dublin (UCD) was listing; they went something like this:

- Summer internships with Ernst and Young: A number of vacancies for students in their penultimate year will be available in the summer for those interested in pursuing a career as a chartered accountant or tax consultant or for those interested in the risk management and risk service areas.
- Emerald Cultural Institute: This language school in Dublin is looking for students to fill roles in the following areas: tour guiding, administration, and sports assistants for summer 2005.
- IBM: Extreme Blue is a three-month summer internship program. IBM is looking for students to work in its Dublin Software Laboratory, one of a number of software development labs within IBM. Students work in a high-performance "biztech" team on various projects. The teams will comprise four students: three technical and one business.

WORK PERMITS

Unless you can claim Irish or other EU citizenship, or qualify for a working visa under the Work Authorization Scheme, you'll need a work permit to obtain paid employment in Ireland. You can't apply for one yourself—work permits are issued only to employers not employees.

Employers have to contact the minister for the Department of Enterprise, Trade, and Employment before any prospective employee arrives in the country. A work permit gets issued only if the ministry is satisfied that an employer has taken all reasonable steps to recruit a suitably qualified person from Ireland or the European Union.

Yes, Americans do work here but most are employed by large U.S. multinationals in positions requiring high levels of know-how. If you're a computer whiz-kid, involved in scientific research, or a manager who has already climbed a good way up the corporate ladder, you're undoubtedly a highly valued member of the workforce. No doubt your skills will be needed for the success of your company's Irish operations and multinational employers no longer have to obtain work permits for those here on terms up to four years. However, even if you already work for a U.S. multinational with an Irish outlet, work permits are *not* issued for more run-of-the-mill jobs outside the technology sector. Numerous overseas companies set up in Ireland to avail themselves of generous grants, incentives, and tax breaks. What Ireland gets from the deal is new jobs for the local workforce. In most instances, if an employer requires manual, clerical, and secretarial staff, and so on, the company must make these positions available to Irish or other EU nationals.

For more information contact the Work Permits Section, Department of Enterprise, Trade, and Employment.

LANDING THE JOB

A traditional curriculum vitae (CV) is not necessary in Ireland. You do not need to include minor details. But you do need to include the major points—your skills, qualifications, a description of your achievements, and necessary personal details. Try to keep your CV interesting. The story of your career should convince the recruiter that you are worth meeting. You need to inform him or her about the context in which your achievements have taken place and what you have to offer in the future. Keep your CV to two pages and concentrate on what you have being doing for the last five years.

When you've made it through the selection process, you need to start preparing for an interview. No matter how well qualified you are, you still need to "interview well." Try to learn something about your prospective employer's business. Be sure you know exactly what the position entails. Present yourself clean and well groomed, and dress appropriately for the position you are applying for and the company it is with. If you are applying for a position with a major company, you can expect the interviewing process to last a couple of weeks. You may well be called for a second interview.

BENEFITS

Although they do not get as much time off as in some other EU countries, Irish workers are legally entitled to four weeks' annual holidays and nine days of public holidays. This applies to all workers, full-time, part-time, temporary, or even casual, who have been employed for more than one year. Entitlements for less than one year of employment are on a pro-rata basis.

> *Although they do not get as much time off as in some other EU countries, Irish workers are legally entitled to four weeks' annual holidays and nine days of public holidays.*

The holiday period varies from industry to industry, but you will generally get two weeks' vacation in the summer months, one in winter, and one in spring. Although four weeks is the legal entitlement, in practice many Irish workers enjoy more than this. For example, it is not unusual for most of the country to be off work from Christmas Eve to January 2.

Highly skilled workers in major companies can expect a range of benefits. These might include payments to a health plan, retirement pension, share options, subsidized travel, or a company car.

Expectant mothers are entitled to 18 weeks' statutory maternity leave, with at least 4 weeks before the birth. The entitlement covers all women employees who are working eight hours per week or more, and who have contributed to the state's pay-related social-insurance scheme. This also applies to self-employed women. You would need to have been contributing for two years to qualify. In either case, 70 percent of reckonable earnings is paid with set minimum and maximum levels.

There is no legal requirement for companies to pay for sick leave, unless it is part of the contract of employment. Sick leave or "disability benefit" is generally paid for by the state. As with maternity leave, you would need to have contributed to the scheme for two years before qualifying. Disability payments are graduated according to your earn-

Trading places, the market square, Roscommon Town

ings, with minimum and maximum levels set. Note that if you are self-employed, you will not be entitled to any disability benefits. You would have to take out a private insurance policy.

Self-Employment

Self-employment is a different kettle of fish entirely. New country, new career? If you have an entrepreneurial flair and like the idea of working for yourself, you can do so. Maybe you've been toying with the notion of going into the antiques trade, starting a boat-building business, or owning a restaurant, coffee shop or pottery studio. Or maybe you're the "crafty" type who could design greeting cards decorated with pressed wildflowers or carve mythical figurines from pieces of bog oak. And here's an idea—how about providing a relocation service for other Americans wanting to move to Ireland?

Anybody out there with a "green thumb?" Well, please come and open a good plant and tree nursery in my locality. Get that permission from the Land Commission to buy a large plot of the Irish countryside and you may even want to consider growing mushrooms on a commercial scale—a Jordanian immigrant in my own area is doing just that. Making a living from the land doesn't have to mean crops and cattle. Agribusiness ventures take in everything from quails' egg production to making goat cheese to running pets' boarding kennels. I know an English couple in Leitrim who make a living from growing herbs and one Swiss lady in Roscommon has set herself up as a traditional harness- and saddle-maker.

Pubs and guesthouses are homes with an obvious built-in business potential. If a home with an income sounds your type of thing, why not consider a small shop? Many retail outlets have owner-accommodation above the actual business premises. You'll be amazed at how many Irish towns are crying out for a health-food store, for instance. At present, shoppers in Boyle and Carrick-on-Shannon have to make a 40-mile round-trip to Sligo to buy Puy lentils and goats' milk yogurt.

Leaving aside the question of whether to buy an existing business or start an entirely new venture, as an American citizen you're first going to have to jump through the bureaucratic hoops. For EU citizens there are no restrictions: any Dutch, German, or British national can start enterprises without having to seek what's known as "Business Permission." So, if you can claim Irish or other EU citizenship, do so—this slashes through all the red tape at a stroke.

OBTAINING BUSINESS PERMISSION

In the tortuous prose of governmental directives, Business Permission is "the permission of the Minister of Justice, expressed in writing, to allow a particular person or group of persons to engage and become established in business in the State for a particular period of time." All non-EU citizens need to obtain such permission.

Business Permission isn't granted automatically and a lot will depend on the nature of any proposed venture. In general, you must satisfy the Ministry of Justice that the granting of approval would:

• Result in the transfer to the state of capital in the minimum sum of an equivalent $332,000. This minimum investment can be waived if:
(a) the minister is satisfied the application is justified for the purpose of pursuing activities as a self-employed person.

Or (b) that you are the spouse or a dependent of an Irish or EU national.

• At the very least, maintain existing employment within an existing business.

• Add to the commercial activity of the state.

• That the business would substitute Irish goods for goods that would otherwise have to be imported.

• Be a viable trading concern and provide the applicant with sufficient income to provide for him-/herself without resorting to noncontributory social welfare or paid employment for which a work permit is required.

All applications for Business Permission need to be accompanied by the following documentation:

• A passport or national identity papers

• A registration certificate if you are already living in the state

• A statement of character from the police authorities of each country in which you have lived for more than six months during the 10 years preceding an application

• A business plan, preferably endorsed by a firm of accountants

Applicants normally receive the minister's decision within one month. On receiving approval, you're allowed to start your business or commence trading immediately, but you will need to register (or renew an existing registration) with the *Gardaí* in the area in which you intend to live and work.

Permission to live in the state is given in conjunction with the validity of business permission, initially a period of one year. One month before your permission expires, you'll need to reapply to the Ministry of Justice to renew your permit and also to submit audited accounts and evidence of compliance with tax laws. If everything is in order, business permission will be renewed for a further five years. You can obtain detailed information about business permission from the Immigration Division at the Ministry of Justice.

Labor Laws

The various employers' organizations in Ireland are forever complaining about the amount of labor regulations they have to comply with. The range is extensive, to say the least. As an example, the Ministry of Labor Affairs publishes a so-called "brief guide" to the labor laws that runs to

81 pages. Just about every aspect of employing an individual is covered by a law. Contracts and terms of employment have to be provided to every worker within two months of starting work. There are laws in place regarding the length of the working week for various categories of work. Laws have to be adhered to when employing young people. Wage laws, safety, health, and welfare at work are all catered for. There are laws relating to the national minimum wage, overtime, sick leave, minimum notice, redundancy, carer's leave, insolvency, and dismissal. The most recent act affecting employers/workers came into force in 2004; there is now a total ban on smoking in the workplace.

WORKERS' RIGHTS

The various labor laws in place ensure that Irish workers are well protected. The large number of organized workers' unions look after the welfare of their members when it comes to workers' rights.

The Terms of Employment Acts 1994 provide that an employer is obliged to provide an employee a written statement of the terms of employment within two months of the commencement of employment. There are numerous official avenues to explore if a worker feels his or her rights have been abused.

MINIMUM WAGE

Despite fierce opposition from most sectors of Irish industry, the country has had a minimum wage law in place for a number of years. It is reviewed regularly and from February 2004 the national minimum hourly rate of pay was set at €7 ($8.70) per hour. The law provides that all experienced adult workers must be paid an average hourly rate of pay that is not less than the national minimum wage.

BAR
TOWELS
95ᵖ
each.

© Steenie Harvey

Finance

Asking how far your money will stretch in Ireland is one of those "how long is a piece of string?" questions. Although there's no escaping the fact that many day-to-day living costs are higher than in the United States, other factors help create some balance. For starters, you won't be paying property taxes or rates (local council taxes). Retirees can take advantage of a valuable free travel concession and free hospital emergency treatment is there for any resident who needs it. And, if you're on a fixed income, it's reassuring to know that Ireland has a relatively low inflation rate—currently 2.5 percent.

As in any other country, much will depend on where you choose to live, the kind of lifestyle you expect to enjoy, and your hobbies and interests. Theater tickets are astoundingly cheap, for example, but computer and good-quality photographic equipment is exorbitantly expensive.

Leaving aside the question of rent or mortgage payments, if you're happy with simple country pleasures—a modest home with all the necessary comforts, a small fuel-efficient car, adequate health coverage, and occasional treats—then $3,000 per month should prove more than ample to cover the cost of living. Obviously if you're the type of person who expects to dine out regularly in top-class Dublin restaurants, drive a Mercedes, belong to an exclusive gym, and own a huge Georgian mansion with equally huge heating bills then you're going to need rather more in the way of funds.

To put the income question into some kind of context, the basic state pension for Irish couples under 80 years of age stands at $1,470 per month; it's $830 for single pensioners. The most recent figures issued by the Central Statistics Office put the average monthly wage at $2,910 for males and $2,020 for females.

Cost of Living

Throughout the world, countless analysts devote their entire working lives to gleaning cost data from numerous cities. Most recent surveys show that Dublin scores better than New York for home services, utilities, entertainment and, somewhat surprisingly, groceries.

Whether that's correct or not, shopping basket items usually provide worthwhile cost comparisons. Although some towns now have branches of discount European supermarkets such as Lidl, prices within standard chains (Tesco, Supavalu, Londis, and Spar) tend to be on a par, although bargain-hunters can often snap up special deals: two chickens for the price of one, a pound of sausages given away with a pound of bacon rashers, and so on. Figures released by the Central Statistics Office show that an average household (two adults, two children) spends around a fifth of its weekly income on food.

Current costs of some basic foodstuffs are as follows:

- 200-gram jar of Nescafé: $6.58
- 1 pound roasting pork: $5.50
- 80 good-quality tea bags: $1.85
- 12 medium-sized eggs: $1.97
- 2 liters of milk: $1.48
- liter of orange juice: $.81
- 454 grams butter: $1.85
- 1 pound sausages: $1.85

Entertainment and Eating Out

Culture is wonderfully accessible with ticket prices for most forms of entertainment very inexpensive. Art exhibitions are generally always free, though the disappointing news is that we keep our livestock in the fields instead of pickling them in formaldehyde. The price of listening to traditional pub music is merely the cost of your drinks—a pint of Guinness costs around $4.50 in most country pubs; though it can be more than $5 in Dublin. Most tickets for classical music concerts are pitched somewhere between €12 and €30 ($15–37). Sometimes you don't even have to pay that. Dublin's Hugh Lane Gallery often has free recitals at noon on Sundays.

Theater is outstanding value and you don't necessarily have to take a trip to Dublin to catch a good play—especially during the summer, theater companies regularly tour the provinces. Two of Dublin's top theaters are the Abbey and the Gaiety; ticket prices are generally €15–30 ($18.50–37) and €25–38 ($31–47) respectively, though you can pay as much as $70 when the Gaiety has an opera performance. There are dozens of smaller performance venues—Bewley's Café Theater, Andrew's Lane Studio—even Mountjoy PrisonĒ the inmates usually put on a performance once a year. In Cork, tickets for the Opera House are €20–30 ($25–37) and the Everyman Palace Theatre is generally €22 ($27). Galway's Town Hall Theatre charges €10–12 ($12–15). Cinema tickets are a real steal. For example, in Dublin's Savoy Cinema, tickets are €6 ($7.50) in the afternoons and €8 ($9.90) after 6 P.M.

Eating-out costs vary, and choice will very much depend upon population size and whether you're living in a touristy area. Wherever you live, there's never any problem in finding old-fashioned cafés serving tea and scones for $2.20 or tucking into a hearty pub lunch for $10–12. Away from larger towns and the better-known tourist routes, the evenings can get a bit more difficult. Small-town Ireland does not really have a dining-out culture and choice is often limited to a hotel dining room, a burger/pizza place, or the local Chinese restaurant. Although a three-course meal will cost only around $25, the chef is more likely to have trained in Sligo's catering college rather than Hong Kong.

Country-house hotels usually have some very innovative menus and are often open to nonguests. However, a meal here is generally in the "treat" category as prices come in at the $60-a-head level, with wine extra.

- 22 pounds potatoes: $5.57
- 1 kilogram sugar: $1.07
- 500 grams cornflakes: $2.50
- 1 pound bananas: $.70
- 1 pound striploin steak: $7.48
- 1 pound cheddar cheese: $6.15

Smokers may decide to quit when they discover a pack of 20 cigarettes costs around $7.60. A bottle of Australian chardonnay costs $7.42 minimum in most stores, while a decent French red such as a Crozes-Hermitage will set you back around $10. A six-pack of beer (Heineken lager or Guinness) costs around $12.30.

Sharp-eyed readers will have noticed that the above shopping list indicates weights by both the imperial and metric standards. Although Ireland theoretically went metric more than 20 years ago, a dual system still operates. In most butchers' shops and greengrocers, foodstuffs continue to be priced by both the kilo and the pound. And while milk is now sold in liters, barmen continue to measure out beer in pints and half-pints.

SALES TAX

Sales tax isn't charged on groceries but nonetheless Ireland does have a general sales tax that applies to numerous goods and services. Known as VAT (value added tax), it's not generally itemized separately, except on utility bills. In all shops, restaurants, and other consumer outlets, the amount you see on price tags and menus is the price you'll pay.

Smokers may decide to quit when they discover a pack of 20 cigarettes costs around $7.60. A bottle of Australian chardonnay costs $7.42 minimum in most stores, while a decent French red such as a Crozes-Hermitage will set you back around $10.

Varying rates of VAT apply to different services and sales. The standard 21 percent rate is charged on things such as telephone bills, new vehicles, petrol (gas), beer, spirits, most household goods, adults' footwear and clothing, and many professional bills, including lawyers' fees. A reduced 13.5 percent rate applies to electricity, fuel for the home, restaurant meals, newspapers, and cinema tickets. VAT isn't a talking point for most consumers as it's an invisible tax—it is only if you intend to provide any services that it need concern you.

HOUSEHOLD GOODS

Many electrical appliances and other household goods are quite expensive, particularly when it comes to good-quality furniture. Furthermore, items such as cookers and iceboxes are like dinky dollhouse pieces compared to what's available in North America. You'll just have to keep telling yourself "small is beautiful."

Hiring Help

Ireland isn't Latin America and you shouldn't come here expecting to find legions of maids, cooks, and gardeners looking for live-in positions. Nor are people prepared to work for a pittance. Although it's common to find Dublin's professional classes employing cleaning ladies, this isn't really the case in the rest of the country. Although nearly all parish priests still have a housekeeper, ordinary mortals would be considered very odd if they advertised for home help nowadays. Most people in rural areas are fiercely independent and it's only the very elderly or housebound who require assistance, in which case it's classed as a social need and provided by the health authorities.

Ireland's strong economy has resulted in a workforce that is picky about the type of work it takes on. Most fruit and vegetable pickers are now brought in from former Eastern European Bloc countries.

That's not to say you won't be able to get paid help, though it will come at a price. High living costs apply to Irish people too and a daily "treasure" will expect at least the minimum adult wage of approximately $8.50 an hour, though you'll certainly not get anybody to work for that sum in Dublin. In countryside areas, persuading a man to come and dig the garden or paint the house will cost at least $60 a day plus materials. If it's a case of occasional help to mow the lawn or weed the flower beds, you should be able to find plenty of willing schoolboys available for weekend and holiday work at around $6 per hour.

Even if you plan to rent rather than buy a property, the cost of furnishings is something you may need to budget for. Although holiday lets and student accommodation almost always have the basics, not all Irish houses for long-term rental are furnished. It isn't possible to rent furniture, though many newer properties will have fitted kitchens and built-in wardrobes. Those on tight budgets should check out local auctions where you can often pick up some great furniture bargains.

If you're buying new, a selection of branded electrical items taken from larger stores is as follows and all prices include VAT:

- Zanussi refrigerator freezer, 4.9 cubic feet: €300 ($372)
- Zanussi 9.8-cubic-foot chest freezer: €380 ($471)
- Tricity Bendix dishwasher: €379 ($470)
- Bosch washing machine: €449 ($557)
- Sharp microwave: €100 ($124)
- Sony 32-inch wide-screen TV: €1,000 ($1,240)
- Electrolux vacuum cleaner: €130 ($161)

- Morphy Richards toaster: €35 ($43)
- Sony DVD recorder: €430 ($533)
- Morphy Richards food processor: €200 ($248)
- Electrolux single-oven cooker: €400 ($496)
- Zanussi tumble dryer: €260 ($322)

It's not worth bringing electrical items with you as the voltage system here is different: 230 volt AC 50 Hz. Plugs are normally of the flat three-pin variety. For the moment, TVs operate on the 625-line PAL system, although the expected digital explosion will bring myriad changes. Don't bring VCR tapes either as they will be incompatible with Ireland's VHS system.

LIGHT AND HEAT

Electricity is supplied by the ESB—the acronym stands for the Electricity Supply Board. Bills arrive every two months and each will include a standing charge of €10.57 and a "public service obligations levy" of €1.92 ($2.38). That's €74.94 ($93) per year even before you've used any electricity. Costs obviously depend upon usage, but estimate around $2,000 annually for a typical cottage. Including VAT of 13.5 percent, my own bills for the November–December, January–February, and March–April periods were €196 ($243), €403 ($500), and €234 ($290) respectively. This covered lighting and the usual electrical items as well as heating.

Natural gas is available only in Dublin and along parts of the east and southern coasts. The rest of the country uses bottled butane gas. Bottles are sold by most supermarkets, village shops, hardware stores, and garages—the price is €20–22 ($24.80–27.30). I use a gas cooker, and a bottle of gas lasts me 5–6 weeks.

If you want a peat (turf) fire, there are two methods. The easy way is to buy bales of peat briquettes, which are again sold by most general stores. They cost around $3.20 per bale, which should be sufficient for a roaring blaze in the sitting room all evening. The alternative is to rent a patch of bog from a farmer during summer and cut and dry your own turf. Believe me, it is filthy, backbreaking work and you'll probably try it only once. Costs depend upon the quality of the turf: I paid around $170 for a supply that lasted most of the winter.

Coal is mostly Texan or Polish. Ireland's coal mines have all closed down, for they yielded only low-grade "brown" coal suitable for industrial use. Twenty-five kilos of smokeless coal for domestic fires costs around $13.65. Like peat, coal can also be used in old-fashioned kitchen ranges, many of which provide hot water as well as cooking facilities.

Banking

Opening a bank account in Ireland is straightforward. There are no exchange controls and no limit on the amount of money you can bring into or take out of the country. If you are buying property, it will be important to have funds transferred as soon as possible. Even if you've chosen to rent a home, you'll almost certainly want to have a current account with a bank near the town where you plan to live. It can be used in conjunction with a cash card, which acts as a check guarantee card and allows holders to draw funds from ATMs (automated teller machines). Through a current account, you can also arrange standing orders to pay off regular bills such as electricity and telephone.

When opening an account, all banks ask you to show a passport or some other form of identification. This is to comply with government legislation (Criminal Justice Act 1994) that was introduced to prevent criminal organizations and drug dealers from using Irish banks as laundry baskets.

The two largest retail banks are Allied Irish Bank (AIB) and Bank of Ireland; both have branches in even the smaller towns. Larger places also usually have branches of National Irish Bank, Ulster Bank, TSB, Irish Permanent, and First Active.

It should come as no surprise to find that banks are out to profit from their customers and most transactions attract charges. All banks apply similar charging structures and their fees shouldn't be a worrying sum for the average spender. On my own recent bank statement, quarterly fees amounted to just over $13.

CURRENCY

Ireland is one of the European member states that replaced its national currency (the Irish punt) with a single shared currency, the euro, on January 1, 2002. The euro (symbol: EUR or €) is divided into 100 cents (1 cent = €0.01). You can now use your Irish notes and coins in 11 other countries—there is no need to change currency. Euro coin and banknote denominations are as follows:

- Bronze-colored metal coins: 1 cent, 2 cents, 5 cents
- Gold-colored metal coins: 10 cents, 20 cents, 50 cents
- Bimetal coins: €1, €2
- Banknotes: €5, €10, €20, €50, €100, €200, €500

Coins have one side common to all 12 countries in the Euro-zone and one side specific to each issuer country. (The other participating countries at this moment are Belgium, Holland, Luxembourg, Germany, Austria, Greece, Ireland, Italy, Spain, Portugal, and Finland.) The common side shows a European map and the denomination of the coin. The country-specific side of Irish coins shows the word Eire plus the national symbol of the harp.

Euro banknotes are identical throughout the Euro Zone and depict architectural styles throughout European history, from ancient on €5 notes to modern on the €500 notes. The designs are allegories of openness (gateways on the face side) and union between peoples (bridges on the reverse side). Dominant colors are €5—gray; €10—red; €20—blue; €50—orange; €100—green; €200—yellow; €500—violet.

At the time of writing, the exchange rate against the dollar was €1 = $1.24.

CREDIT CARDS

Visa and/or MasterCard are probably the most useful credit cards to have in Ireland. Although American Express and Diners Club cards are accepted in many shops, hotels, gas stations, and supermarkets, they're not nearly as commonly accepted as Visa or MasterCard.

They're undoubtedly convenient, but having a full deck of credit cards will cost you dearly in Ireland. With tax revenue falling during the recent economic slowdown, the government decided to boost its income by imposing an annual tax (for each credit card held) of €40 ($49.60). Interest rates are high too. One of the most competitive is MBNA, which has an interest rate of 16.9 percent APR (variable) on its standard Visa card and 14.9 percent on its gold Visa card. With Bank of Ireland, interest rate on the standard MasterCard/Visa is 18.8 percent.

Taxes

IRISH TAXES

The question of taxation is horrendously complicated and much will depend on your personal circumstances. For instance, are you planning to become a permanent resident or just spend the summers in Ireland? Are you contemplating self-employment or simply planning to enjoy a well-earned retirement? Do you intend trading on the Irish stock market? The list of financial activities that can result in having to take care of a tax liability is extensive, but the basic rule is that *all* income arising from Irish sources is subject to Irish income tax. That's unless you are an artist or writer—Ireland can be a wonderful financial haven for creative types as royalties and sales of works considered worthy of artistic or literary merit are tax-exempt.

As regards income from sources outside Ireland, the state has a double taxation agreement with a number of countries, including the United States. In essence, this ensures that you'll not be taxed twice on the same income, such as monies from a company or social security pension (which can be paid to you in Ireland). You'll receive a credit to cover the tax that's already been paid in your country of origin, which you must produce when submitting tax returns within Ireland. Citizens of the United States will obviously have to obtain this proof from the Internal Revenue Service.

To be classed as a resident for tax purposes within Ireland, you need to spend 183 days in the state during a tax year. Spend fewer than 183 days in Ireland and the revenue commissioners deem you to be a visitor and no part of your income from non-Irish sources is subject to personal taxation. If a visit falls across two separate tax years, the number of days for tax residency purposes is 280.

For more extensive information on the tax residency laws, contact the revenue commissioners. A useful free booklet is "RES 1," which details the tax liabilities of foreigners living in Ireland.

Income tax provides around 38 percent of the government's total tax revenues. The system covers PAYE (pay as you earn), which employers are obliged to deduct from workers' salaries and also includes self-assessment. In both cases, everyone is entitled to certain allowances and reliefs and people whose income falls below a certain level aren't taxed at all. Current income tax exemption rates for individuals are €5,210 ($6,460) for those under the age of 65. For married couples the exemption rate is doubled. Thus, couples who are both aged under 65 are allowed an income of \$12,920 before they start paying tax.

After allowances have been deducted, the rates on taxable income for single people are 20 percent for the first €28,000 (\$34,720) of earnings and 42 percent on the remainder. A 42 percent top rate of tax may seem shocking, but it has come down from the 65 percent levels of the 1980s. One-parent families are allowed to earn €32,000 (\$39,680) before entering the top-rate tax band; a married couple with only one income, €37,000 (\$45,880).

If applicable, you can also claim relief on things such as mortgage interest repayments, health insurance premiums, charitable donations. and, if in employment, contributions to pension schemes.

Unless you become self-employed or find paid employment within Ireland, PRSI (Pay Related Social Insurance) contributions won't apply. The PRSI tax is an additional tax on wage-earners that goes toward state contributory pensions, unemployment benefits, disability allowances, and so on. The PSRI system is complex with differing levy rates, but most workers pay 6 percent on their weekly incomes. Again, you can obtain more information from the revenue commissioners.

The rate of capital gains tax (CGT) stands at 20 percent with an annual exemption of just over €1,270 (\$1575) per individual. Investments that may attract capital gains tax include directly held equities, bonds, and certain types of property. The sale of the principal family home is exempt from CGT, as are lottery winnings and bets.

Capital acquisitions tax (CAT), probate tax, and inheritance planning are a minefield for the layperson. If you have substantial assets, it's vital to discuss the subject with a solicitor or a financial adviser who specializes in inheritance laws. While the revenue commissioners do produce guidance on these taxes, the language is arcane and blood relationships are subject to all kinds of provisos. The situation is especially tricky for cohabiters who are deemed "strangers in law" in the matter of inheritance rights.

CAPITAL ACQUISITIONS TAX (CAT)

Capital aquisitions tax covers both gifts and inheritances. The rate of CAT is 20 percent. Apart from tax-free thresholds, there are a number of important exemptions and reliefs. These are:

• The first €3,000 of gifts received by a donee from any one donor in a calendar year

- Gifts and inheritances between spouses is exempt from CAT
- A gift or inheritance consisting of a house that is the only/main residence of the beneficiary is, subject to certain conditions, exempt from CAT
- Gifts or inheritances for public/charitable purposes

If you die intestate (without making a will), your estate gets divided according to guidelines in what's termed the Succession Act. Although not everybody feels comfortable about making a will, it's the only way of ensuring your wishes will be carried out. A straightforward will costs in the region of $200; details of solicitors in your own locality can be had from citizens' advice bureaus, law centers, or the Law Society of Ireland.

AMERICAN TAXES

As a U.S. citizen resident in Ireland, the bad news is that you will still have a legal obligation to file U.S. tax returns annually on your worldwide income. It can be a complex issue, and if you are in any doubt at all about your tax liability, you should seek the advice of a global tax expert.

Basically, if you are a full-time resident in Ireland for a full calendar year, or you live here for 330 days out of any consecutive 12-month period, then the good news is that you can exclude up to $80,000 of earned income from U.S. income taxation. If you are married, and both of you earn income and live here, you can also exclude up to another $80,000 of your spouse's income from taxation. These exclusions can be claimed only by filing tax return Form 2555, and they are not automatic if you fail to file your Form 1040 for the year it applies. You may also be able to claim an additional exclusion or deduction for your Irish housing expenses.

More bad news is in store if you are self-employed. Unfortunately the foreign-earned income exclusion does not apply to the U.S. self-employment tax. This means that if you have your own business overseas or are an independent contractor, you will still be required to pay self-employment tax on your net earnings. You will need to file a Schedule C with your U.S. tax return and pay any due self-employment tax. Net earnings are income after all your legal business expenses have been deducted and must include the income earned both in Ireland and the United States.

The deadline for the April filing can be extended for either two or four months. You will be allowed the two-month extension if on the regular due date of your return you are living outside of the United States and your main place of business is outside the United States. You need to attach a statement to your return to that effect to qualify for the extension. For the four-month extension, you will need to file Form 4868 with your return.

Investing

Although Ireland's economy has turned in a stellar performance in recent years, relatively few outsiders associate the Emerald Isle with major profits and prosperity. Yet for the last decade, this has been one of Europe's fastest-growing economies, recording double-digit growth figures in the late 1990s. The pace slowed in the last two years, but estimates issued by the Irish Economic and Social Research Institute predicted that the average percentage GNP growth for 2005 would be 4.7 percent.

Although Ireland's economy has turned in a stellar performance in recent years, relatively few outsiders associate the Emerald Isle with major profits and prosperity.

Since joining the EU, the structure of the Irish economy has experienced dramatic changes. During the late 1980s and throughout the 1990s, the manufacturing sector came to be dominated by information technology companies, many foreign-owned. Consequently Ireland's fortunes are entwined with what happens in the rest of the world.

INVESTMENT OPTIONS

A thriving economy goes hand in hand with rising house values and as is pointed out in the property sections of the book, the Dublin housing market has delivered huge windfalls for property investors who got in on its recent soar-away act. Can these massive rises continue? Isn't the bubble going to burst? Well, the pundits have been asking those questions for the last five years, but my own view is that buying Dublin property solely for its investment potential is only for the brave.

However, with deposit interest rates likely to remain low, you may be looking for a more rewarding investment than what is on offer through high-street savings institutions. An obvious alternative is the stock market, which has the potential to offer greater returns.

Irish Stock Market

New York has the Dow Jones, London has the FTSE, Paris has the CAC-40, and Dublin has the ISEQ. The base figure for the ISEQ Index is 1,000, which was set on January 4, 1988.

Ireland's Top 10 Companies

The website of the Irish stock exchange, www.ise.ie, contains stock prices and summaries of business news from publicly traded Irish companies. Based on market capitalization on November 30, 2004, Ireland's top 10 companies were as follows:

Company	Value in Euros (Millions)	Sector
Allied Irish Banks PLC	12,662	Banks
Bank of Ireland	11,094	Banks
C R H PLC	10,084	Building materials
Elan Corporation PLC	7,672	Pharmaceuticals
Anglo Irish Bank Corporation PLC	5,701	Banks
Ryanair Holdings PLC	3,839	Airlines
Irish Life And Permanent	3,503	Banking and insurance
Kerry Group Plc	3,211	Food
Independent News and Media PLC	1,656	Newspapers and media
Grafton Group PLC	1,623	Building materials

The Irish index, in common with stock markets globally, has fallen back considerably in the past few years. However, there was a partial recovery in 2003, and at the time of writing the index stood at 6,166, an increase of 25.3 percent since the beginning of the year.

Over the long term, equities have outperformed other types of investments such as property, bonds, and savings accounts. However, nothing can ever be taken for granted and you should always remember that shares can go down as well as up.

HOW TO INVEST

There are a number of ways to buy Irish equities. The first, direct investment in a company, is when a stockbroker buys a designated amount of shares on your behalf. As most Irish stockbrokers also deal on the London market, you're not necessarily limited to the small amount of stocks that make up Dublin's ISEQ Index. Indeed, some home-grown companies have bypassed the Irish marketplace completely and gone instead for a sole London listing.

Dealing costs vary widely. Any transaction, no matter how small, costs a minimum of €32 ($40) in commission fees if done through any branch of the Allied Irish Bank, which has its own stockbroking arm. On the other hand, if you choose an execution-only broker, dealing costs can be less expensive. The brokerage company I use is Fexcom which charges commission fees of €25 ($31) on deals of up to €2,000 ($2,480). There are a number of other Dublin-based stockbrokers who welcome small investors.

Despite the risk factor of equities, the government also takes a bite out of your investment. Stamp duty is 1 percent and so on a $2,000 deal you pay tax equivalent to $20. When selling shares, you'll be subject to capital gains tax (CGT) on any profits made. Current rate of personal CGT is 20 percent, but you're allowed an annual allowance of €1,270 ($1,575) before paying tax. If you've made losses on other shareholdings during the tax year, these can be offset against a CGT bill. More tax is due if a company pays shareholders dividends—either 20 percent or 42 percent, depending on your income tax bracket.

SPREADING THE RISK

An alternative to direct-equity investment is pooled investments. You may already be clued in to these by holding U.S. mutual funds. In Ireland, mutual funds are called unit trusts and unit-linked funds. The money paid in by investors is pooled together in units in the investment company's assets, which can include property, equities, and government gilts (see *Gilts and Bonds* section) from both Ireland and overseas. With these types of investments, the tax liability on profits is paid by the investment fund and you won't have to meet a personal CGT bill. In general, banks, building societies, and life assurance companies sell pooled investments. Some funds concentrate solely on holding Irish assets while others hold baskets of British, continental European, or worldwide stocks.

Although most life assurance companies have a minimum level of €2,000–5,000 ($2,480–6,600) for investors looking to stash away a lump sum in unit-linked funds, Bank of Ireland and Allied Irish Bank also have plans whereby you can make minimum monthly investments of €100 ($124 per month minimum). This is a good way to invest for the long term because if the stock market heads south, your monthly investment buys more units. Recommended holding term is seven years at least, but there's nothing to stop you cashing in units earlier.

Seeking the right product in what can seem a bewildering financial maze does take time. One of the most tax-efficient packages on offer is a PIP: a personal investment plan. Similar to a unit trust in that it holds a broad mix of stocks, you can realize greater profits with a PIP because the fund pays a lower 10 percent rate of tax on profits. To qualify for this special tax rate, at least 55 percent of the fund has to be invested in Irish equities, 10 percent of which must be in stock of developing companies. Again, you can alleviate the horror of finding you've put a lump sum into a plunging stock market by making monthly investments: €75 ($93) per month minimum with Allied Irish Banks and €60 ($75) per month minimum with the Educational Building Society (EBS).

TRACKER BONDS

Another type of stock market–related investment is a tracker bond. Most (but not all) trackers carry a two-pronged guarantee, the most important being that your original capital is returned after the set term of the investment. Any guarantee on profits depends on the rising of the index (or indices) that the bond is "tracking" —should the chosen stock market commit suicide, at least you get your money back. However, capital isn't always guaranteed, so make sure you know what you're getting into before investing. The term of a bond can be from 18 months to 5.5 years and will be linked to the performance of one or more of the world's bourses (stock exchanges) such as the DAX Index in Frankfurt or the FTSE 100 in London. Again, all major banks and assurance companies market tracker bonds.

GILTS AND BONDS

Government gilts and bonds are another kind of investment product that can be bought by individuals. A bond is a fixed-interest investment. Basically it's a certificate of debt issued by the government or a company guaranteeing repayment of the original investment plus interest by a specified future date.

Gilts are issued by the government and offer a fixed-interest payment twice yearly, with your money back at the end of the investment term. They are traded in a similar fashion to shares, and the price can fluctuate daily, thus affecting the effective return. Contact a broker for more information on these.

Cill - Dá - lua, An P
KILLALOE
POST

Communications

Forget all those old jokes about the pony express and pigeon post. Ireland has a modern and efficient communications system, with lots of cell phone options, broadband, etc. The media includes many regional radio and TV stations including satellite and cable TV.

Telephone Service

A telephone will be indispensable to most homeowners. The republic's major domestic service is provided by Eircom, a former state-owned company with one of the world's most up-to-date digital systems. Like most former monopolies it's fairly expensive, but deregulation in telecoms is opening the market to competition.

Nowadays Eircom rarely takes longer than seven days to install a telephone. Costs of connection depend upon whether it's a first-time installation or if the line is already in place. If you are an existing customer moving house, the reconnection service is free. A first-time connection is charged at €130 ($161)—this includes both line connection and a telephone set with features such as call-waiting and three-way calling. Prices include VAT sales tax.

There are 18 telesales centers around the country—simply dial 1901 within Ireland for more information about getting connected.

Bills arrive at two-monthly intervals, each one carrying a line charge of €44.18—approximately $55. That's $330 per year before you've even made a single call. And I'm afraid there's some more unwelcome news—Ireland doesn't have any such thing as a free call. Unlike in the United States, gossiping to new friends and neighbors down the road will come at a cost. The number of units used determines actual cost of calls. Each unit buys a certain amount of time—how much depends upon the time of day, whether it's a weekday or a weekend, and also the destination of the call. Prices have come down in recent months, and for some strange reason it's cheaper to phone North America than Europe. Calls at different times of the day from private phones are charged by the following method:

• Calls within Ireland are charged by the minute. Local rates are daytime $.061; evening $.015; weekend $.015. Rates for national calls are daytime $.103; evening $.061; weekend $.015. Calls *to* Irish cell phones vary according to the network you are calling. Rates run daytime $.28–.36; evening $.22–.24; weekend $.14–.19.

• International calls are also charged by the minute. Rates to the United States and Canada are daytime $.24; evening $.19; weekend $.19. Rates to Britain are daytime $.19; evening $.18; weekend $.15. Rates to near Europe are $.30 anytime.

British Telecom, in partnership with ESAT, entered the Irish market within the last few years and is now providing some welcome competition to Eircom. Its charge for a call to the United States or Canada is approximately $.10 per minute anytime.

First-time connection fee with EsatBT is €130 (approximately $161).

There has also been an avalanche of new telephone resellers appearing on the market. Each offers a bewildering array of packages that can cut the cost of your telephone bill. You will not have to go looking for these servers; regular mail in your post will let you know they are there. Using these call suppliers means having to first dial a prefix code and then your telephone number.

How to Make Calls

Within Ireland, telephone numbers are quoted with subscriber trunk dialing (STD) codes given first in brackets. These are the equivalent of area codes. For example, the STD code for Dublin is 01; for Galway it's 091. Say you were in Dublin and wished to call Galway's tourist office (tel. 091/537700). The digits given are those you would dial. If, however, you were calling from within Galway itself, simply ring 537700.

When phoning from the United States, you first need to dial the international access code (011) followed by the country code for Ireland (353). And although Galway's STD code is 091, that initial "0" is dropped when phoning from abroad. Thus, to reach Galway's tourist office, dial 011-353-91/537700.

As another example, say you want to call the Revenue Commissioners at Dublin Castle (tel. 01/878-0000). That's the number you call if phoning on an Irish phone from outside Dublin. Within Dublin you would ring 878-0000. If calling from the United States, you would dial 011-353-1/878-0000.

To call the United States from Ireland, first dial the access code (00), followed by the country code (1), followed by the area code and then the local number. The Irish Embassy's number in Washington, DC, is tel. 202/462 3939. To call from Ireland, dial 00-1-202/462-3939.

Public Phone Boxes

Making international calls from public pay phones can be very costly. Charges, per minute, to the United States and Canada are $1.76 per minute anytime. Making a call to Hong Kong or Japan would cost $2.48 per minute.

Public pay phones accept either coins or calling cards, which are sold at post offices, petrol stations, newsagents, and most grocery stores. Calling cards are available in units of 50 ($6.20); 70 ($8.68); 100 ($12.40); 150 ($18.60); and 200 ($24.80). Pay-phone units are charged at different rates depending on whether a coin phone or card phone is used. A $.20 coin buys a two-minute local call but the cost is fractionally reduced if using a 50-unit calling card.

Emergency Calls

In an emergency, dial either 999 or 112. Calls are free and you must ask the operator for the service you want: fire brigade, *Gardaí* (police), ambulance, lifeboat, or mountain rescue. When the emergency service answers, state the address or location where help is required.

CELLULAR PHONES

The number of people who own a cell (mobile) phone in Ireland is estimated at 3.5 million. The Irish commission for communications regulation (COMREG) reported recently that the percentage of Irish people who use cell phones rose to 89 percent by the middle of 2004. It gives the average spent by mobile-phone users in Ireland as €47 ($58) per month.

Cell phones range in price from $12 to more than $200 when you buy a "prepay" phone or commit to a yearly contract. Buying a phone (SIM Free) without a prepay or monthly contract is likely to cost from $200 to more than $520.

There are three cell-phone networks in Ireland operated by Vodafone, O2, and Meteor. All three operators offer the choice of connecting to their networks through either a yearly subscription or a prepaid package. Prepaid packages would suit individuals who would rarely use a cell phone. With outlets nationwide, it is easy to buy call credit as and when you need it. Subscriptions are generally for a year and vary significantly depending on the network and package chosen.

The Irish commission for communications regulation (COMREG) reported recently that the percentage of Irish people who use cell phones rose to 89 percent by the middle of 2004.

All three networks claim to cover roughly 98 percent of the population and have roaming agreements with more than 100 countries, including the United States. Sounds good, but population isn't territory and mountains tend to have an unfortunate effect on mobile phone transmissions. Technology meets its match in west Kerry, Connemara, and parts of Donegal. You may even encounter problems around Dublin because of the Wicklow Mountains.

Analog cellular phones will not work in Ireland. Dual-mode digital GSM phones that support 900MHz will work. You will need a SIM card from a network that has a roaming agreement with an Irish network.

Meteor

With 6 percent of the market, Meteor is the smallest network operator. It offers a choice of "pay later" 12-month contracts. The cheapest has a monthly charge of €25 ($31). Included in that price is 75 minutes of "free talk time" and 75 free text messages.

Calls to other Meteor numbers through its prepaid service cost $.20 per minute anytime. Calling the United States or Canada would set you back €.50 ($.62) per minute anytime.

O2

O2 accounts for about 40 percent of the mobile market in Ireland. There is a choice of three subscription packages with this operator. Choosing the option with the lowest subscription charge will cost you €15 per month. Calls with this choice cost:

- $.19 per minute (off peak) to other O2 or fixed-line numbers
- $.37 per minute (off peak) to Meteor/Vodafone numbers
- $.62 per minute at peak times to any mobile network or fixed line in Ireland
- $1.14 per minute to the United States or Canada at peak times

The cost of calls reduces should you choose a higher monthly subscription.

There are two options with prepaid call credit on the O2 network. Depending on when you are most likely to use your cell phone, you can choose from a daytime-option price plan, "Early Bird" (7 A.M.–5 P.M.), or an evening plan, "Night Owl" (6 P.M.–7 A.M.). Making calls within the time frame you choose will cost:

- $.15 per minute to any Irish mobile or fixed-line number—weekends
- $.78 per minute to Vodafone/Meteor numbers—weekdays (6 P.M.– 2 A.M.)
- $.68 per minute to O2 mobiles or fixed-line numbers—weekdays
- $1.49 per minute to the United States or Canada—calling them on your prepaid mobile would be very expensive

Vodafone

The most popular network in Ireland with 54 percent of the market, Vodafone has six pay-monthly options. At the "light user" end of the scale, €20 ($24.80) monthly includes 50 minutes of free off-peak call time. Using this plan, calls cost:

- $.19 per minute (off peak) to other Vodafone or fixed-line numbers
- $.38 per minute (off peak) to other Irish mobile networks
- $.38 per minute (peak) to other Vodafone numbers
- $.62 per minute (peak) to other mobile network or fixed-line in Ireland
- $.95–1.14 to the United States and Canada, depending on the time you call

As with its competitors, a higher monthly subscription gives you reduced rates and more "free" or inclusive call time. Vodafone also gives you the option of choosing a prepaid or "ready to go" service. Call rates with this choice are:

- $.19 per minute (off peak) to Vodafone or Irish fixed-line numbers
- $.38 per minute (off peak) to other Irish mobile network numbers
- $.62 per minute (peak) to Vodafone or Irish fixed-line numbers
- $.81 per minute (peak) to other Irish mobile network numbers

Email and Postal Service

INTERNET ACCESS

Ireland has a reasonable choice of service providers if you need to be connected to the Internet. You can choose between free- or subscription-paid service providers. Free-service providers are popular with experienced users and individuals who use the Internet purely for email. Most free servers will let you have more than one email address, although not all will allow you free web space.

All of the free-service providers now offer unlimited access through local call numbers, which basically means that your only outlay is for the cost of a local telephone call. The disadvantages of using free-service providers are speed and access. Connection is via a standard modem and you will sometimes fail to connect because lines are busy. If you're willing to pay for premium services, basic yearly subscriptions start at around €183 ($227). As with the free service, access is unlimited although you will still have to pay for the cost of a local telephone call. Most subscription services offer technical support (at local call rates), additional email addresses, and free web space of between 50 and 100 megabytes.

Broadband Access

Ireland's largest Telecoms operator, Eircom is continuing to introduce broadband access to different areas of the country. The advantages of broadband access are:

• Download speeds that are about 30 times faster than normal modems
• A permanent connection to your service provider, so you don't need to "dial up" each time you want to connect
• Voice and data together—you can surf the net and make/receive call at the same time

Broadband access is more expensive. Monthly subscription rates through Ireland On-Line (IOL) start at €39 ($48.50) with Eircom packages starting at €40 ($49.60).

If you must have broadband access but live in a rural area that does not have the coverage, you can connect via satellite. Digiweb offers a service that is totally independent of your telephone line. Having an "always-on" Internet connection by this method does not come cheaply. The monthly fee is €99 ($122.80).

If you don't own a computer, you can log on to the Internet at some public libraries or in one of the growing number of cybercafés. Charges are around $5.50 per hour, though in some cases there's limited free access if you become a library member. You'll now find cybercafés in most sizeable Irish towns too.

POST OFFICES AND COURIERS

Ireland's state-owned postal service is run by An Post. According to its own figures, more than 560 million letters are delivered annually with more than 87 percent achieving next-day delivery. Main post offices generally are open 8:30 A.M.–5:30 P.M. on weekdays; 9 A.M.–noon on Saturdays. Along with handling mail, they pay out state pensions and unemployment benefits; sell TV licenses, lottery tickets, and prize bonds; stock travel pass and passport application forms; operate currency-exchange facilities and various savings schemes.

Village post offices don't offer as extensive a range of services and most close for lunch. However, as the local post office is often the village grocery store too, it's usually possible to buy stamps after the mail counter has officially closed. To catch the last post you'll need to check locally as every postbox has its own particular collection time.

Within Ireland itself, postcards and standard letters under 100 grams cost an equivalent of $.60 to mail. Heavier items are charged by weight. A flat package weighing 250 grams–500 grams costs $1.79; a two-kilogram package $8.10.

Airmail deliveries to the United States generally take 5–7 days. Letters under 50 grams cost $.81 and are again then scaled by weight. A 250-gram package costs $4.35; a 900 gram package $12.40. Economy surface rates are far cheaper than airmail and that same 900-gram package costs only $9.92. The major drawback is that it could take as long as 15 weeks to reach its destination.

If posting important documents or valuables within Ireland, you can send them by basic registered mail for an additional fee. There are four minimum rates for letters/large envelopes: $4.84, $5.46, $6.63, and $9.30, with the cost depending on weight. A two-kilogram package costs a minimum of $11.78 to register. Should a package get lost, you can claim compensation of up to €320 ($397). You can buy extra insurance for more valuable packages. It's also possible to register mail destined for the United States but the maximum compensation allowed falls to a paltry €35 ($43.40).

A Poste Restante service allows visitors to have mail sent to a local post office. It's free and can be availed of for up to three months. You can also rent a private box number at head post offices, delivery depots, and certain other post offices around the country. In towns, An Post charges €220 ($273) per annum for letters, €440 ($546) to include parcels as well.

Most major international courier services are represented in Ireland and have collection depots around the country. Quotes for sending a one-kilo (2.2-pound) document package to the United States were $65 with FedEx and $80 with DHL. However, I've found the cheapest to be SDS—$54 for the same weight package—and you can hand over packages at main post offices. For local offices look under "Courier Services" in the telephone directory's Golden Pages.

Media

NEWSPAPERS AND MAGAZINES

The republic's two main broadsheet dailies are the *Irish Times* and the *Irish Independent;* both cost €1.50 ($1.86). The *Irish Times* has quite a serious outlook, while the *Irish Independent* carries more gossipy lifestyle features. Both have good business coverage and special weekly property supplements (Thursdays for the *Times,* Fridays for the *Independent.*)

Published in Cork, the *Examiner* is another daily but its sale is not that widespread outside the southern half of the republic. If your taste runs to tabloids, there are special Irish versions of British dailies such as the *Sun, Mirror,* and *Star.* All carry a relentless cavalcade of celebrity gossip and scandal and not very much in the way of news.

On Sundays you can choose from the *Sunday Independent, Sunday Business Post, Tribune,* and an Irish edition of Britain's *Sunday Times.* The *Sunday World* is rather more down-market and celebrity-oriented but it's undeniably popular. There are also a substantial number of provincial newspapers, which are published on a weekly basis and concentrate mainly on local issues and events.

As far as U.S. publications are concerned, *Time, Newsweek,* and the *International Herald Tribune* are usually on sale in larger newsagents. If you want regular copies, your local newsagent will be able to order them for you. Don't, however, expect to get any papers or magazines through your letterbox—Ireland doesn't have newspaper delivery boys and girls.

> *One of the best reads for potential new residents is a quarterly subscription magazine,* Inside Ireland. *Most of its readership is American and it contains lots of valuable practical advice along with quirky features and lifestyle articles by folks who have already bought a home here.*

Many of Ireland's local newspapers are flown out to U.S. cities with sizable populations of Irish-Americans. You'll certainly be able to buy the *Sligo Champion* or the *Longford Leader* in New York and Boston. It's also worth looking at magazines such as *World of Hibernia* or *Ireland of the Welcomes,* both of which carry plenty of travel and general-interest features.

One of the best reads for potential new residents is a quarterly subscription magazine, *Inside Ireland.* Most of its readership is American and it contains lots of valuable practical advice along with quirky features and

Ireland on the Web

For those who already have computers with an Internet connection, there's an amazing amount of information available on all things Irish. For example, ask a search engine to come up with details on Irish travel and you'll be overwhelmed with a choice of thousands of sites varying from corporate golfing holidays to cottages for rent in County Clare. Many Irish-interest websites are actually based in the United States but there are some interesting homegrown ones too. Have a browse around some of these:

www.irlgov.ie
The Irish government's official website with links to various departments such as Foreign Affairs, Health, Justice, the Revenue Commissioners, and so on. Although visiting the taxman isn't exactly an entertaining experience, you can download comprehensive files on everything from vehicle registration tax to self-employment requirements.

www.luminarium.org/my thology/ireland
An absolutely fascinating site of myth, folklore, and stories containing heaps of esoteric material. Did you know that *caisean uchad* was a kind of Celtic pass-the-parcel game in which a burning sheep's head was passed around a group of revelers?

www.mayo-ireland.ie
Here you'll find Comhaltas Ceoltori Éireann, Ireland's main organization for keeping the flame of traditional culture alight. Plenty of information on festivals, music teaching, music publications, and local branches.

www.ceolas.org
Another Irish music site with sound clips and a wealth of information on traditional music and dance.

www.macnas.com
All about Galway's community-based arts and street theater group with clips of the annual madcap parade during Arts Week.

www.iavi.ie
Real estate through members of the Irish Auctioneers and Valuers Institute. Some members are better at keeping their listings up-to-date than others, but it's a good indication of countrywide property and prices. You'll find everything from cottages to farmhouses, pubs to hotels, Georgian mansions to urban apartments.

www.ireland.travel.ie
The official site of Bord Fáilte, the Irish Tourist Board. All the basic need-to-know information about hotels, restaurants, sights to see, and things to do. Plus, if you're seeking a special-interest vacation, check out its searchable database. It came up with 148 suggestions for an equestrian holiday.

www.irish-times.com, www. ireland.com
All the daily news and views from one of Ireland's top broadsheet newspapers. The site includes a genealogical gateway where you can discover the history behind many Irish sur-

names or embark upon a search for your own Irish ancestors.

www.finfacts.ie
Extremely useful site for current information on economic indicators, savings options, best airfares, and so on.

www.hookemacdonald.ie
If you're looking for a house or apartment to rent in the Dublin area, check out Hooke and MacDonald's "Let on the Net" site. When I looked it had a good range of available properties, including a furnished one-bedroom apartment in the Rathmines area for $950 per month.

www.wow.ie
WOW means What's on Where. If you want nationwide listings for films, music, theater, and gallery openings throughout Ireland, this site should fit the bill.

www.jesuit.ie
Need some spiritual guidance? Although not everyone will want to pray in front of a computer screen, Ireland's Jesuit priests are now o-line. Their website includes a "Sacred Space" with a daily prayer.

www.nationalarchives.ie
Ireland's National Archives now has a searchable database. It includes the Ireland-Australia transportation index, complete with names, trial dates, and crime descriptions. I discovered numerous Harvey namesakes who made the journey "down under" on convict ships. In 1838, an unfortunate 22-year-old named Thomas Harvey from Louth was sentenced to seven years' transportation for stealing a plate.

www.rte.ie
Up-to-date Irish news, radio programs, plus daily TV and radio listings from RTE, the state-owned broadcaster.

http://foxleap.fortunecity.com/irishlyrics
Who will plow the fields all day and who will thresh the corn? That's the first line of "The Bantry Girl's Lament." Or maybe you want to know the words to "The Wild Colonial Boy"? You'll find the lyrics to more than 100 traditional Irish folk songs here.

www.iha.ie
Irish racehorses—an investment or a gamble? Run by the Irish Horseracing Authority, this is an informative site for those who want to buy a thoroughbred or simply check out the fixture list calendar for race meetings.

www.golfclubireland.com
Golf enthusiasts will want to experience the rub of the Irish green. This site includes pars for various Irish golf courses, green fees, club memberships, and much more besides.

www.ostlan.com
Go to Ostlan for a guide to pubs and restaurants. The site includes a review section—you can write your own review or see what previous happy (and disgruntled) diners have said about Irish establishments.

lifestyle articles by folks who have already bought a home here. You can obtain a free sample copy by email through the website.

TELEVISION AND RADIO

The public television service consists of RTE 1, RTE 2, and an Irish-language station, TG4. An independent station, TV3, also broadcasts. Home-produced programs that are very popular include *Fair City,* a soap opera about Dublin families, and *The Late, Late Show,* claimed to be the world's longest-running chat show. Many other programs (around 60 percent of output) are brought in from Britain, Australia, and the United States, so if you're pining for familiar fare, you'll be able to keep up with what's happening with the Simpsons, who's chatting with Oprah, and even tune in to the U.S. Masters golf tournament.

Sports coverage on public TV is good—although you'll rarely catch baseball, there's more than enough Gaelic games, soccer, golf, tennis, snooker, horse racing, and Formula One to keep even the most fanatical sports addict satisfied. If you want live North American sports, there are cable TV and satellite channels such as Sky and NTL. Through Sky Digital or NTL cable you will be able to subscribe to NASN, the North American Sports Channel (www.nasn.com). The subscription rate for this channel is €15.99 ($19.83) per month, with a one-time connection fee of €6 ($7.44).

An important point to note is that you need a license to watch TV. It costs €152.00 ($188) annually and you obtain one from the post office. If a detector van comes around and you cannot produce a license, you will be taken to court and fined as much as €634 ($786) for a first offense. The money garnered from license-payers goes to fund the making of RTE programs.

Ireland's three national radio stations are supplemented by a plethora of independent regional stations. Like everywhere else in the Western world, some offer wall-to-wall pop, others a mix of music, chat, and phone-ins. One of the most entertaining phone-in programs, on which everything and anything is up for discussion, is the *Gerry Ryan Show.* It is broadcast on weekdays 9 A.M.–noon on RTE 2FM (FM 90.4—97MHz; MW 612, 1278 kHz). Opera—including performances from the New York Met—and classical music can be found on Lyric FM (FM 96—99 MHz).

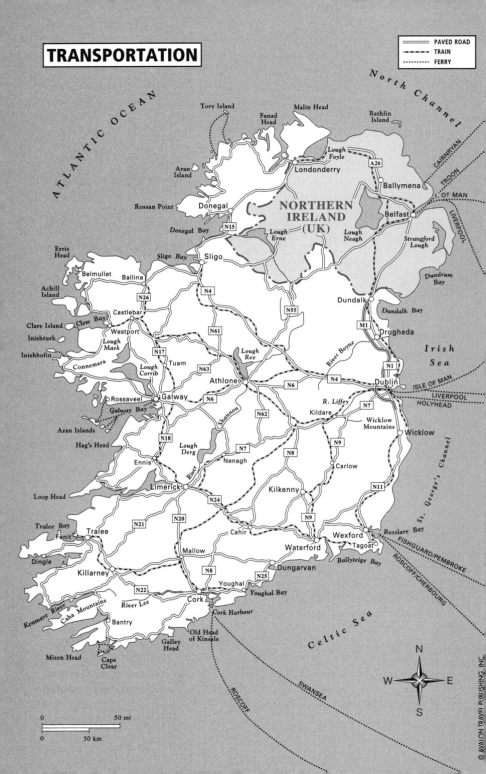

© Steenie Harvey

Travel and Transportation

You'll have to drive on the other side of the road, and you may have to hop a ferry to get where you're going, but you'll soon find getting around in Ireland is no hassle at all.

By Air

Deregulation in the air-travel business has brought much-needed competition to the skies above Ireland. Airlines now fly direct to more than 70 scheduled destinations and every year brings increasing numbers of holiday charter flights to North America, the Caribbean, and popular Mediterranean hotspots.

With 15.9 million passengers annually, the country's main international gateway is Dublin Airport. Shannon Airport, 15 miles from Limerick, lost much of its business with the abolition of the so-called "Shannon stopover," a ruling that all incoming and outgoing transatlantic flights had to touch down there. However, Shannon still offers limited services to the United States and also has good connections to U.K. destinations. There are also limited services to Belgium, Germany, Portugal, and Spain.

The range of overseas flights from Cork is expanding on a yearly basis. It's now possible to fly direct to Spain, Italy, Malta, and the Czech Republic. The majority of the flights operating out of Cork, though, are to U.K. destinations. Over the border in Northern Ireland, Belfast's airport provides another overseas gateway. It's worth considering if you're seeking budget charter fares to Canada—returns to Toronto can sometimes be had for under €395 ($490).

Ireland's network of small domestic airports connects Dublin to the provinces and provides limited flights to the United Kingdom. Most are served by Aer Arann. They also provide services between, Cork, Galway, Donegal, the Isle of Man, Derry in Northern Ireland, and eight destinations in the United Kingdom. Domestic flight times are under 40 minutes but fares are astonishingly expensive for the relatively short distances covered. For example, return flights between Dublin and Sligo cost €65 ($80). Note that it isn't possible to fly direct between provincial airports—all journeys necessitate a changeover in Dublin.

In general, high summer and the Easter, Christmas/New Year holiday periods are the most expensive times to fly to and from the States as there's always increased demand from visiting friends and relatives.

County Mayo's Knock Airport is also served by Ryanair flights from London. It gets quite busy in summer with charter flights of pilgrims bound for the Marian shrine in Knock village.

On the transatlantic route, Aer Lingus flies direct to four U.S. destinations: New York JFK, Chicago, Los Angeles, and Boston. Its North American flying partner is American Airlines, which connects Ireland with more than 240 U.S. cities. As part of its expansion program, Continental Airlines has also entered the Irish marketplace, providing onward connections to a range of U.S. cities. Flight times between Ireland and the U.S. Eastern Seaboard cities average eight hours.

Transatlantic fare structures are constantly changing and invariably subject to seasonal differences. In general, high summer and the Easter,

Christmas/New Year holiday periods are the most expensive times to fly to and from the States as there's always increased demand from visiting friends and relatives. Much depends on how flexible you can be and how far in advance you can book. Although cut-price economy returns to New York are sometimes advertised from $282 ($350), the reality is likely to be in the region of at least €532 ($660) for a return over the Easter period.

At the time of writing, Aer Lingus's best available deal was a midweek economy return on its Dublin-Chicago route for $360, through January–February 2005. The price of a midweek return with Continental from Dublin to Newark in January was €290 ($370). Just as in the States, it pays to shop around and keep your eyes peeled for special promotional offers in the media, travel agents' windows, or on the Internet.

The real bonanza for Ireland's air passengers is on the Dublin-Britain routes, where competition ensures rock-bottom return fares starting as low as €40 ($50). It's a great opportunity for you to travel farther afield—not just to London, but also to cities such as historic Edinburgh, the Scottish capital. Fly to Leeds/Bradford and you're at the gateway to medieval York and the Yorkshire Moors—remember *Wuthering Heights* and the Brontë sisters? Or, for an authentic insight into blue-collar English culture, join the legions of Irish fans who regularly fly to northwest England to watch soccer teams such as Liverpool and Manchester United!

Looking at other European destinations, the most affordable cities to reach are Paris, Brussels, and Dusseldorf—economy returns can be had for €120 ($150). As regards other European cities, they're not particularly cheap to get to from Ireland—especially when compared to the flight deals that are available to North America. (The blame is put on high taxes and landing fees.) A sample of the lowest-priced returns with Aer Lingus include: Amsterdam €140 ($174); Zurich €193 ($240); Madrid €156 ($194); and Rome €161 ($200).

To cut costs when traveling to Europe, I often fly to Britain first. Sure, traveling via London adds time, but it can save you a great deal of money. For example, this summer I was to visit the Italian island of Sardinia. Total cost for my return ticket Dublin-Stansted-Alghero with Ryanair is €175 ($217).

All travel agents sell air tickets, but they are now losing quite a bit of their business to agents on the web. Two of the biggest sites are www.ebookers.ie and www.gohop.ie. Although I haven't personally used Ebookers, I had no problems when booking a flight to Cyprus through Gohop.

By Ferry

Apart from the Aran Islands, which have their own airstrips, the only way to reach the 18 inhabited islands off Ireland's coastline is by ferry. They are mostly run by small, private concerns with some boats able to take only 12 passengers. Larger vessels are equipped to carry cars but these aren't superferries—the Arranmore ferry takes only eight cars at a time. Sailing schedules vary and there are always more crossings between Easter and late September to cater for tourists.

Ferries are the traditional way to reach Inishmore, Inishmaan, and Inisheer, the three Aran Islands. Depending on your embarkation point (Galway, Rossaveal, or Doolin in County Clare) and eventual destination, journey times take 30–90 minutes. A number of ferry companies serve the islands, though some operate only during summer. Aran Island Ferries runs an all-year service to each island with return fares from €19 ($23.50).

At the southern end of the country, in County Cork, Cape Clear Island copes with an estimated 20,000 annual visitors. Many come for the bird life, for this is one of the main passageways for summer migrants. Sailing time from Baltimore village on the mainland is 45

© Steenie Harvey

the Tipperary shore of Lough Derg

Free Travel for Retirees

Regardless of citizenship or income, all residents over the age of 66 are entitled to free travel on the road and rail services of Dublin Bus, Bus Éireann, Irish Rail, the DART, and certain other private bus and local ferry services. There's no limit to the amount of free travel that you can enjoy, though some restrictions apply to city bus services during peak travel times.

The free travel pass can also be used for cross-border journeys to and from Northern Ireland. In addition, Aran Islands residents can claim up to six free return flights to the mainland every year. Another benefit is that your spouse doesn't have to pay when traveling with you, even though he or she may not yet be a retiree. Applications for travel passes can be picked up at post offices or your local social-welfare office.

minutes. Return adult fares are €11.50 ($14.25). It makes a nice day trip—you leave Baltimore at 11 A.M. and depart Cape Clear at 4 P.M.

In County Mayo, Clare Island was the old stamping ground of Ireland's infamous pirate queen, Grainne Uaille. It has 150 permanent residents and it can be reached from Roonagh Quay, 12 miles from Westport town. Fares are €15 ($18.60) return. Another island worth exploring is Inishbofin, the "Island of the White Cow" in County Galway. Sailings leave from Cleggan village; fares are €15 ($18.60) return.

Should you want to cross the Irish Sea to Britain, there are a reasonable number of day and nighttime ferries. Services to Holyhead in North Wales are operated by Stena Line, from Dun Laoghaire and Dublin ports, and by Irish Ferries, from Dublin port. Prices with both are similar and rise dramatically in high season. With Irish Ferries, a five-day return for car and driver costs €230 ($285) in low season but €360 ($446) in July. Additional passengers are charged €14 ($17.50) each way. Depending on whether travel is by high-speed catamaran or traditional ferry, crossing time is between 1 hour, 40 minutes and 3.5 hours.

The main crossing point for ferries to South Wales is Rosslare in County Wexford. Again Stena and Irish Ferries share the route. With Irish Ferries, returns for foot passengers cost €26.50–54 ($33–67); if taking a car, prices vary €230–480 ($285–595), depending on season and length of stay. Again, extra passengers are charged €14 ($17.50) each way and the crossing time averages four hours.

If you've the stamina for a 16-hour-minimum sea crossing, bowls of milky coffee and fresh buttery croissants await in France. Irish Ferries sails to both Roscoff and Cherbourg; single tickets cost €50–121 ($62–150) for foot passengers and there is a range of deals if you want to take the car and stock up the trunk with inexpensive wine. Nine-day spring and fall specials start at €348 ($432) return.

By Bus

In general, all towns of any size are on a bus route with regular links to Dublin or the nearest city. It's possible to travel between most places, though not always by the direct route. Journeys may involve changes and sometimes a wait in midland transport hubs such as Longford.

Villages, especially those west of the River Shannon, are not particularly well served. Some rural communities have only a once-a-week service; many don't even have that. There are numerous localities where catching the bus means first having to undertake an 8–10-mile trek to the nearest main road.

The country's national bus service is Bus Éireann, its logo a friendly-looking Irish setter. Fares are less expensive than with the train, though buying a one-way ticket isn't substantially cheaper than buying a return. If you're planning just a one-day trip, ask about special day-return offers as these are usually good value. Ordinary weekday return fares to selected destinations are as follows: Dublin-Cork €16 ($20); Dublin-Tralee €22.50 ($28); Dublin-Galway €13 ($16); Dublin-Ballina €12 ($15). Services are quite frequent—for example, seven buses travel daily to Tralee.

Competition is provided by numerous local operators whose coaches usually provide services to destinations that Bus Éireann does not. Depending on local need, services generally vary between twice a day to once a week. In the little County Leitrim town of Drumshanbo for instance, there's one early morning bus every weekday taking workers to Sligo. Shoppers can use the service, but it means spending all day in Sligo town as the coach doesn't return until after 6 P.M. and all the regulars are on board.

Most buses leaving for the provinces depart from Dublin's central bus station, Busaras. On the north side of the River Liffey, it's less than a five-minute walk from Connolly Railway Station. Within the capital, a fairly comprehensive service is provided by Dublin Bus. As well as linking the city to suburbia and the greater Dublin area, it runs frequent services to the airport, ferry ports, and the two main railway stations. The average fare is €1.45 ($1.80), and make sure you have the exact

The Age of Steam

Steam engine buffs should make tracks for the Shannonside village of Dromod where enthusiastic volunteers are gradually rebuilding the Cavan and Leitrim Railway. First opened in 1887, it was built to the Irish narrow gauge of three feet. In those early years, transportation of livestock was the backbone of the service as the sparsely populated countryside delivered few human passengers. The line's later traffic mostly consisted of coal from the mines of the nearby Arigna Mountains.

By the time the last trains ran in 1959, the line's locomotives were virtual museum pieces. Happily a lifted track was relaid and a project to restore the railway started in 1993. If you've a taste for nostalgia, short-haul passenger services now run on Saturday and Sunday afternoons between May and October. Kiddies always look forward to the end of the season and the Halloween special, when they can ride a "Ghost Train" past a haunted graveyard, Dr. Frankenstein's workshop, and all kinds of other spooky places. Volunteer helpers are always needed during winter, the maintenance season. Contact the Cavan and Leitrim Railway, Dromod, County Leitrim; tel. 071/963-8599.

amount—drivers no longer give change. What happens if you overpay? You're issued a voucher—repayable at the Dublin Bus office on Upper O'Connell Street. The fare to the airport, 10 kilometers (6.2 miles) north of the city, is €5 ($6.20) from Busaras or Heuston stations. In other cities, Bus Éireann provides the city-to-suburbs service.

By Rail

The Republic's rail service is called Iarnród Éireann. Although trains are faster than buses, the network is by no means extensive—for example, you cannot reach anywhere in counties Donegal, Cavan, and Monaghan. Nor can you travel to the seaside towns of west Cork, Kerry's Dingle Peninsula, or the far western corners of County Clare.

For journeys originating in Dublin, Connolly Station is the departure point for trains north to Belfast, northwest to Sligo, and down the east coast route passing through Wicklow to Rosslare Harbor. Heuston Station is where to board for Cork city, Limerick, Galway, Tralee, and a number of other towns in the south, southwest, and west. (The stations are connected by the No. 90 Dublin Bus service.)

As with buses, day-return tickets represent the best value in what is rather a complex fare structure of off-peak returns, weekend specials, midweek returns, and so on. The staff are normally very helpful in advising what would be the best-priced ticket to suit your plans. Traveling second-class, some sample five-day return fares are as follows: Dublin-Athlone €31.50 ($39); Dublin-Galway €37 ($45.90); Dublin-Belfast €48 ($59.50); Dublin-Cork €54.50 ($67.50); Dublin-Tralee €55.50 ($68.90).

Dublin also has the DART, an acronym for Dublin Area Rapid Transport. An electric rail system with several stations within the capital, it plies between Howth on the north County Dublin coast and Bray in County Wicklow. Fares range €1.05–3.35 ($1.30–4.15).

Dublin's Luas is a brand-new light rail transit system. The Green Line connects Sandyford to Saint Stephen's Green in approximately 22 minutes. The Red Line connects Tallaght to Connolly Railway Station in approximately 43 minutes. There are a number of different fare structures: A one-journey adult return from Sandyford to Saint Stephen's Green costs €3.80 ($4.70).

By Car

Driving in Ireland can be both a pleasure and a penance. Yes, it's true that many roads are blessedly quiet and free of other motorists. It's also true that it's perfectly safe to stop and ask locals for directions if you get lost. Although there have been improvements in recent years, the typical country road can be a bit of a nightmare. Many are pitted with potholes or awash in winter floodwater and—just when you want to use it—being used as a private gathering place by beasts of the field.

Not that we country folk envy city motorists. Peak time in Dublin is an abysmal snarl-up—this was a city built for the horse and carriage trade, not juggernauts, buses, and commuter traffic. Even the brand-new motorway link to the west is subject to frequent tailbacks and delays. Just to add insult to injury, the price of petrol (gasoline) is enough to make you weep. Most major oil companies are represented here but there is little variation on prices within cities. However, you can pay a lot more in remote rural areas where there is no competition. Regular unleaded petrol costs €.94–1.01 ($1.16–1.25) per liter; it's a few pence less for diesel.

Yield! Major road ahead.

RULES OF THE ROAD

For first-time visitors from North America, the golden rule to remember is that Ireland drives on the *left*. Other things to get used to are overtaking on the right and giving way to traffic approaching on your right at roundabouts. Car-rental companies usually recommend that you try to avoid country roads for the first day or so until you're familiar with the car and the new driving environment.

Their advice makes lots of sense. When you first encounter a boreen (a narrow, rutted track with grass growing up the middle), you may well wonder how you are expected to keep to the left-hand side of the road when it's barely wide enough for one vehicle, let alone two. Panic-stricken by seeing a tractor hurtling toward them, some foreign motorists head straight for "the soft margin," better known in other countries as "the ditch." The trick to driving safely along boreens is to keep your speed down and be constantly on the watch for likely passing places such as farm gateways.

Helped by EU grants, Ireland has made heroic efforts to improve its road network but there's still a long way to go. While there are short sections of motorway around Dublin, they're nothing like the freeways of North America. Unless otherwise indicated, motorway and dual carriageway speed limits are 70 mph (112 kmph); direction signs are white on a blue background. Tolls are payable at only two points within the country, both in the Dublin area. One is on the M50 ring road between the airport and N4 interchange to the west. The other is on the R131 East Link Bridge—in both cases the toll for cars is €1.20 ($1.50).

Between most towns you're likely to be driving on "N" roads: national primary routes. Here the general speed limit is 60 mph (96 kmph) until entering a built-up area, where it reduces to 30 mph (48 kmph). Direction signs have white or yellow lettering on a green background. Unless indicated otherwise, the same speed limit applies to "R" roads: secondary routes where signs have black lettering on a white background. Then, of course, there are the boreens, where direction signs of any kind at all are largely conspicuous by their absence. If you're lucky enough to find a signpost at a country crossroads, it's not an exaggeration to suggest that the fingerpost might be pointing in the wrong direction.

On newer signs, and by the end of 2005, all distances and speed limits were to be displayed in kilometers, even though most Irish people continue to think in terms of mileage. Older signs carry distances in miles. To further confuse the visiting motorist there is also such a thing as an "Irish mile," which is slightly shorter than a conventional mile. Thankfully the Irish mile is a rarity nowadays and usually spotted only on centuries-old stone markers hidden in hedgerows. More confusion waits in Gaeltacht areas, where road signs are entirely in the Irish language. The most important direction sign to watch for is a red-bordered triangle carrying the words Géill Slí. This indicates a major road ahead and you must give way to traffic on it.

The minimum driving age is 17 and it's compulsory to wear seat belts in both the front and rear of the car. Children under 12 aren't permitted in front seats. Documents that should be carried when driving are a valid driver's license and the vehicle log book or your rental agreement; insurance and road tax discs also have to be displayed on the front windscreen. All cars over three years old must also have an NCT disc displayed. This is "The National Car Test" disc that indicates your vehicle is roadworthy. If you or another party is involved in an accident, then the Gardaí (police) must be informed.

DRIVER'S LICENSES

As a visitor, you're allowed to drive on your American or an international driver's license for up to 12 months. After that, unfortunately for Americans, yours is not one of the licenses that can be exchanged for an Irish one. Residents are required to obtain a provisional license and then sit the driving test. It's fairly rigorous and the pass rate remains static at around 50 percent.

Issued by the motor tax offices of local authorities, a provisional license costs $18.60 and is valid for two years. Application forms need to be accompanied by a birth certificate, two passport-sized photos, and an eyesight report from your doctor or optician. All applications for a first provisional license must also be accompanied by a "theory test certificate." If you haven't passed the driving test within the two-year time span, you can obtain another provisional license upon producing a notice of failure from the driving test center.

The law requires provisional drivers to be accompanied by a qualified driver, though this rule is often blatantly ignored. Curiously enough, there are some Irish drivers who have never sat the test yet legally hold a full license. During the late 1970s the wait for driving tests was so lengthy that the government simply gave up and issued full licenses to all and sundry on the list. It's unlikely to happen again as the wait for a test is not as long nowadays: around 6–8 weeks in the provinces, a little longer in Dublin.

No matter how highly you rate your driving skills, it's advisable to take a few lessons with an instructor before sitting the Irish driving test. The instructor will know the local test routes and what a particular examiner is likely to ask you to do. Driving lessons average around €36 ($45) per hour. Most people take lessons in the instructor's car, which can also be used for the test. Sitting the driving test costs €38 ($47.50) and the ordeal lasts for around 45 minutes. Once the test is over, you're told immediately whether you've passed or failed.

If you pass, you'll then have to buy a full license. These are valid for 1, 3, or 10 years and cost €5 ($6.20), €15 ($18.60), and €25 ($31) respectively. Drivers aged 67 or over are issued 3-year licenses only. If you are over 70, you can apply for a 1- or 3-year license, subject to certification of fitness to drive by your doctor.

Driving schools can be found through your local telephone directory's Golden Pages but make sure they belong to an accredited body such as the DIR (Driving Instructor Register) or ACDI (Association of Certified Driving Schools).

BUYING A CAR

Unless you opt for city life, it will be extremely difficult to get by in Ireland without a car. Although new car sales are at an all-time high, prices are very high because of the tax regime. One of the smallest cars on the road, the Fiat Panda, retails for €11,300 ($14,000). Roomier midrange cars can be had for around €17,000 ($21,000): Opel Astras start at €18,000 ($22,300), Toyota Corollas €19,000 ($23,560). A Volvo S401.6 saloon will cost at least €28,500 ($35,340), and the cheapest BMW (316I model) retails for €45,800 ($56,800). A good website for checking out what kind of car you can get for your money is www.motorweb.ie.

Second-hand cars are rather more affordable, but still not cheap. For example, €2,900 ($3,600) buys a 1995 Nissan Sunny. Obviously price depends on the age and make of car: You can spend anything from €3,950 ($4,900) for a 10-year-old Opel Corsa to €15,000 ($18,600) for a nearly new Toyota Corolla, one of Ireland's most popular cars. Other favorites are the Ford Fiesta and Ford Escort—around €4,700 ($5,800) for a five-year-old model. The vast majority of garage owners who sell second-hand cars are trustworthy—not fly-by-night characters who'll sell you a mechanically unsound heap of rust. After all, garage owners are part of the local community too and there's no profit in rooking the people you have to live with!

CAR TAX AND INSURANCE

All cars on the Irish road need to be taxed and insured. Levied annually (or if you wish by the quarter), the state road tax operates on a sliding scale based on the size of a car's engine. A car with a 950 cc engine such as a Ford Fiesta is taxed at €152 ($189) annually. A bigger car, say a Peugeot with a 1400 cc engine, attracts a levy of €314 ($389). Road tax is paid at your local motor-tax office.

The law also compels you to have motor insurance. Get caught without it and you'll be taken to court and given a heavy fine—persistent offenders are often jailed. Cost varies enormously depending on whether you take out fully comprehensive coverage or opt for just third-party insurance. Factors such as age, driving record, type of car, and whether you hold a full or provisional license are also taken into account. For example, full insurance coverageon a one-year-old Volkswagen Golf, driven by a mature driver who has never submitted a claim, is likely to be in the region of €450–1,150

Unless you opt for city life, it will be extremely difficult to get by in Ireland without a car.

($558–1,426), depending on where you live. (Dublin has a growing reputation for car thefts so premiums for city residents are higher.) If you live in a country area, third-party coverage is likely to cost around 25 percent less.

A host of insurance companies operate in Ireland—Hibernian, Irish National, and Guardian PMPA to name but a few. Instead of spending hours on the phone getting quotes, it's far simpler to visit an insurance broker who'll do the job for you. You'll find brokers in every town. Alternatively, contact the Irish Brokers Association for a list of members.

Service and maintenance costs also need to be budgeted for. Large garages linked to specific dealerships may charge you as much as €350 ($434) for an annual service. In contrast, a one-man-band local garage may charge only half that for the exact same work. If you're happy with your local garage then use it.

THE NCT TEST

January 2000 ushered in bad news for all of us who owned old bangers. Under pressure from Europe, the Irish government decreed that all cars over three years old would have to be mechanically tested and carry proof of roadworthiness: the NCT (National Car Testing) Certificate. Your car now has to pass an NCT competence test every two years. It is an offense to drive an uncertificated car.

There are 43 testing centers around the country. There is no need to go looking for one—they find you from the registration records at the Motor Taxation Office. When your car is due for its NCT test, you'll be sent an appointment 6–8 weeks beforehand.

You have to pay a €50 ($62) fee to have the car tested. If it fails, you must take it to a garage and get the faults put right, then pay another €27 ($34) for a retest. The only ways of avoiding the NCT test are to own a car that's classed as "vintage" or to keep your car on an island that isn't linked to the mainland by a road bridge.

CAR RENTAL

Major international rental firms such as Hertz, Avis, and Budget are all represented in Ireland and their desks are almost the first things that greet you in the arrival hall at Dublin and Shannon airports. You'll also find outlets in all major towns—look in the telephone Golden Pages under "car hire."

If you leave booking until you arrive in Ireland, weekly rental rates are punitive: around €300 ($372) in high season for a small car such as an Opel Corsa; around €430 ($533) for a larger model such as a Ford Mondeo. These rates include fully comprehensive insurance coverage, VAT, and unlimited mileage. Out-of-season rates are lower, but you'll probably get much better deals if you book from within the States.

To hire a car, it's essential to have a valid driver's license from your country of origin and it normally must have been held for at least two years. Age requirements are generally 23–70 or 75—you'll find it almost impossible to hire a car if you fall outside these limits. All major credit cards are accepted; with the international firms you should be able to rent models that have automatic rather than the normal manual transmission.

Most Irish rental firms have recovery service agreements with the AA (Automobile Association—not Alcoholics Anonymous!). Unlucky drivers who break down should contact the rental company as soon as possible.

TAXI SERVICE

In Dublin, Cork, Galway, and Limerick, taxis are metered. It's rare to come across cabs cruising for passengers: The best places to find them are at official taxi ranks and bus or rail terminals. Alternatively, you can ring a particular company's central operations depot for a pick-up. In Dublin, minimum taxi charges are €2.75 ($3.41) for the first half mile and then €1.35 ($1.67) per subsequent mile. Extras include a hiring charge of €.50 ($.62) and the same price for each piece of luggage or extra passenger. These are minimum charges. You can expect to pay about 33 percent more on Sundays, holidays, and 10 P.M.–8 A.M.

In many small provincial towns there may be only one or two firms, usually family-owned businesses for which the sons and nephews do the driving. If you've a train to catch, don't leave phoning until the last minute. You may find somebody else has just booked the last available cab.

Taxis throughout provincial Ireland aren't metered, so it's normal to agree the fare beforehand. As a rule of thumb, average rates are €1.45–1.75 ($1.80–2.20) per mile. As with city cabs, it's usual to tip around 10 percent. Do beware, though, that long-distance cab rides can be very expensive, as most drivers will calculate a price to compensate for their return trip.

Housing Considerations

Whether you aim to rent or buy, Irish property comes in a myriad enticing guises, from traditional farmhouses to cozy modern bungalows and rambling Georgian mansions clad in skeins of ivy. You can even buy a plot of land in a glorious location and build that dream home you've always had in mind. The republic's 26 counties offer a treasure chest of beguiling ideas, though some areas are a lot more expensive than others. The east coast in particular has seen a phenomenal rise in house values in the past few years—and prices are still rising. Space is rapidly running out and many new homes built in the past few years have been apartments.

Renting

Are you a student? A computer expert sent over to Ireland on a yearlong assignment? An adventurous spirit who simply wants the experience of living here for a couple of years? If so, you'll probably be thinking of renting a property.

Bear in mind that the country's slow pace of life won't suit everybody. Nor will the climate—the winter skies of northern Europe can often be gray and dreary.

Perhaps you don't fit into those categories at all. It could be that you've long dreamed of owning here and nothing is going to deter you. Well, although you may have already made up your mind that you want to buy, there are two main reasons why you should also consider rental options.

The first is financial. Unless you've been holed up in a cave for the past few years, you'll know Irish real estate prices have shot into the stratosphere. While the rate of increase has slowed in recent months, that doesn't mean house values are plummeting.

And there's always the possibility that Ireland and the Irish lifestyle might not meet your expectations. Living in a foreign country is always very different from spending a vacation there. If Ireland is completely new

© Steenie Harvey

Many Irish families prefer modern rather than 'traditional' properties.

to you, it certainly makes sense to rent a property for an initial 6- or 12-month period so you can get to know the country and its people.

Even if you do eventually intend buying or building a home, renting allows ample time to visit different counties and find the right property at—you hope—a reasonable kind of price. You don't want to be rushed into a hasty decision you might later regret—it's all too easy to do if you're here on a two-week summer vacation when skies are that special shade of duck-egg blue, roses are in full bloom, and everywhere looks its idyllic best.

Bear in mind that the country's slow pace of life won't suit everybody. Nor will the climate—the winter skies of northern Europe can often be gray and dreary. Buying a house isn't like buying a new pair of drapes: It's a major financial commitment. By renting a property initially, you'll be able to ensure that the Emerald Isle is the ideal home for you in January as well as in flaming June.

LONG-TERM RENTALS

Ireland has a mix of both furnished and unfurnished rental properties, so it's unnecessary to buy furniture if you don't want to. Although renting here isn't complicated, be warned that in the long term, it can also work out to be fairly expensive. Certainly so if you were thinking of living in Dublin.

The country's rate of home ownership is put at 83 percent, one of the world's highest, so there's never a huge glut of rental property available. In some areas rents have almost tripled in recent years. The booming housing market has led to an increased clamor for affordable accommodation, particularly from young Dubliners on modest incomes. However, supply can't always meet demand, and thus the rents keep on rising.

Within Dublin, both private landlords and real estate agents advertise in the classified sections of newspapers such as the *Irish Independent, Irish Times,* and *Evening Herald.* As well as handling property sales, some real estate firms such as Sherry Fitzgerald, Hooke and Macdonald, and Lisney have their own rental departments. Plus there's a host of agencies dealing with rentals that also advertise in the above-mentioned newspapers.

In provincial towns and cities, the best way of finding rental properties is to scan the classified sections of local newspapers or contact agents in an area that appeals to you. Although the vast majority of provincial real estate agents don't have specific letting departments, most generally have a handful of rental properties on their books. Outside of Dublin, you should certainly be able to find a 1- or 2-bedroom furnished apartment for around €500 ($620) per month in most provincial towns.

Most long-term rentals will require you to sign a lease for a year. Providing the rent is paid, tenants are well protected under Irish law. The landlord is obliged to provide a rent book or written lease that includes the duration of the tenancy, the amount of rent, when payment is to be made, and by what means—cash, standing order, check, and so on. The terms of the lease should also include arrangements regarding utility bills, the amount and purpose of the deposit, and whether pets are allowed.

Signing a lease legally obliges you to pay the rent for any agreed period, regardless of whether you move on within the next few weeks. An aggrieved landlord is within his rights to track you down and demand any missing payments if you decide to leave early. Of course, it's quite likely that you'll be able to come to an amicable arrangement should you find a suitable property to buy before the rental lease expires.

SHORT-TERM AND VACATION RENTALS

If you're thinking of renting for a couple of months rather than a year, you may have to settle for a holiday let. However, I have seen properties advertised for lease periods of 4 and 6 months—the best thing to do is to contact some of the larger agencies with your requirements.

To rent a vacation property in the summer is fairly expensive, but low season rates fall dramatically. It may even be possible to negotiate an advantageous 2- or 3-month rental deal with the owner—you'll never know until you ask.

A good place to start is with the Irish Tourist Board's self-catering accommodation guide—you can see its descriptions of rental homes, prices, and contact details through the website at www.ireland.ie. As all properties marketed through Bord Fáilte must meet certain standards, you can be sure that these homes will be warm and well decorated with all necessary conveniences. It may seem an obvious thing to mention, but in case you are wondering—all vacation properties are furnished. And prices are per property, not per person.

For example, in the tranquil green fields of County Cavan, you could rent a modern bungalow with angling, golf, and forest walks on the doorstep. Sleeping nine, and with everything supplied, it rents for €190–295 ($242–366) per week.

Think grand walks, a pretty harbor town with excellent seafood restaurants, and lungfuls of ozone-laden air. In County Mayo, Westport is an attractive town with golf courses, a sailing club, and the Croagh Patrick pilgrimage mountain. Here a traditional cottage sleeping five rents for €225–450 ($279–558) per week.

Another example of vacation rental properties available through the Irish Tourist Board website comes from the peaceful heart of County Kilkenny—a 200-year-old house sleeping six. This rents for €250–350 ($310–434) per week.

There is also a wide range of agencies, though high-season prices tend to be higher than if you make a private arrangement. The Rent-an-Irish-Cottage company has small cottage complexes in Cork, Kerry, Clare, and many other scenic locations. Many cottages are thatched and often have open peat fires. At Terryglass in County Tipperary, for example, a cottage sleeping six rents for €250–610 ($310–757) weekly depending on time of year. On Lough Derg, Terryglass is a pretty village with a marina and pubs that serve meals as well as offering entertainment. Portumna Castle and Forest Park are nearby and the village is a good touring base if you want to combine Tipperary with day trips into the counties of Galway, Limerick, and Clare.

This company also offers traditional-style terraced cottages at Durris, a village in west Cork. A stone's throw from Dunmanus Bay, one of Ireland's most beautiful bays, Durris is on the Sheep's Head Peninsula, which has magnificent scenery and walks. Rented on a weekly basis, these cottages also sleep six. Price ranges from €205 ($254) in January to €685 ($850) in July and August.

July and August are peak months for vacations in rural Ireland. For cottages in the most popular counties—Cork and Kerry—the rule is to book as far ahead as you can. Donegal is also fairly busy during these months. Many Irish families (and many more from across the border in Northern Ireland) plump for holidays in the republic's wildest and most northernmost county. At this time of year, you'll invariably need to book for a week minimum. It's generally Saturday to Saturday, though there are exceptions. At other times of year, you can usually opt for long weekends or 3- or 4-day midweek stays.

Turf smoke, peaceful walks, deserted beaches, wildflowers, rare bird life, friendly people—if you like the sound of County Donegal, Irish Cottage Holiday Homes has thatched cottages sleeping seven on Cruit Island, joined by a bridge to the mainland. Just down the road is a golf links and there are plenty of opportunities for shore and deep-sea angling. The cottages rent for €350 ($434) per week in winter, €995 ($1,233) per week in July and August.

Irish Cottage Holiday Homes acts as a central booking point for numerous small, privately owned cottage complexes. Also try Trident Holiday Homes and Self Catering Ireland—both have a wide selection of vacation properties throughout the country.

Dublin? Although you don't usually have to book months in advance to stay in a vacation apartment in Ireland's capital, I'd advise allowing at least a 6- to 8-week time scale to make sure of getting somewhere nice and centrally located. Vacation rentals through Trident Holiday Homes start at €400 ($496) weekly for an apartment sleeping two in the Rathmines neighborhood. Overlooking the River Liffey and Charlotte Quay, another small apartment is €600 ($744) weekly. For the firm's Dublin apartments, prices do not depend on season.

Another option is Jacobs Apartments, in the heart of Dublin city center's financial district. The apartments sleep either two or four people and are only a short walking distance from the main shopping areas, Connolly Station and the central bus station. Weekly prices range €550–750 ($682–930).

How to Book a Vacation Rental

All owners and rental companies have their own ways of doing things, but in many cases the procedure is to pay around 30 percent of the rental price when you place a booking. The balance may be due 4–6 weeks before the start of the hire date, or on arrival. Electricity, heating, and bed linen are often included in the price, though in some homes you may have to feed coins into a meter for electricity. You may also have to pay extra to hire bed linen and towels. Some property owners also request damage deposits.

If an agency or privately owned establishment is geared up to take credit cards, you can normally pay the deposit by this method. Visa and MasterCard are the most widely used cards in Ireland. The other main method of making payment is to go to your own hometown bank and obtain a foreign currency draft for the required amount against a recognized bank (e.g., a check in euros drawn against the Bank of Ireland in Dublin). You then send this draft to your chosen agency or individual to be cashed—for peace of mind, send it by registered or certified mail.

Personal checks in dollars are not really acceptable. Although Irish banks take them—I sometimes pay U.S. dollar checks into my own bank—they

Jargon Busting

Auctioneer--one of the titles by which real estate agents are known in Ireland. They handle straightforward property transactions as well as auctions.

Building survey—a detailed surveyor's report on a property that will indicate any potential problems.

Conveyancing—the legal work carried out in either the sale or purchase of a property.

Deeds—legal documents that show ownership of a property.

Detached—a property that stands alone.

Development—a newly built property or housing estate.

Dormer home—a house with extra rooms built into its roof space.

Flat—an apartment.

Gazumping—when the seller receives and accepts a higher price on the property despite having already accepted a previous offer before any contracts have been signed.

Listed building—a building with specific architectural or historic interest. It cannot be altered in any way without planning permission.

Period property—a Georgian Period property will have been built between 1714 and 1830 under the reign of Kings George I, George II, George III, and George IV. Victorian Period property describes properties constructed under the reign of Queen Victoria, 1837–1901. Edwardian Period property denotes properties built under the reign of King Edward VII, 1901–1910.

Semidetached—a property which is joined to one other property.

Solicitor—the attorney who acts on behalf of the buyer or seller in sale or purchase of a property.

Terraced house—a property that forms part of a connected row of houses.

take a devil of a long time to clear. Even in this supposedly electronic age, I've been told to allow up to 20 days for payment to clear.

Buying Property

The cost of buying a home has become the biggest downside to the country's recent economic success. Wealthy Irish city-dwellers are still in the market for second homes in scenic areas and fierce competition continues to drive prices skyward, especially for refurbished homes around the most sought-after villages. Fifteen years ago, you were spoiled for choice if you wanted to buy a sound little cottage on an acre of land for under $25,000. Unfortunately, those days have long since passed into the history books.

Where should you be looking? Really, the answer has to be whatever corner of Ireland you fall in love with. There are no real purpose-built

© Steenie Harvey

Property values in Dublin have soared—an 1890s artisans cottage can easily achieve over $240,000.

communities where little knots of Americans, Germans, or Brits have created a home-from-home expatriate lifestyle such as you find in places such as Mexico's Lake Chapala, Portugal's Algarve, and the Costa del Sol in Spain. Buy a house in Ireland and you really are buying into the local community.

(You'll find lots of information about property prices in the *Prime Living Locations* chapter, but this section concentrates on the practicalities of buying a home.)

BUYING A SITE AND BUILDING COSTS

If it's the case that you've found the perfect location but no properties on the market suit your requirements, you may want to buy a plot of land and have a house built to your own specifications. An important point to note is that all buyers, whatever their nationality, must obtain planning permission from the local authority before starting building work. Once you start scouring the listings of sites for sale, you'll notice that the more expensive sites are in highly desirable scenic areas and carry the magic words "with full planning permission approved."

Just because a site is for sale doesn't necessarily mean you'll be given the green light to build upon it. Ireland now has rigorous planning laws and flouting of the regulations can lead to heavy fines. Lax standards in the past resulted in some charmless areas of "ribbon development," whereby a number of coastal areas got brutalized by a seemingly endless string of houses of very dubious architectural merit. Traveling the coast road approaches to Galway city can be a shock to those who remember the days when local people lived in simple cottages instead of huge Spanish-style haciendas complete with incongruous Georgian porticos.

Although it's possible to make a planning application yourself, the devil is always in the details and a fair amount of specialist knowledge is required. Most people leave it in the hands of an architect or builder—your estate agent will introduce you to firms he or she has dealt with before. One of the first things the firm will do is check that building proposals don't conflict with the local authority's development plan, which lays down guidelines pertaining to the area. After submitting plans, they then either seek outline planning permission (OPP), which essentially establishes approval as to the general nature of the project—OPP for a three-bedroom residence, for example. Alternatively, they can apply straightaway for the most common type of permission—full planning permission, which entitles the applicant to start building his or her new home. They (or you) will also need to have a notice of the proposals published in the local newspaper as well as on a board beside the site. This is to give any interested parties warning of your plans and to allow them the chance to object.

Once full planning permission has been obtained, it generally applies for a term of five years. If the house hasn't been completed within this time span, it's necessary to make a renewed application for planning permission.

The cost of having a house built obviously depends on the type of residence you have in mind. Current estimates for building costs are approximately €110 ($137) per square foot. For a typical three-bedroom bungalow-style home of 1,100 square feet, you're looking at a figure of around €121,000 ($150,000). The cost of the land that you aim to build on is another matter entirely. Land zoned for development carries

The Dos and Don'ts of Property Buying

DO thoroughly investigate an area where you intend buying and visit it at different times of year—not just in summer.

DO talk to locals—they'll know what similar houses in the locality are selling for.

DO visit a number of estate agents to compare properties and prices.

DO use professionals and have legal title to a property approved by a solicitor.

DO remember you haven't legally secured a property until both buyer and seller have signed formal contract documents. Oral agreements count for nothing.

DO arrange insurance coverage. Ideally it should be in place on the day you visit the solicitor's office to sign the final contract.

DO ensure money is transferred through correct banking channels with a proper record of the transaction.

DO make sure sufficient funds are available if buying at auction—successful bidders have to pay 10 percent of the purchase price on the day of sale.

DON'T buy sight (or site) unseen.

DON'T buy when on holiday—arrange a proper house-hunting trip. An even better idea is to rent a house before you buy.

DON'T write to estate agents asking for details of "quaint little cottages in western Ireland." They'll require you to be far more specific regarding locality and price range.

DON'T be unrealistic. You're not going to find a chocolate-box thatched farmstead for $25,000.

DON'T shave on costs—get that surveyor's report.

DON'T forget to allow for additional fees and charges.

DON'T go building your dream home without first obtaining planning permission.

DON'T even think about attending an auction if you're one of life's impulsive characters.

a far higher price than farmland. (You will not usually get planning permission to build upon farmland.)

If you want Atlantic views, serviced sites of less than a quarter of an acre now sell for more than €100,000 ($124,000) in the south coast counties of Waterford and west Cork. On the other hand, you can buy a half-acre site with full planning permission to build a bungalow in a County Donegal valley for €45,000 ($56,000).

As with secondhand properties, it all comes down to location. A site in County Meath—on the east coast and within easy commuting distance of Dublin—will cost more than 10 times the price of a site in landlocked County Roscommon.

Around Dublin's satellite counties, vendors can practically name their price for prime sites in the right location. A .2-acre site with planning permission for a three-bedroom house in County Wicklow recently sold for €300,000 ($372,000). Just to reiterate—that price was for the site alone; to actually build the house would be extra.

It's also necessary to obtain planning permission if you intend to do major work on an existing building—for example, adding an extension or converting old stables into a residence. Once alterations are complete, you must make sure your builder gives you a certificate of compliance to show that planning permission had been granted and work was carried out according to any specific regulations laid down. Keep this certificate with the property deeds: It's an important document that needs to be produced should you eventually wish to resell.

Planning application fees to build a house are €65 ($81). Plenty of information can be obtained from local authority offices. If you want to discuss ideas with an architect, lists of accredited members for a particular locality can be had from the Royal Institute of Architects of Ireland.

NON-NATIONALS BUYING PROPERTY

There's nothing to stop you as an American from buying a house or site in Ireland providing that the amount of land amounts to less than two hectares (five acres). If, however, the property comprises more than five acres and is outside the boundaries of a town or city, you'll need to seek the consent of the Land Commission. This is a government body, which is part of the Department of Agriculture and Food.

These regulations apply to all non-EU nationals. Although each situation is considered on its merits, permission is not always forthcoming, particularly if it concerns the sale of a large tract of good-quality farmland. On the other hand, if a property includes a substantial acreage of "wilderness" land, you shouldn't encounter any problems. Basically it comes down to what the land was previously used for and what you, the prospective new owner, intend to do with it.

Those who hold dual Irish nationality or can claim citizenship of any other EU country may buy as much land as they wish in any area whatsoever without seeking government permission. Once you have been resident in Ireland for seven years, you are also exempt from these regulations. Another point to note is that the proviso doesn't apply to any house with a large acreage that falls within a town's boundaries.

LEGAL TITLE OF PROPERTY

Most residential properties in Ireland are registered as freehold. This means that title to the property can be held forever and is entirely free of rent. Whether you eventually sell a property or bequeath it to your heirs, its legal title always remains as freehold.

You're more likely to come across leasehold titles in relation to city-center houses or commercial properties. A leasehold title can be set at anything from 250 years to 999 years and usually comes with an annual ground rent that is payable to the title-holder. The number of years that are left to run on any lease invariably affects the price of a property, but it's occasionally possible to buy out the lease and obtain freehold title. As leasehold titles can be complicated, seek legal advice before signing any contracts.

HOW TO BUY PROPERTY

Irish properties are mostly sold through estate agents, also called auctioneers. Unfortunately there is no real multiple-listings system like that in the States and most agents have their own particular little cache of properties. This means buyers have to do a lot of legwork getting around the vari-

Raising Home Finance

Banks, building societies (mutuals), and mortgage brokers are the principal sources of home financing in Ireland. Banks and building societies sell their own mortgages; mortgage brokers arrange finance on behalf of a range of banks and building societies. Subject to income, status and good references from your home bank, some newcomers to Ireland may be able to raise up to 70 percent of the purchase price from an Irish lending institution. Note, "some." Unless it's a short-term mortgage (5–10 years), individuals over 50 years of age usually find it difficult to obtain finance.

Mainly because of the high cost of property, Irish buyers can sometimes borrow as much as 92 per-

cent from a lender. Much depends on personal financial circumstances. In general, though, lenders take earnings into consideration when determining how much you can borrow. A working individual can usually borrow 2.5 times their annual income. If your spouse also has an income this can increase the amount you can borrow, normally by a multiple of one. As an example, a couple earning €60,000 and €40,000 respectively should be able to borrow €190,000 ($236,000).

There are dozens of mortgage packages on the market, with both fixed and variable interest rate options. All financial institutions will provide advice and explain the options that are open to you.

ous offices. Most agents belong to professional bodies such as the IAVI (Irish Auctioneers and Valuers Institute) or IPAV (Institute of Professional Auctioneers and Valuers). Members must adhere to certain standards of practice and are bonded by deposit-protection funds. As a buyer, you aren't liable for the estate agent's fee for selling a property. This is met by the vendor and generally amounts to 2.5–3.5 percent of sale price.

The main method of sale for residential properties is through "private treaty," whereby a suggested price level is placed on the property. This is only a guideline price and a property may eventually change hands for more or less than the price you'll see advertised in an estate agent's window or a newspaper. It's quite acceptable to make an offer, particularly if a house has been on the market for some time—the owners may be prepared to accept a lower sum than the guideline price.

A guideline price isn't binding on the vendor so ensure any agreement is put in writing. Oral deals are not legally enforceable. Have you heard the term "gazumping"? What it means is the acceptance of a higher offer by the seller, despite having verbally agreed to sell the property to someone else. Gazumping does happen, particularly in today's market where house values are continually rising.

Secondhand properties are sold according to the principle of *caveat emptor*—buyer beware. So, do make sure that any contractual agreement you sign is "subject to surveyor's report." Whether you're interested in a $150,000 cottage or a million-dollar mansion, it would be senseless to go ahead and buy without first engaging a surveyor or architect to check for structural defects. A surveyor's report may save you a lot of money as well as a lot of heartache in the long run.

Do *you* know if a house's foundations are crumbling away? The vendors (and their estate agent) are under no legal obligation to tell you so. Should a surveyor actually uncover a horror story, you're entitled to withdraw your offer and get your deposit back—that's if you've insisted that the contract covers this eventuality, of course. Surveyors' fees average €250 ($310) and a list of members can be obtained from the Society of Chartered Surveyors.

Before agreeing to buy any property, and pay the usual 10 percent deposit, it's wise to consult an Irish solicitor (attorney) of your own to ensure that your interests are properly protected. Although it's not essential, most buyers use a solicitor to handle the actual conveyancing of a property—i.e., drawing up a formal contract and getting the deeds transferred into their names.

As well as helping with negotiations on the purchase price, the deposit, the date you can take possession, and any special contract conditions, your solicitor will check to ensure the title of the property is free and clear. If necessary, he or she can also obtain permission for the sale from the Land Commission.

The entire process normally takes 6–8 weeks. The balance of the purchase price is paid only when your solicitor is satisfied that you are acquiring good and marketable title to the property. Your estate agent should be able to point you in the direction of a local solicitor. Alternatively, get a list of members from the Law Society of Ireland.

Solicitors no longer have a fixed rate of charges for conveyancing, but the Law Society recommends its members charge 1.5 percent of the purchase price plus €126.97. A VAT (sales tax) of 21 percent is also payable on legal fees. It all sounds horribly baffling and expensive but on a €100,000 property, fees would be €1,500 + €126.97 = €1,626.97. The VAT amounts to €341.66. That makes a total of €1,968.63 ($2,441).

AUCTION SALES

Around 6 percent of Irish properties are sold at auction. In general, the type of properties that come under the hammer include a varied selection of Dublin houses, large country mansions and estates, farms with a substantial acreage of grazing land, and business concerns such as busy town-center pubs or hotels in well-known tourist locations.

In the past, some vendors sold at auction because their houses had languished on the market for years and any sale price was better than none at all. Nowadays things are different.

Auction properties are advertised 4–6 weeks in advance of the sale date, which gives time for potential buyers to evaluate a property and get a surveyor's report. In the past, some vendors sold at auction because their houses had languished on the market for years and any sale price was better than none at all. Nowadays things are different. In an ever-soaring market, it can be difficult to put a value on certain types of property and auctioneers are achieving fantastic results for clients who choose to sell by this method, often 20 percent and more above guideline prices. Astute vendors are also aware that people tend to get carried away at auctions, often bidding more than what a property is really worth.

The "reserve" placed on a property is the minimum price a seller will accept. Reserve prices can differ from advertised guideline prices, as the

Home Sweet Home

Some Irish real estate agents have a passion for purple prose. Others—well, let's just say a few have been known to be somewhat economical with the truth. So, beware of what all those enticing descriptions may *really* mean.

"Uninterrupted views" (Of the gasworks/abattoir/lunatic asylum)

"Garden requires a little attention" (Welcome to Ireland's version of the Amazon rainforest)

"Oozing with old-fashioned charm" (Plumbing dates from the 1740s)

"Perfect for a handyman" (Completely derelict)

"Must be seen to be believed" (I can't believe that this dump costs $100,000 either)

"Wonderfully compact" (How tall are you?)

"Very secluded location" (25 miles from anywhere)

"Renowned wildlife habitat" (House infested with mice, cockroaches, and death-watch beetles)

"Ready to walk into" (No front door, no back door, cows using the kitchen as a byre)

"Fishing on the doorstep" (Area prone to flooding)

"Awaits a discerning buyer" (Nobody else has been fool enough to make an offer)

"Cliff-top cottage--attractively priced for quick sale" (Due to fall into the ocean within the next two years)

"Totally unvamped" (Wood-wormy floorboards, dry rot behind the plasterwork)

"Tastefully decorated" (If your tastes run to shocking-pink decor and mirrors on every ceiling)

"With some unusual features" (Such as the gaping holes in the roof)

seller isn't obliged to decide what the reserve price is until the actual day of the auction. An IAVI directive states that the guideline figure should be within 10 percent of what the auctioneer reckons the reserve price will be. As this doesn't always happen, some would-be buyers suffer immense disappointment when the prize property sells for far more than they anticipated. To rub salt in the wounds, nobody is going to refund their out-of-pocket expenses for valuation and surveyor's reports.

Should you buy at auction and your bid proves to be the highest acceptable offer, the purchase contract must be signed there and then. You must also pay a 10 percent deposit immediately. The balance becomes due when all legalities have been completed, usually 6–8 weeks afterward.

Unlike with private treaty sales, you cannot contract to buy subject to a surveyor's report's being satisfactory. This should have been done before the sale date and you bid unconditionally. If, for any reason, you cannot complete the sale, you can wave farewell to your 10 percent deposit.

OTHER CHARGES

Along with solicitors' and surveyors' fees, a number of other outlays are involved in house purchase. Registration fees can be of two types and your solicitor will advise you which one is appropriate. For most homes the registration fee is €375–500 ($465–620).

STAMP DUTY

This is essentially a government purchase tax. If you've owned property anywhere in the world before, the rates in last column will apply to you (see sidebar *Stamp Duty on Residential Property*). First-time buyers means first-time global buyers. Just because you've never owned a home in Ireland doesn't mean you're classed as a first-time buyer.

The stamp duty fees, payable through your solicitor, are made on the day when final contracts are exchanged.

APPLICATION FEE

This will only concern you only if you've arranged finance or a mortgage to buy property. Charged by banks and building societies, it's sometimes levied as a percentage of the loan (typically .5 percent) or a flat fee of €125 ($155).

MORTGAGE STAMP DUTY

Borrowers pay an additional government levy on all mortgages of more than €254,000 ($315,000). Duty is charged at €1 for every €1,000 borrowed.

HOUSE INSURANCE

For peace of mind, get your house insured. You should arrange coverage from the moment you sign the final contract. In general, premiums are lower in rural areas where rebuilding costs are cheaper and the risk of burglaries is far less than in the cities.

As a reflection of how house prices (and building costs) have risen, the minimum coverage you can take out with Bank of Ireland Insurance Services is €105,000 ($130,000). A home with a thatched roof will be seen as being at greater risk from fire damage than a modern bungalow. Similarly, a house with a cellar that is sited beside a river could carry a fair risk of flood damage. Thus it will undoubtedly attract higher premiums than a similar house perched on top of a hill.

It's impossible to give exact quotations for the entire country. However, insuring a 750-square-foot cottage in County Clare for €115,000 rebuilding costs, plus household contents coverage of €30,000, will result in an annual premium of around €200 ($248).

As with car insurance, the umbrella organization for brokerage firms is the Irish Brokers Association.

PROPERTY TAXES

Even if you own a mansion, property taxes aren't something you need to worry about. Ireland does not have them. Rates (local authority charges) apply only to commercial property, not the residential sector.

Water is there for the taking, unless you belong to one of the country's very small number of private water schemes. But unless you are comfortable with the idea of buying a trailer and hauling all your household rubbish along to the local tip, you'll have to pay for refuse collection. Charges set by local authorities/private contractors are levied at an annual rate of around €250 ($300).

UTILITIES

Both newly built properties and old cottages where no utilities existed before will need connecting to water and electricity supplies. One-time connection charges apply in both instances. Water connection charges are usually in the €650–750 ($806–930) range. Unless the property is very remote, electricity connection is around €1,050 ($1,300).

In towns and some villages, sewage and wastewater gets piped into a main sewer that leads to a community sewage treatment plant. However, in many rural areas, no such facilities exist. Homeowners need to install a septic tank costing approximately €2,600 ($3,225). Tanks need emptying every 10 years or so. I had my own emptied a couple of years ago and it cost €150 ($186).

© Steenie Harvey

Resources

Contacts

Consulates and Agencies

UNITED STATES

Embassy of Ireland
2234 Massachusetts Avenue NW
Washington, DC 20008
tel.: 202/462-3939
fax: 202/232-5993
www.irelandemb.org

Consulate General of Ireland
Ireland House
345 Park Avenue, 17th Floor
New York, NY 10154-0037
tel.: 212/319-2555
fax: 212/980-9475

Consulate General of Ireland
400 North Michigan Avenue,
Suite 911
Chicago, IL 60611
tel.: 312/337-1868
fax: 312/337-1954

Consulate General of Ireland
100 Pine Street, 33rd Floor
San Francisco, CA 94111
tel.: 415/392-4214
fax: 415/392-0885

Consulate General of Ireland
535 Boylston Street
Boston, MA 02116
tel.: 617/267-9330
fax: 617/267-6375

IRELAND

U.S. Embassy
42 Elgin Road, Ballsbridge
Dublin 4
tel: 01/668-8777
fax: 01/668-9946
www.dublin.usembassy.gov

Tourist Information Offices

UNITED STATES

Irish Tourist Board
345 Park Avenue
New York, NY 10154
tel: 212/418-0800 or
800/223-6470

IRELAND
Dublin
Tourist Office

Baggot Street Bridge
Dublin
Callsave tel.: 1-850/230330

The Western Seaboard
Tourist Office
Eyre Square
Galway
tel.: 091/537700

Tourist Information
James Street
Westport
County Mayo
tel.: 098/25711

Tourist Office
Arthur's Row
Ennis
County Clare
tel.: 065/682-8366

The Southwest
Tourist Information
Beech Road
Killarney
County Kerry
tel.: 064/31633

Tourist Information Office
Aras Fáilte
Grand Parade
Cork
tel.: 021/425-5100

The Southeast
Tourist Office
Shee Alms House
Rose Inn Street
Kilkenny
tel.: 056/776-0933

Tourist Office
Crescent Quay
Wexford town
County Wexford
tel.: 053/23111

Tourist Information Office
1 Arundel Square
Waterford city
County Waterford
tel. 051/875788

Tourist Information
Sarsfield Street
Clonmel
County Tipperary
tel.: 052/22960

The Northwest and Lakelands
Tourist Office
Temple Street
Sligo
tel.: 071/916-1201
This office also maintains information on counties Roscommon and Leitrim. For County Cavan information, call the Dublin office.

Tourist Information Office
Derry Road
Letterkenny
County Donegal
tel.: 074/912-1160

Making the Move

U.S. CONTACT GROUPS

A list of affiliated clubs and societies with American links can be had from the American Embassy.

Irish-American Society
Contact: Joan Hanley
16 Dargle Wood, Templeogue
Dublin 16
tel.: 01/494-4091
U.S. expatriates can touch home base through this support group offering advice, get-togethers, business contacts, and so on. One red-letter day in its calendar is Thanksgiving with a dinner hosted by the U.S. ambassador to Ireland. Independence Day is another: The society holds a barbecue, barn dance, and fireworks display at Dun Laoghaire, County Dublin.

American Legion
Contact John N. Power, Adjutant
11 Skiddy's Homes, Pouladuff Road
Cork
tel.: 021/314188
Ex-servicemen and women can join the American Legion, which has branches in Dublin, Claremorris in County Mayo, and Killarney in County Kerry. They'll keep you informed on U.S. government policy toward veterans and pension entitlements and also about various legion get-togethers.

American Women's Club of Dublin
40b Dartmouth Square
Dublin 6
tel.: 01/676-6263
The club produces a monthly newsheet for members and organizes lectures, tours, and courses on different aspects of Irish culture.

American Chamber of Commerce Ireland
Heritage House,
23 Saint Stephen's Green
Dublin 2
tel.: 01/661-6201
Depending on business interests, you may want to contact this group, which promotes cultural and commercial exchange between the two countries.

IMMIGRATION AND CITIZENSHIP

Department of Justice, Immigration and Citizenship Division
72/76 Saint Stephen's Green
Dublin 2
tel.: 01/678-9711 or 01/602-8202

Irish Citizenship Through Grandparent

Applications are processed through the local Irish embassy or consulate, or (once you are resident in Ireland), through:

Department of Foreign Affairs,
Consular Section
72/76 Saint Stephen's Green
Dublin 2
tel.: 01/478-0822

CUSTOMS AND EXCISE

Revenue Commissioners,
Customs and Excise
Information Office
Castle House

South Great George's Street
Dublin 2
tel.: 01/679-2777

PET QUARANTINE

Lissenhall Quarantine Kennels
and Catteries Lissenhall, Swords
County Dublin
tel.: 01/840-1776
fax: 01/840-9338

Language and Education

Foras na Gaeilge
7 Merrion Square
Dublin 2
Callsave tel.: 1-850/325325
eolas@forasnagaeilge.ie
www.forasnagaeilge.ie

Gael Linn
35 Dame Street
Dublin 2
tel.: 01/675-1200
fax 01/670-4180
eolas@gael-linn.ie
www.gael-linn.ie

Oideas Gael
Gleann Cholm Cille
Dhun ha nGall
tel.: 074/973-0248
fax 074/973-0348
oifig@oideas-gael.com
www.oideas-gael.com
(About the address—that's how
Irish speakers write "Glencolmcille,

County Donegal," and postmen
need to recognize both forms.)

Áras Mháirtín uí Chadain
(the Irish Language Center of
University College Galway)
An Cheathrú Rua
Co na Gaillimhe
tel.: 091/595101
fax 091/595041
caitriona.uichualain@oegaillimh.ie
www.gaeilge.nuigalway.ie

The Department of
Education and Science
Marlborough Street
Dublin 1
tel.: 01/889-6400
fax 01/878-6712
info@education.gov.ie
www.education.ie

THIRD-LEVEL EDUCATION

Major Irish universities that accept foreign students include:

National University of Ireland—University College Dublin
Belfield
Dublin 4
tel.: 01/716-7777
info@ucd.ie
www.ucd.ie

National University of Ireland—University College Cork
Cork
tel.: 021/490-3000
isoffice@ucc.ie
www.ucc.ie

National University of Ireland—Galway
University Road
Galway
tel.: 091/524411
international@nuigalway.ie
www.nuigalway.ie

National University of Ireland—Maynooth
Humanity House
NUI Maynooth
Maynooth
County Kildare
tel.: 01/708-3420
International.Office@nuim.ie
www.nuim.ie/international/main

University of Dublin—Trinity College
Trinity College Dublin
College Green
Dublin 2
tel.: 01/608-1000
admissns@tcd.ie
www.tcd.ie

University of Limerick
Limerick
tel.: 061/202414
Admissions@ul.ie
www.ul.ie

Dublin City University
Glasnevin
Dublin 9
tel.: 01/700-5953
international.office@dcu.ie
www.dcu.ie

Royal College of Surgeons
www.rcsi.ie
All students from America and Canada must apply through the Atlantic Bridge Program in the United States:
Peter Nealon, Director
Atlantic Bridge Program
3419 Via Lido, PMB 629
Newport Beach, CA 92663-3908
tel: 949/723-6318
info@atlanticbridge.com
www.atlanticbridge.com

National College of Art and Design
100 Thomas Street
Dublin 8
tel.: 01/636-4200
fios@ncad.ie
www.ncad.ie

PRIVATE COLLEGES
American College Dublin
2 Merrion Square
Dublin 2
tel.: 01/676-8939
degree@amcd.ie
www.amcd.ie

Griffith College Dublin
South Circular Road
Dublin 8
tel.: 01/415-0400
international@gcd.ie
www.gcdinternational.ie

LINKS WITH U.S. UNIVERSITIES AND ORGANIZATIONS

It is not possible to list the several hundred links that exist between North American and Irish educational establishments. Students should check with their own university or college for links to Irish counterparts.

NAISA
http://www.naisa.com

University of Notre Dame
Notre Dame, Indiana
www.nd.edu/international

Lynn University
Boca Raton, Florida
www.lynn.edu

www.studenttraveler.com
General information for students traveling abroad.

Health

Voluntary Health Insurance Board (VHI)
Lower Abbey Street
Dublin 1
Callsave tel. 1-850/444444
from outside Ireland
tel.:056/775-3200
www.vhi.ie (for online quotes)

BUPA Ireland
2 Fitzwilliam Square
Dublin
Callsave tel. 1-890/700890
from outside Ireland
tel.01/662-7662
www.bupaireland.ie (for online quotes)

Hibernian Life and Pensions
60/63 Dawson Street
Dublin 2
tel.: 01/617-8000
www.hibernian.netsource.ie

ALTERNATIVE THERAPIES
Delphi Mountain Resort and Spa
Leenane
County Galway
tel.: 095/42987
delphigy@iol.ie
www.delphiescape.com

PREVENTIVE MEASURES

**Irish Family
Planning Association**
60 Amiens Street
Dublin 1
tel.: 01/806-9444
post@ifpa.ie
www.ifpa.ie

Kilcullen's Seaweed Baths
Enniscrone
County Sligo
tel.: 096/36238

**Lisdoonvarna Spa
Wells Centre**
Lisdoonvarna
County Clare
tel.: 065/707-4023
(June–September only)

Employment

JOB LISTINGS

Skills Shortages
Fas
www.fas.ie
Details of national skill shortages
and vacancies

Health Service Executive
www.careersinhealthcare.ie

Newspaper Websites

Irish Examiner
www.examiner.ie

Irish Independent
www.unison.ie

Irish Times
www.ireland.com

Sunday Business Post
www.sbpost.ie

Sunday Tribune
www.tribune.ie

INTERNSHIPS

IAESTE—The International
Association for the Exchange of
Students for Technical Experience
iaeste@aipt.org
www.iaeste.org
Note that IASTE accepts only
online applications.

IAESTE—United States
10400 Little Patuxent Parkway,
Suite 250
Columbia, MD 21044-3510

IAESTE—Canada
P.O. Box 1473
Kingston
Ontario K7L 5C7

ONLINE RECRUITMENT AGENCIES
www.monster.ie
www.jobs-ireland.com
www.irishjobs.ie

www.job2job.ie
www.job.ie
www.nixers.com
www.mrs.ie (medical)

WORK PERMITS

Work Permits Section, Departartment of Enterprise, Trade, and Employment
Room 105, Davitt House,

Adelaide Road
Dublin 2
tel.: 01/631-3333

BUSINESS PERMISSION

The Immigration Division, Department of Justice
13-14 Burgh Quay
Dublin 2
tel.: 01/616-7700

Finance

BANKING

For information on bank services call into any local branch or contact the following:

AIB Bank Headquarters
Bankcentre, Ballsbridge
Dublin 4
tel.: 01/660-0311

Bank of Ireland Head Office
Lower Baggot Street
Dublin 2
tel.: 01/661-5933

First Active
First Active House,
Leopardstown
Dublin 18
tel.: 01/207-500

IPermanentTSB
56/59 Saint Stephen's Green
Dublin 2
tel.: 01/212-4101

National Irish Bank
Head Office
7/8 Wilton Terrace
Dublin 2
tel.: 01/638-5000

Ulster Bank
33 College Green
Dublin 2
tel.: 01/608-4000

TAXES

Revenue Commissioners
Dublin Castle
Dublin 2
tel. 01/878-0000

Law Society of Ireland
Blackhall Place
Dublin 7
tel.: 01/671-0711

BUILDING SOCIETIES

**EBS Building Society
(Head Office)**
2 Burlington Road
Dublin 4
tel.: 01/665-8081

STOCKBROKERS

Fexco
Fexco House, Ely Place
Dublin 2
tel.: 01/637-3080

BCP Stockbrokers
72 Upper Leeson Street
Dublin 4
tel.: 01/661-7111

Bloxham Stockbrokers
2/3 Exchange Place
Dublin 1
tel.: 01/829-1888

Dolmen, Butler, and Briscoe
3 College Green
Dublin 2
tel.: 01/633-3800

Goodbody Stockbrokers
122 Pembroke Road,
Ballsbridge Park
Dublin 4
tel.: 01/667-0400.

Communications

TELEPHONE

Land Lines
Eircom
Saint Stephen's Green
Dublin 2
tel.: 01/671-4444
www.eircom.ie

Esat Bt, Head Office
Grand Canal Plaza
Dublin 4
tel.: 1-800/923923
www.esatbt.com

Cellular Phones
Meteor Mobile Communications
Kingswood Avenue, Citywest
Business Park, Naas Road

Dublin 24
tel.: 01/430-7000
info@meteor.ie
www.meteor.ie

O2 Ireland
McLaughlin Road, National
Technological Park
Limerick
tel.: 061/203737
customer.care@02.ie
www.o2.ie

Vodafone
Mountain View, Leopardstown
Dublin 18
tel.: 042/932-6745
www.vodafone.ie

INTERNET SERVICE PROVIDERS

Free

www.eircom.net
www.oceanfree.net
www.indigo.ie

Subscription

www.eircom.net
www.iol.ie
www.indigo.ie
www.utvinternet.ie

Satellite Broadband

www.broadband.digiweb.ie

Cable TV Connection

www.cablenet.ie

POSTAL SERVICE

**National Postal Service—
An Post Head Office**
Post Office, O'Connell Street
Dublin 1
tel.: 01/660-0311

INTERNATIONAL COURIERS

FedEx
within Ireland
tel.: 1-800/725725

DHL
within Ireland
tel.: 1-800/535800

SDS
tel.: 01/459-1133

MEDIA

Inside Ireland
P.O. Box 1886
Dublin 16
tel.: 01/493-1906
www.insideireland.com

The Western Seaboard

Connacht Tribune
Galway
www.connacht-tribune.ie

Western People
Mayo
www.westernpeople.ie

Clare Champion
Barrack Street
Ennis, Co. Clare
tel.: 065 682 8105
fax: 065 682 0374
editor@clarechampion.ie
www.clarechampion.ie

The Southwest

The Kerryman
Tralee, Co. Kerry
tel.: 066 71 45500
fax: 066 71 45572
dmalone@kerryman.ie
www.unison.ie/kerryman

The Corkman
The Spa
Mallow, Co Cork
tel.: 022 42394
newsdesk@corkman.ie
www.unison.ie/corkman

The Irish Examiner,
Academy Street,
Cork,
tel.: 021 4272722.
jill.osullivan@tcm.ie.
www.irishexaminer.com

The Southeast

Wexford People,
Channing House,
Rowe Street,
Wexford
tel.: 053 40100
fax: 053 40191/2
ann.jones@peoplenews.ie
www.peoplenews.ie

Waterford News
25, Michael St.
Waterford,
tel.: 051 874951
fax :051 855281
editor@waterford-news.ie
www.waterford-news.com

Nenagh Guardian
13 Summerhill,
Nenagh,
Co. Tiperary,
tel.: 067-31214
fax: 067 33401
info@nenagh-guardian.ie
www.unison.ie/nenagh_guardian/

The Northwest and Lakelands
The Sligo Champion
Finisklin Road
Sligo
tel.: 071 9169222
fax: 071 9169833
editor@sligochampion.ie
www.unison.ie/sligo_champion

Donegal Democrat
Derry Journal,
Buncrana Road,
Derry BT48 8AA
tel.: 028 7127 2200
fax: 028 7127 2218
www.donegaldemocrat.com

Leitrim Observer
St.Georges Terrace,
Carrick-on-Shannon,
Co.Leitrim.
tel.: 071 96 20025
fax: 071 96 20112
info@leitrimobserver.ie
www.leitrimobserver.ie

Roscommon Herald
St Patrick's Street,
Boyle,
Co Roscommon,
tel.: 071 96 62004
fax: 071 96 62926
editor@roscommonherald.com
www.roscommonherald.ie/

Travel and Transportation

AIRPORTS

Dublin Airport
tel.: 01/814-1111

Shannon Airport
tel.: 061/712000

Cork Airport
tel.: 021/431-3131

Belfast Airport
tel.: 01849/422888

Knock Airport
tel.: 094/67222

AIRLINES

Aer Arann Head Office
(domestic and UK)
The Atrium
Dublin Airport
tel.: 01/844-7700
www.aerarann.ie

Aer Lingus
(domestic, European, and
transatlantic)
Dublin Airport
tel.: 01/886-8844
www.aerlingus.ie

Continental Airlines
(transatlantic)
tel. 1-890/925252

Delta Airlines
(transatlantic)
tel. 1-800/768080

Ryanair (domestic and European)
Dublin Airport
tel.: 01/609-7800
www.ryanair.com

FERRIES
Domestic Services

Aran Island Ferries
4 Forster Street
Galway
tel.: 091/561767 or 091/568903
www.aranislandferries.com

Cape Clear Ferry
(contact Coiste Naomh Ciaran for
schedules)
tel.: 028/39119

Clare Island Ferry
tel.: 098/25711

Inishbofin Ferry
tel.: 095/44642

United Kingdom
and France

Stena Line
tel.: 01/204-7700

Irish Ferries
tel.: 01/638-3333

BUS SERVICES
National
Bus Éireann
tel.: 01/836-6111
www.buseireann.ie

Dublin
Dublin Bus
tel.: 01/873-4222

The Western Seaboard
Galway
Bus Éireann Travel Center
Galway Ceannt Station
Galway
tel.: 091/562000

County Mayo
Bus Éireann Travel Center
Ballina
tel.: 096/71816

County Clare
Bus Éireann
The Railway Station
Ennis
tel.: 065/682-4177

The Southwest
County Kerry
Bus Éireann offers services to
many destinations from
Tralee
tel.: 066/712-3566

Killarney
tel.: 064/30011

Cork
Bus Éireann offers services to most
Irish cities and large towns
tel.: 021/450-8188

The Southeast
Kilkenny
Tourist Office (for timetable
information)
Shee Alms House, Rose Inn Street
Kilkenny
tel.: 056/776-0933
Bus Éireann offers services to
Dublin, Cork, and Waterford

Wexford
tel.: 053/33114
Bus Éireann offers services to
Dublin, Rosslare Harbour, Gorey,
Limerick, and Killarney in Kerry

J. J. Kavanagh
tel.: 056/883-1106
Private buses to Enniscorthy and
County Carlow

Waterford
Bus Éireann offers services to
Dublin, Cork, Limerick, Galway,
Kilkenny, and Rosslare
tel.: 051/879000

Tipperary
Bus services between most Tipperary towns and Dublin, Cork,
and Limerick
tel.: 01/836-6111

J. J. Kavanagh runs a service to and from Dublin Airport, calling at Roscrea and Nenagh
tel: 056/883-1106

The Northwest and Lakelands

Sligo
Bus Éireann
Macdiarmada Station
Sligo
tel.: 071/916-0066
Services to Dublin, Galway, Ballina, and Derry in Northern Ireland; also Lakelands bus services

Donegal
Bus Éireann
Letterkenny
tel.: 074/912-1309
Buses to Dublin, Cork, and Galway and points in between, to Northern Ireland, and a number of local routes including Killybegs and Bundoran

TRAINS

Iarnród Éireann—Irish Rail
Connolly Station, Amiens Street
Dublin 1
tel.: 01/836-6222

Dublin

Trains from Connolly Station to Belfast, Sligo, and many parts of the midlands, and from Heuston Station to Galway, Westport, Kilkenny, Waterford, Cork and Kerry.
Both stations
tel.: 01/836-6222

The Western Seaboard

Galway
Iarnrod Éireann (Rail Services)
Galway Ceannt Station
Galway
tel.: 091/561444

County Mayo
Ballina
tel.: 096/71818

Castlebar
tel.: 096/71818

Claremorris
tel.: 094/71011

Westport
tel.: 098/25253

County Clare
tel.: 065/684-0444
Rail services to Dublin via Limerick from Ennis

The Southwest

County Kerry
Rail services to Dublin from Tralee
tel.: 066/712-3522

Killarney
tel.: 064/31067

Cork
Rail services direct to Dublin,
indirect routes to Waterford and
Killarney
tel.: 021/450-4888

Southeast
Kilkenny
Rail services to Dublin and
Waterford
tel.: 056/772-2024

Wexford
Rail services to Dublin, Rosslare Harbour, Enniscorthy, and
Wicklow
tel.: 053/22522

Waterford
Rail services to Dublin, Kilkenny,
Limerick, and Rosslare
tel.: 051/873401

Tipperary
Tipperary Station
tel.: 062/51206

Limerick Junction
tel.: 062/51406

Nenagh
tel.: 067/31232

Thurles
tel.: 0504/21733

Clonmel
tel.: 052/21506

The Northwest and Lakelands
Sligo
Rail services to Dublin, stopping
at Longford, Mullingar, and a
number of other stations from
Macdiarmada Station
Sligo
tel.: 071/916-9888

County Roscommon
Train services to Dublin from Boyle
tel.: 071/966-2027

Castlerea
tel.: 094/962-0031

Roscommon town
tel.: 0906/626201

County Leitrim
Rail service to Dublin from
Carrick-on-Shannon
tel.: 071/962-0036.

DRIVING
**Driver Testing Section—
Department of Transport**
Government Buildings
Ballina, Mayo
tel.: 096/24200

www.motorweb.ie
Car price information

INSURANCE COMPANIES
Hibernian Insurance
Haddington Court, Haddington
Road

Dublin 4
tel.: 01/607-8000

Allianz, Head Office
Burlington House, Burlington Road
Dublin 4
tel.: 01/613-3000

Irish Brokers Association
87 Merrion Square
Dublin 2
tel.: 01/661-3067

CAR RENTALS
Avis
1 East Hanover Street
Dublin 2
tel.: 01/605-7500
www.avis.ie

Budget
Athlone Road
Roscommon
tel.: 0906/627711
www.budget.ie

Hertz
149 Upper Leeson Street
Dublin 2
tel.: 01/676-7476
www.hertz.ie

CAR ASSISTANCE
The Automobile Association
23 Suffolk Street
Dublin 2
tel.: 01/617-9900
www.aaireland.ie

Housing Considerations

SHORT-TERM RENTALS
Rent-an-Irish-Cottage
51 O'Connell Street
Limerick
tel.: 061/411109
fax: 061/314821
info@rentacottage.ie
www.rentacottage.ie

Trident Holiday Homes
15 Irishtown Road, Irishtown
Dublin 4
tel.: 01/668-3534
fax: 01/660-6465

reservations@tridentholidayhomes.ie
www.tridentholidayhomes.ie

Irish Cottage Holiday Homes
Bracken Court, Bracken Road,
Sandyford
Dublin 18
tel.: 01/205-2777
fax: 01/293-3025
cottage@irishcottageholidays.com
www.irishcottageholidays.com

Self Catering Ireland
Kilrane
Rosslare, County Wexford
tel.: 053/33999
www.selfcatering.ie

**Jacobs Apartments,
Booking Office**
21-28 Talbot Place
Dublin 1
tel.: 01/855-5660
fax 01/855-5664
jacobs@isaacs.ie
www.isaacs.ie

USEFUL CONTACTS
Society of Chartered Surveyors
5 Wilton Place
Dublin 2
tel.: 01/676-5500
fax 01/676-1412
info@scs.ie
www.scs.ie

The Law Society
Blackhall Place
Dublin 7
tel.: 01/672-4800
fax: 01/672-4801
www.lawsociety.ie

**Royal Institute of
Architects of Ireland**
8 Merrion Square
Dublin 2
tel.: 01/676-1703
fax 01/661-0948
info@riai.ie
www.riai.ie

Irish Brokers Association
87 Merrion Square
Dublin 2
tel.: 01/661-3067
fax 01/661-9955
info@irishbrokers.ie
www.irishbrokers.com

Real Estate Agents

DUBLIN
Sherry Fitzgerald (City Center)
24 Mountjoy Square East
Dublin 2
tel.: 01/856-1428
fax 01/856-1433
info@sherryfitzgeraldsheehy.ie
www.sherryfitz.ie

Hooke and Macdonald
118 Lower Baggot Street

Dublin 2
tel.: 01/661-0100
fax 01/676-6340
sales@hookemacdonald.ie
www.hookemacdonald.ie

Lisney
24 Saint Stephen's Green
Dublin 2
tel.: 01/638-2700
fax 01/676-6540

dublin@lisney.com
www.lisney.com

WESTERN SEABOARD
County Galway
Homeseekers
The Old Malte, 17 High Street
Galway
tel.: 091/563225
fax 091/565891
info@homeseekers.ie
www.homeseekers.ie

Matt O'Sullivan
The Square
Clifden
County Galway
tel./fax: 095/21066
property@mattosullivan.com
www.mattosullivan.com

County Mayo
Brendan Tuohy
North Mall
Westport
County Mayo
tel.: 098/28000
fax 098/26728
btuohy@iol.com
www.iavi.ie/propertyireland/
btuohy

County Clare
Philip O'Reilly
22/24 Abbey Street
Ennis

County Clare
tel.: 065/684-4448
fax 065/682-0496
info@philiporeilly.com
www.philiporeilly.com

Green Valley Properties
Caherhurley
Bodyke
County Clare
tel./fax: 061/921498
greenvalley@eircom.net
www.gvp.ie

THE SOUTHWEST
County Kerry
Sean Daly
34 Henry Street
Kenmare
County Kerry
tel.: 064/41213
fax 064/41717
info@seandaly.com
www.seandaly.com

Ted O'Connor
Green Street
Dingle
County Kerry
tel./fax: 066/915-1533
conprop@iol.ie
www.dingleproperty.com

County Cork
Sheehy Brothers
Market Street

Kinsale
County Cork
tel.: 021/477-2338
fax 021/477-2472
info@sheehybrothers.com
www.sheehybrothers.com

Sherry Fitzgerald O'Neill
37 North Street
Skibbereen
County Cork
tel.: 028/21404
fax 028/22551
info@oneillproperty.ie
www.oneillproperty.ie

Key Properties
Bantry
County Cork
tel.: 027/50111
fax 027/51601
tom@keyproperties.net
www.corkkerryproperties.net

THE SOUTHEAST
County Kilkenny

SF McCreery
40 Parliament Street
Kilkenny
tel.: 056/772-1904
fax 056/776-3499
info@sfmcreery.com
www.sherryfitz.ie

County Wexford

Corish's
The Crescent Mall

Wexford town
County Wexford
tel.: 053/22577
fax 053/22974
jcorish@propertypartners.ie
www.propertypartners.ie

Wexford Property Management
Saint Peter's Square
Wexford town
County Wexford
tel.: 053/21525
fax 053/44187
info@wexfordpropertymanage
ment.com
www.wexfordpropertymanage
ment.com

County Waterford

O'Shea and O'Toole
11 Gladstone Street
Waterford city
County Waterford
tel.: 051/876757
fax 051/876506
info@osheaotoole.com
www.osheotoole.com

County Tipperary

Shee and Hawe
62 Main Street
Carrick-on-Suir
County Tipperary
tel.: 051/640041
fax 051/641009
sheeandhawe@propertypartners.ie
www.propertypartners.ie

THE NORTHWEST AND LAKELANDS

Sligo Real Estate Agents

Schiller and Schiller
Ardtarmon Castle
Ballinfull
County Sligo
tel.: 071/916-3284
fax 071/916-3860
schiller@iol.ie
www.irelandproperties.com

Remax Property Centre
5a Bridge Street
Sligo
tel.: 071/914-4446
fax 071/914-7247
www.remax-ireland.com

Donegal

McCauley Properties
Market Square, Malin Road
Moville
County Donegal
tel.: 074/938-2110
fax 074/938-2664
sales@mccauleyproperties.com
www.mccauleyproperties.com

Lakelands

Vincent Egan
Elphin Street
Boyle
County Roscommon
tel./fax: 071/966-2464
www.vincentegan.net

DNG Farrell
Riverview House, Landmark Court
Carrick-on-Shannon
County Leitrim
tel.: 071/962-0976
fax 071/962-0844
liamfarrell@wfarrell.ie
www.dng.ie

Suggested Reading

Dames, Michael. *Mythic Ireland.* Thames and Hudson, 1996.

De Paor, Liam. *The Peoples of Ireland: From Prehistory to Modern Times.* University of Notre Dame Press, 1990.

Foster, R. F., ed. *Oxford Illustrated History of Ireland.* Oxford University Press, 1991.

Grenham, John. *Tracing Your Irish Ancestors.* Genealogical Publishing, 1993.

Kinsella, Thomas, trans. *The Tain* (from the Irish epic *Tain Bo Cuailnge.* Oxford University Press, 1983.

Pennick, Nigel Campbell. *Celtic Sacred Landscapes.* Thames and Hudson, 1996.

Smith, C. B. F. Woodham. *The Great Hunger: Ireland 1845—1849.* Penguin USA, 1995.

Trevor, William. *Writer's Ireland: Landscape in Literature.* Thames and Hudson, 1986.

Yeats, W. B., ed. *Fairy and Folk Tales of Ireland.* Simon and Schuster, 1998.

Index

A

abortion: 36, 43–44
Achill: 122
agriculture: 117, 222
airmail: 258
air pollution: 217
airports: 310
air travel: 265–267, 310
alcohol consumption: 15–16
alternative health care: 212–213
Americans, Irish attitudes towards: 18–19
Anglo-Norman invasions: 27
animals: 14–15
appliances, electrical: 71, 238–240
Aran Islands: 76, 117–119
archaeological sites: County Clare 127;
    Newgrange 22; Ring of Kerry 131
architecture: 54–55
Ardara: 84, 170
arts, the: 52–57; architecture 54–55;
    dance 44–46; fine art 53; literature
    55–57; metalwork 9; music 44–45;
    storytelling 46
auction sales, real estate: 294–295
automobiles: see cars

B

Ballina: 123
Ballinasloe: 119
Ballinspittle: 137
Ballsbridge: 103
Ballydehob: 138
Ballyhogue: 149
Ballyshannon: 168
Ballyvaughan: 126
Baltimore: 79, 138
banking: 241–242
banshees: 163, 196

Battle of Boyne: 28
Beltane: 23
benefits, employee: 228–229
"Big Fella, The" (Michael Collins): 136
bird life: 15
bird-watching: 125, 138
Blarney: 139
Bloom, Leopold: 102
bonds: 249
Boru, Brian: 26, 127
Boyle: 173
broadband access: 257
building costs, home: 288–291
BUPA Ireland: 211
Burren: 126
businesses, Ireland's top 10: 247
Business Permission: 230–231
bus travel: 270–271, 311

C

calendar, Celtic: 23
Cape Clear Island: 138, 268–269
capital acquisitions tax (CAT): 244–245
Carrick-on-Shannon: 84, 174
Carrick-on-Suir: 157
cars: 272–278; driver's licenses 275; insur-
    ing 276; purchasing 276; renting 277–
    278; resources 314; road rules 273–274
Cashel: 82, 156
Castlebar: 120
castles: 54
Castletown House: 55
Catholicism: 51–52
Cavan, County: 171, 176
CCE (Comhaltas Ceoltoiri Éireann): 46
cellular phones: 254–256
Celtic culture: 9, 21–24
children, moving with: 188–189
Christianity, arrival of: 24–25

citizenship: 183–187; by descent 184; dual 187–188; by marriage 185–186; rights and obligations of 188
Claddagh rings: 115
Clare, County: 76–77, 124–127
Clare Island: 269
Claremorris: 123
Clifden: 115
Cliffs of Moher: 125
climate: 14, 215
Clonakilty: 79, 137
Clonmel: 82, 157
clothing: 70–71, 181
coal prices: 240
Cobh: 78, 136
codes, phone: 253
colleges and universities: 201–203; resources 305; Trinity College 101
Collins, Michael: 136
commerce: 37–38
communication, social: *see* language
communications: 251–262, 308–309
Connacht Province: 12
Connemara: 76, 114–116
consulates: 300
Cork City: 78, 135–136
cost of living: 236–241
County Cavan: 171, 176
County Clare: 76–77, 124–127
County Cork: 134–139; general discussion 8; coast 136–139; exploratory trips to 77–81; real estate prices 134–135, 136–139; rental homes 137, 285; transportation 266
county divisions: 11–12
County Donegal: 83, 165–171
County Galway: 112–119
County Kerry: 130–134; general discussion 13; exploratory trips to 77–81; Killarney Town 130; lakes 131; north Kerry 133–134; Ring of Kerry 131–133; Tralee 130
County Kildare: 75
County Kilkenny: 142–146

County Leitrim: 171, 174–176
County Mayo: 77, 119–123
County Meath: 75
County Roscommon: 171, 172–174
County Sligo: 83, 162–165
County Tipperary: 154–159
County Waterford: 150–154
County Wexford: 146–150
County Wicklow: 75
courier services: 258
credit cards: 72, 242
crime: 19, 217–218
Croagh Patrick: 51, 119
Cromwell, Oliver: 28
crystal, Waterford: 151
Cult of the Head: 23–24
culture shock: 180–181
currency: 71–72
customer service: 18
customs, social: 48–49
customs, and immigration: 72, 191, 303

D

Dalkey: 106
dance: 44–46
DART (Dublin Area Rapid Transit): 109
dental care: 211–212
Dingle Peninsula: 80, 134
Dingle town: 134, 196
dining: costs 237; gratuities 89
disabilities, access for people with: 217
disease: 215–216
divorce: 16, 43–44
doctors: 207–208
Donegal: 167–168
Doolin: 126
Doolough tragedy: 122
Downings: 169
dress: 181
drinking culture: 15–16
driver's licenses: 275
drug addiction: 217–218

Drumcondra: 107
dual nationality: 187–188
Dublin: 95–109; general discussion 5,
    63; accommodations 84–85; climate
    12; dining 90; exploratory trips to
    74–75; geography 96–97; immigra-
    tion 181; maps 94, 100; north side
    106–108; real estate agents 315; real
    estate costs 97–98, 99–108; rental
    homes 98–99, 286; south side 101–
    105; transportation 108–109, 267,
    271–272
Duncannon: 149
Dunfanaghy: 169
Dungarvan: 154
Dunmore East: 82, 153
duty-free imports: 191
duty-free shopping: 71

E

Easter Rising: 33
economy: 37–38, 222–224
education: 199–205; adult 201; public
    curriculum 199; resources 303–305;
    school year 199–200; student intern-
    ships 225–226; third-level 201–203
Eircom: 251–252
Éire, creation of: 34
elders, honoring: 49
elections, participating in: 188
electricity costs: 240
email: 256–257
emergency help: 218, 254
employment: 221–232; benefits 228–229;
    hiring household help 239; internships
    225–226; IT sector 224; job applica-
    tions 227–228; labor force 223–224;
    labor laws 231–232; minimum wage
    232; permission, to establish business
    230–231; resources 306–307; self-em-
    ployment 221, 229–231, 245; students,
    working 225; unionization 223; visas
    224, 227; worker's rights 232; work
    ethic 49
Ennis: 124
Enniscrone: 165
Ennistymore: 126–127
entertainment costs: 237
ethnicities: 41–44
Europe, transportation to: 267
European Union, membership in: 37–38
euros: 71–72, 241–242
excise tax: 191
exports: 37, 38
expressions, common Irish: 198–199

F

fairies: 163
fairy spells (pishogues): 163
family importance: 49
fauna: 14–15
ferries: 268–270, 310
festivals: ancient traditions behind 9;
    Celtic 23; Cork 8; Great October Fair
    119; music 45; Orange Order Parade
    168; Rose of Tralee 130; Saint Ste-
    phen's Day 47; Wexford Opera Festival
    148; see also specific place
finance: 235–249; banking 241–242; credit
    cards 242; currency 71–72, 241–242; in-
    vesting 246–249; living costs 236–241;
    resources 307–308; taxes 243–246
fishing: Aran Islands 117; County Mayo
    120
flag, symbolism of the: 52
flora: 14–15
flowers: 15
folklore: Celtic 22–24; County Sligo 162;
    fairies 163; medicinal 155, 208–209;
    online resources 260
food: 236–238
Forty Foot pool: 105
freehold titles: 292
furnishings, cost of: 238–240

G

Gaeilge (Irish): 193
Gaelic sports: 43
Gaeltacht areas: 195–196
Galway, County: 118–119
Galway City: 8, 112–114
gas, cost of natural: 240
gasoline prices: 272
gay culture: 50–51
gender roles: 50
genealogy: 184–185
geography: 11–14
gilts, government: 249
Gladstone, Prime Minister: 32
Glasnevin: 107
Glencolumbcille: 84
Glengarriff: 139
goldsmithing: 115
golf: 42
government: 35–37
gratuities: 89
Great Hunger (1940s): 31, 122
Great October Fair: 119
gypsies: 19

H

Ha-penny Bridge: 102
health care: 207–217; alternative 212–213; dental 211–212; employment providing 224–225; general practitioners 207–208; insurance 210–211, 213; medicinal herbs 215; pharmacies 213–214; preventative 214–216; public vs. private 209–211; resources 305–306
heating costs: 240
herbs, medicinal: 215
hired help: 239
history: 21–35; Christianity 24–25; English colonization 27–28; Great Hunger (1940s) 31; independence, struggle for 32–33; Irish Free State creation 34; Irish Republican Army (IRA) 33–34; Middle Ages 26–27; penal law 29; prehistory 22; twentieth century 32–34; Viking invasions 24–25; Waterford City 151–152
HIV/AIDS: 215–216
Holycross: 157
Holy Island: 127
Home Rule Bill: 32–33
horseback riding: 42
horse fairs: 119
housing: building costs 288–291; jargon 287; purchasing 287–297; rentals 282–287; resources 314–315
Howth: 108
hunting: 5

I

Iar Connacht: 116–117
Imbolc: 23
immigration: 72, 181–183, 302
information technology sector: 222
Inisfallen Island: 131
Inishcealtra: 127
Inisheer: 117
Inishmaan: 117
Inishmore: 117
Inishowen Peninsula: 84, 170
Inistioge: 146
insect bites: 214–215
Insula Viventium: 155
insurance: auto 276–277; critical illness 213; health 210–211; home 296
Internet access: 256–257, 309
Internet resources: 260–261
internships: 225–226
investments: 246–249; attracting 222; bonds 249; foreign 37; how to 247–248; options 246–247
Ireland's Eye: 108
Irish language (Gaeilge): 193
Irish Republican Army (IRA): 33–34

Island of the Living: 155
itineraries, fact-finding: 73–84

JK

Joyce, James: 102, 105
Joyce, Richard: 115
jury duty: 188
Kells Priory: 145
Kenmare: 79
Kerry, County: *see* County Kerry
Kildare, County: 75
Kilkenny, County: 142–146
Kilkenny town: 142–146
Killahoey Beach: 169
Killaloe: 127
Killarney Town: 80, 130
Killiney: 106
Killkenny City: 81
Kilmore Quay: 82, 149
Kinsale: 79, 136–137
Knock: 121
Kyteler, Alice: 143

L

labor laws: 231–232
"Lady Betty": 173
Lahinch: 126
Lakelands, the: 171–176
language: common expressions 198–199,
    287; Gaeilge (Irish) 193; place-names
    198–199; resources 303; schools
    196–198; word differences, common
    194–195
Leitrim, County: 171, 174–176
Lenister Province: 12
Lent: 49
leprechauns: 163
lesbian culture: 50–51
Liberties quarter: 104
lifestyle changes: 180–181

Liffey River: 13, 96
Liscannor: 126
literature: 55–57
living costs: 236–241; entertainment and
    dining 237; food prices 236–238; fur-
    nishings, cost of 238–240; rental homes
    282–287; utilities 240; value added tax
    238; *see also* housing; real estate
Lough Corrib: 76
Lough Derg: 166–167
Lough Key: 84
Lough Rynn: 175
Lughnasa: 23

M

MacMurough, Dermot: 26–27
"mad cow disease": 216
magazines: 259
mail services: 190–191, 257–258
Malin Head: 167, 170
marriage, citizenship through: 185–186
Mayo, County: 77, 119–123
McCarrick: 165
Meath, County: 75
media: 259–262
medical care: 207–217
medications: 71, 213–214
medicinal herbs: 215
Merrion Square: 103
metalwork: 9
Meteor: 255
metric system: 238
Midleton: 139
migrants: 19
minimum wage: 232
minority faiths: 52
Mizen Peninsula: 79
mobile phones: 254–256
Monaincha: 155
monasteries, early Christian: 24
money: *see* finance
"moral" issues: 16

mortgages: 292
Muckross Lake: 131
Munster Province: 12
Murrisk: 121
music: 44–45, 53
mutual funds: 248
myths: 8–9

N

naturalization, citizenship through: 186–187
NCT (National Car Testing) Certificate: 277
Nenagh: 158
Neolithic tribes: 22
Newgrange: 22
newspapers: 259
Nire Valley: 154
Nore Valley: 81
Norris, David: 50
Northern Ireland: 11, 35
Northwest and Lakelands: 161–176; general discussion 66–67; accommodations 88–89; County Donegal 165–171; dining 92–93; exploratory trips to 83–84; Lakelands, the 171–176; map 160; real estate agents 318
nurses, employment for: 224–225

OP

O'Connell, Daniel: 30–31
Oireachtas: 35
Opera Festival, Wexford: 148
Orange, William of: 28
O2 phone company: 255
packing: 70–71, 190–191
Parliament, national: 35
Parnell, Charles Stewart: 32
passports: 71, 73
peat (turf) costs: 240

peat bogs: 13–14
periodicals: 259
"Permission to Remain" visa: 181–182
permits, work: 227
petrol prices: 272
pets, moving with: 189–190, 303
pharmacies: 213–214
phone services: 251–256
pilgrimages: 119, 166–167
place-names, Irish: 198–199
plane travel: 265–267
Plantation of Ulster: 27–28
plant life: 14–15
poetry: 57
politics: government bodies 35–36; political parties 35, 36; pub "surgeries" 49; relations with Northern Ireland 35; in social conversation 18
Pollard: 158
pollution: 217
porters, tipping: 89
possessions, shipping: 190–191
post offices: 257–258
potato famine: 31
prejudice: 18
prescription drugs: 213–214
preventative health care: 214–216
Prospect Cemetery: 107–108
Protestant colonization: 27
provincial divisions: 11
PRSI (Pay Related Social Insurance): 244
publications: 259
public phones: 253–254
public transport: 10
pubs: 45, 49

QR

quarantine: 189–190, 303
Quiet Man, The: 120
racism: 18
radio: 262
railways: 271–272

rainfall: 14
real estate: 287–297; agents 315–318; appointments 70; auction sales 294–295; building costs 288–291; citizenship concerns 291; dos and don'ts 290; financing 292; holidays for agencies 72; how-to 292–294; installing utilities 297; insurance 296; online resources 260; prices 287; taxes 297; titles 292; *see also specific place*
refugees: 18–19
religion: 51–52; banishment of Catholic 28, 29; Catholicism 24–25, 51–52; Celtic 22–23; Croagh Patrick pilgrimage 119; Daniel O'Connell's Catholic Association 30–31; Knock shrine 121; Lough Derg pilgrimage 166–167; minority faiths 52; Protestant colonization 27
rental homes: 282–287
Republic of Ireland: 11
Ring of Kerry: 79, 131–133
rivers: 13
road rules: 273–274
Roaringwater Bay: 138
Romanian gypsies: 18–19
Roscommon, County: 171, 172–174
Rosses Point: 165
rural lifestyles: 180–181

S

safety: 217–218
Saint Columbcille: 169
Saint Patrick: 24, 26, 119
Saint Patrick's Purgatory: 166–167
Saint Stephen's Day: 47
Saint Stephen's Green: 103
sales tax: 238
Samhain: 23
Sandycove: 105
schools: 199–205; language 196–198; school year 199; *see also* education
Schull: 138

self-employment: 229–231, 245
senior citizens, free travel for: 10, 269
sexually transmitted infections (STIs): 216
shamrock, the: 44
Shannon River: 13
Sheep's Head Peninsula: 79, 138–139
shipping: 190–191, 257–258
sick leave: 228
Sinn Féin: 33–34, 35
Skibbereen: 79, 138
Slieve League Peninsula: 169
Sligo, County: 83, 162–165
Sligo Town: 83, 162–164
Smithfield: 107
smoking, ban on public: 217
society: 15–18; community importance 49; conversation 48; culture shock 180–181; customs 48–49; gay and lesbian 50; gender roles 50; migrant 19; prejudice 18–19; pub society 45, 49; social class 43; traditional 44–48; traditions 4; views on American 18–19
Southeast: 141–159; general discussion 65–66; accommodations 87–88; County Kilkenny 142–146; County Tipperary 154–159; County Waterford 150–154; County Wexford 146–150; dining 92; exploratory trips to 81–83; map 140; real estate agents 317; real estate prices 144–146, 156–159
Southwest: 129–139; general discussion 65; accommodations 86–87; climate 129; County Cork 134–139; County Kerry 130–134; dining 91–92; map 128; real estate agents 316; real estate prices 130, 131–134
spa treatments: 212–213
sports: 42–43, 189
statistics: geographical 11; trade 37
steam trains: 271
stock market, Irish (ISEQ): 247–248
storytelling: 46
Strandhill: 83, 165

student immigrants: 182
studying abroad: 203–205, 225
Sugrue, Elizabeth: 173
surfing: 165
sweaters, Aran: 118

T

taxes: auto 276–277; capital acquisitions tax (CAT) 244–245; capital gains 248; import 191; income 243–244; Irish 243–244; low corporation 222; PRSI (Pay Related Social Insurance) 244; real estate 296, 297; sales 238; U.S. 245–246
taxi drivers, tipping: 89
taxis: 278
teenage drinking: 189
telephone services: 251–256, 308
television: 262
temperatures: 14
Temple Bar: 102
tetanus shots: 214
Thomastown: 145
tinkers: 19
Tipperary: 155–156
Tipperary, County: 154–159
tipping: 89
Tone, Wolfe: 29–30
tourist information: 300–301
tourist seasons: 71
tracker bonds: 249
trade statistics: 37
traditional culture: 44–48
train travel: 271–272, 312–313
Tralee: 130
Tramore: 153
transportation: 265–278; air travel 265–267, 310; bus travel 270–271, 311; car rentals 73; car travel 272–278, 314; ferries 268–270, 310; map 264; resources 310–314; taxis 278; train travel 271–272, 312–313

Trinity College: 101, 204
tuition fees, third-level: 202
turf (peat): 13–14, 240

UV

Ulster Province: 12
Ulster Volunteer Force: 32–33
Ulysses: 102, 105
unemployment: 223
unionization: 223
universities: 201–203, 305
University College Dublin: 204
U.S. tax: 245–246
utilities, cost of: 240
vacation rentals: 284–286
vacations: 16–17, 228–229
Valentia: 13
VAT (value added tax): 238
Viking invasions: 24–25
Virginia: 176
Virgin Mary, apparitions of the: 121
visas: 181–183; "Permission to Remain" 181–182, 183; for short trips 73; student 182; worker's 224, 227
Vodafone: 256
voltage: 71
Volunteer Health Insurance Board (VHI): 210–211
voting: 188

WXYZ

wage, minimum: 232
Waterford: 8
Waterford, County: 150–154
Waterford City: 82, 150–152
Waterford Crystal: 151
wealth: 17, 43
weather: 14, 70
Western Seaboard: 111–127; general discussion 64–65; accommodations

85–86; Connemara 114–116; County Clare 124–127; County Galway 112–119; County Mayo 119–123; dining 90–91; exploratory trips to 75–77; Galway City 112–114; Iar Connacht 116–117; map 110; real estate agents 316; real estate prices 122–123, 124–127

Westport: 120–121

Wexford, County: 146–150

Wexford Town: 82, 147

Wicklow, County: 75

wildlife: 14–15

witch, Kilkenny: 143

work: *see* employment

worker's rights: 232

work ethic: 49

Wren Boys: 47–48

Yeats, William Butler: 162, 164–165

Youghal: 78, 136

youth culture: 16, 49

U.S.~Metric Conversion

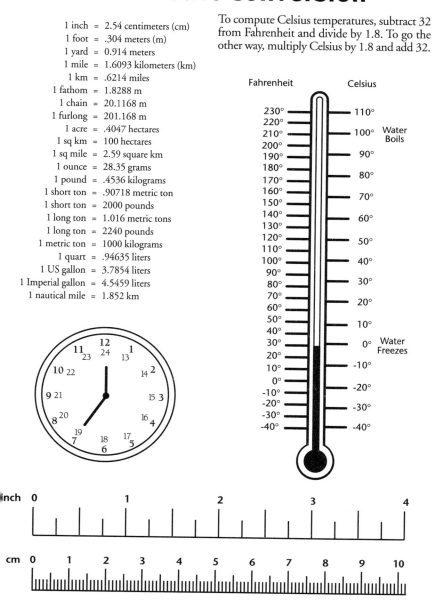

1 inch = 2.54 centimeters (cm)
1 foot = .304 meters (m)
1 yard = 0.914 meters
1 mile = 1.6093 kilometers (km)
1 km = .6214 miles
1 fathom = 1.8288 m
1 chain = 20.1168 m
1 furlong = 201.168 m
1 acre = .4047 hectares
1 sq km = 100 hectares
1 sq mile = 2.59 square km
1 ounce = 28.35 grams
1 pound = .4536 kilograms
1 short ton = .90718 metric ton
1 short ton = 2000 pounds
1 long ton = 1.016 metric tons
1 long ton = 2240 pounds
1 metric ton = 1000 kilograms
1 quart = .94635 liters
1 US gallon = 3.7854 liters
1 Imperial gallon = 4.5459 liters
1 nautical mile = 1.852 km

To compute Celsius temperatures, subtract 32 from Fahrenheit and divide by 1.8. To go the other way, multiply Celsius by 1.8 and add 32.

Fahrenheit   Celsius

230° — 110°
220°
210° — 100°   Water Boils
200°
190° — 90°
180°
170° — 80°
160°
150° — 70°
140° — 60°
130°
120° — 50°
110°
100° — 40°
90°
80° — 30°
70°
60° — 20°
50°
40° — 10°
30°
20° — 0°   Water Freezes
10°
0°
-10° — -10°
-20° — -20°
-30° — -30°
-40° — -40°

Inch 0   1   2   3   4

cm 0 1 2 3 4 5 6 7 8 9 10

Living Abroad in Ireland
Avalon Travel Publishing
1400 65th Street, Suite 250
Emeryville, CA 94608, USA
www.livingabroadin.com

Editor: Christopher Jones
Series Manager: Erin Raber
Design: Jacob Goolkasian, Justin Marler,
 Amber Pirker
Copy Editor: Karen Bleske
Graphics Coordinators: Deborah
 Dutcher and Stefano Boni
Production Coordinator: Tabitha Lahr
Map Editor: Kevin Anglin
Cartographers: Kat Kalamaras, Amy Tan
Indexer: Rachel Kuhn

ISBN-10: 1-56691-921-5
ISBN-13: 978-1-56691-921-0
ISSN: 1555-9750

Printing History
1st edition—October 2005
5 4 3 2 1

Text © 2005 by Steenie Harvey
Maps © 2005 by Avalon Travel
Publishing, Inc.
All rights reserved.

Avalon Travel Publishing
An imprint of
Avalon Publishing Group, Inc.

AVALON
publishing group incorporated

Some photos and illustrations are used by permission and are the property of the original copyright owners.

Front cover photo: © Lonely Planet Images

Printed in the USA by Berryville Graphics

Keeping Current

Although we strive to produce the most up-to-date guidebook that we possibly can, change is unavoidable. Between the time this book goes to print and the time you read it, the cost of goods and services may have increased, and a handful of the businesses noted in these pages will undoubtedly move, alter their prices, or close their doors forever. Exchange rates fluctuate—sometimes dramatically—on a daily basis. Federal and local legal requirements and restrictions are also subject to change, so be sure to check with the appropriate authorities before making the move. If you see anything in this book that needs updating, clarification, or correction, please drop us a line. Send your comments via email to atpfeedback@avalonpub.com, or write to the address above.